the quick guide to home organizing

Books by Sandra Felton and Marsha Sims

Organizing Your Day

5 Days to a Clutter-Free House

the quick guide to home organizing

sandra felton

Published by Revell
a division of Baker Publishing Group
P.O. Box 6287, Grand Rapids, MI 49516-6287
www.revellbooks.com

Spire edition published 2014

ISBN 978-0-8007-8823-0

Previously published under the title *Organizing Magic*

Printed in the United States of America

The authors of any unattributed quotations are unknown.

15 16 17 18 19 20 7 6 5

contents

acknowledgments

Thanks to the following for making this book a reality:

As always, to Ivan, supporter extraordinaire at home and in life. Kisses to you!

To Nanette Holt, remarkable editor and hard worker who strengthened the book with her outlook and experience. Wonderful guidance!

To Lonnie Hull DuPont for her faith and encouragement in moving this book into being at Revell. Many thanks!

To Revell, my publisher for the past quarter of a century. Wow!

introduction

I have loved magic since childhood. And I know I'm not alone.

Many of us have vivid memories of watching Cinderella, sitting in ashes, sad and in disarray. She never had fun and always worked hard. Even so, she was powerless to improve her condition. (Sounded like me when I looked around my messy house.)

But then we rejoiced when she found the prince who whisked her off to a beautiful castle, where she never had to turn her hand to work again. Wow! Can't beat that!

And who brought about the wonderful transformation? Why, the fairy godmother, of course!

For years I waited for my fairy godmother to show up, wave her magic wand over me, and magically change my mess into glorious order, my frustration into joy.

It never happened. The fairy godmother never came to my house. Nor did the elves who worked for the shoemaker while he slept. Nor did the prince, with the reviving kiss, or any of those other magic, fairy-tale people on whom I had subliminally pinned my hopes.

Then I learned where the magic really is—and it changed my life.

In this book I share with you the organizing basics I learned after long ignoring them, waiting for outside help. The information in each chapter contains a little magic dust. Rightly used, you will find your house being slowly—but surely!—changed into the neat, orderly, elegant, comfortable castle of your dreams. And you will be the princess, more relaxed and unhurried, finally able to enjoy your domain.

But *you* must wave the wand. *You* must sprinkle the magic dust. Don't worry—I'll tell you how, step-by-step, walking you through the transformation that will change your life.

Here's your part: Read each chapter carefully. Zero in on how each can help you improve your situation. Note the steps you need to take to create the solutions that apply to you. Then start waving that wand, your treasure trove of solutions. And watch. The magic will come.

Often in fairy tales, like those about Snow White or Sleeping Beauty, a kiss awakens the princess to her new life. So it is with us.

As you follow the hints, tips, suggestions, and encouragements in these pages, always remember to apply them using the magical kiss of organization:

KISS (keep it super simple)

Say it to yourself, when you're tempted to make things more complicated than they need to be. Whisper it again and again. It's an endless source of organizing magic.

Focus on the few changes that work well for you and do those consistently. You'll be surprised at the change that happens. Now get ready for an enchanting journey with me. Our coach awaits . . .

how to use this book

A few useful ideas rightly applied can make a significant change in your life. But it is easy to lose track of them. They tend to drift away unless nailed down on the spot as you read. Here are some suggestions on how to hold on to those ideas that relate to your interests and needs.

1. Underline and write notes in the margin when you see or get an interesting idea. (Unless, of course, this is a borrowed book.)
2. Mark important places you want to remember with a small annotated sticky note so you can find it again easily. This works better than turning down corners.
3. Immediately do the easy step that will make a significant improvement in your life, like calling the phone number that will take you off the calling list of telemarketers.
4. Commit to long-term change where you see the need, such as working to change one bad habit or unproductive behavior. Work on one at a time.
5. Keep a running list of things you need to buy on a sticky note attached to the book so it won't get lost while you read. You can then easily take the note to the store later.
6. Write a to-do list in the back of the book (projects and such) as action ideas occur to you.

ready, set, go!

When I was younger, I embraced many ideas I gleaned from tip books—even the ones that weren't very good. Why? I thought the "expert" who wrote the book was smarter than I was and surely wouldn't lead me wrong. But if I had stuck with all those suggestions, you'd see the following when visiting my house:

- Salmon poached in the dishwasher. It may work, but is it really a good idea to go that quirky route? (Unless your stove is out of order, of course, in which case using this method might make you look like a genius.)
- Nail polish and pantyhose stored in the fridge. They'll keep "fresh" longer there, but do we really want to dress out of our appliances?
- Homemade soap-on-a-rope, created with soap slivers stuffed into the toes of pantyhose.
- Onions kept fresh by suspending them in legs of pantyhose straddling a door.
- Still more discarded pantyhose, recycled as pillow stuffing. (Pantyhose, for some reason, seemed the solution to nearly any household problem.)

Smart Thinking!

How you think affects how organized you are—and how organized you will become. Try reprogramming yourself to become more organized by meditating for a few minutes daily on these positive statements:

1. I am too smart to create a mess. Therefore, I put things where they belong immediately after using them.
2. I am too smart to let the kids make a mess. Therefore, I spend the time and energy to train them to keep things orderly.
3. I am too smart to do everything myself. Therefore, I create a team of family, friends, and hired help to call on when I need assistance.

I Wised Up

It took me some time to wise up a tad. Now I've learned to avoid introducing things into my life that are far out of the pattern that already exists. If a new idea is not easy to incorporate and easy to follow as a regular part of my life, I reject it. What a relief to have finally found that I don't have to integrate all great ideas into my life—I need only the ones that will make *my* life easier.

In this book you'll find many suggestions, strategies, and tips. Employing well-chosen tips will free up your life—now and for years to come. Happily embrace those.

A few you'll try now and perhaps abandon later. But don't cheat yourself by not trying at least a few new things, even if you're not sure they'll work for you. Some of the ideas I thought originally were the poorest, like grouping my clothes in the closet according to category and color, have proven to be lifelong time-savers. Had I not tried them, despite my doubt, I never would have known!

Sometimes you will see what seem to be contradictions. This is often true with words of advice. Tradition tells us that

> **Organizing is not nearly as important as many other things in life. But what it delivers often is priceless.**
>
> Sandra Felton, The Organizer Lady

you can't tell a book by its cover. Yet we're also admonished that first impressions are the most important. We're told to look before you leap. But we're also warned that he who hesitates is lost. Which of the truths in each pair is correct? Both are—but they apply in different circumstances. For instance, sometimes you should be impatient with clutter and take bold steps to move forward. At other times you need to be patient when it comes to moving forward, even when you become discouraged with how slow the improvement seems.

Never fear. I'll help you sort out how to tell the difference.

I define organizing as doing something smart—proactively—to make life easier and more productive. That may include setting up an organizational plan such as the

> If you follow appropriate tips in this book, your organizational life will improve significantly.

Messies Anonymous Flipper, found at www.messies.com. Perhaps it's making a chore chart for your children. It may be clearing out the house, so there isn't as much to dust. It may be giving up some less important responsibilities, so you can narrow your focus on more significant areas of your life.

What Do Tips Have to Do with It?

The purpose of this book is not to ratchet up the details of your life a notch or two. It's not designed to help you fly higher and longer, to be more of a hardworking perfectionist. You're probably already expending most of your time and energy and don't want to expend any more.

This book will help you work less and still accomplish your aims—maybe even better than before and certainly more efficiently. As you read, you'll see tips that will work for you, helping you simplify what you do and how you do it. These tips are proven strategies for getting and staying organized.

Some tips require time and energy—for you, they may take more effort than they're worth. You may have already tried and rejected some of my suggestions. But keep an open mind.

> When you choose the behavior,
> you choose the consequences.

You may decide that tips you once knew and have forgotten, or had earlier rejected, may be useful to you now.

Does this book cover all of the tips and strategies you will ever need? Unlikely. But I *can* promise you this: if you follow appropriate tips in this book, your organizational life will improve significantly. You will be amazed.

So how do you know when to use a tip? Listen to your instincts and your emotions.

Some tips will meet an immediate need. Some will provide a great solution for the future. Ignore the ones that will never be useful for you. Each tip is designed to help you find order and beauty in your life. And like tools, they require intelligent handling to work well.

> **There are no shortcuts to any place worth going.**
>
> Beverly Sills, opera singer

Your education won't stop here. I warmly invite you to join us daily at www.messies.com. It will provide a springboard into a whole ocean of help from people struggling with, and overcoming, the same problems you're facing.

Forty Days to Fabulous

There are forty chapters in this book, all designed to help you radically improve your life in forty days—just maybe not consecutively. What I mean is this: to make this book work for you, you need to pace yourself. You may be tempted to race ahead, reading more than one chapter a day. But that won't give you the time you need to really put the tips in place.

I'm not suggesting you drag your feet. But we're aiming for big changes. Some chapters involve simply learning to see solutions in a new way. With those your progress will likely be immediate. But the solutions in other chapters may take some time to set up. Don't feel as though you've failed if you halt for a day or two and take time to fully implement tips from those chapters before moving on to the next.

Above all, know that you're not alone. I'm still smoothing out the rough spots that crop up in my own life, even after being known for decades as The Organizer Lady.

So, welcome! I'm so glad to have you coming along with me on this journey.

envision your goals

It's time to get excited about what your house can be. Frustration may have started you on the road to change, but excitement will take you even farther than you ever dreamed you could go.

Bring That Dream into Focus

You can't go in your everyday life where you haven't gone in your dreams. When you start daydreaming in detail, it becomes planning.

You can stimulate your dreaming by looking around at the lives of friends you admire, the ones who really seem to have their act together. Think back on how Mom did things, if that's the life you want for yourself. Read decorating magazines.

> **I want peace. I want to see if somewhere there isn't something left in life of charm and grace.**
>
> Rhett Butler, in the movie *Gone with the Wind*

> You can stimulate your dreaming by looking around at the lives of friends who really seem to have their act together.

Visit model homes or open houses. See, feel, smell what you want your house to be.

Read over the statements below and spend a moment thinking about each. Check those that apply to you. You may even have your own to add.

__ I want to be happy when I step into my house.

__ I want my home to reflect my personality and my style.

__ I want my home to be a good launching pad for my family and me.

__ I want to be free from the stress that clutter causes.

__ I want to use my house to meet the needs of others.

__ I want to be able to find things easily.

__ I want to spend less time struggling to stay organized.

__ I want my house to be beautiful.

__ I want a place to train my kids to be responsible, organized adults.

__ I want ______________________________.

__ I want ______________________________.

The Big One

It is your pleasure, your privilege, your high calling, to set goals, to envision a dream. Make it a big one. *The* Big One.

Nothing short of bold vision will be enough to propel you to create the home you envision for your family and to maintain it that way in the years to come. Let me say *for* you what you may not have the boldness to say for yourself: "I want a house that is beautiful, clean, even shining. I want it to be neat and tidy and *stay* neat and tidy. I want to welcome unexpected guests with joy, because I can bless them with the atmosphere of my home, and I can meet their needs there. Houseguests will share themselves with us, and we with them, in the comfort of our house.

> This book is about defining your dream and setting a pace to pursue it.

"I want . . . no, I *need* a house that is easy to live in. It supports me in what I do because things are easy to find and easy to get to. I don't have to struggle to move forward in my projects in this house.

"My family is proud of our home—so proud that they want to be part of keeping it clean and in order. Their friends are welcomed, and they enjoy what we have to offer them here.

"My habits and their habits keep the house nice—consistently—not perfectly but consistently. I want to feel in control of my belongings, papers, and finances, so that area of my life does not become chaotic, frustrating, and even scary. I work smoothly—without wearing myself out in this quest—because I have developed a system that works.

Order is the shape upon which beauty depends.

Pearl S. Buck, author and winner of the Pulitzer Prize and Nobel Prize

"The words *dignity, serenity,* and *harmony* are not strangers in my house. Is it dusty from time to time, or are there things out of place? Perhaps. But never so much that the integrity of what I, or we, have created is lost.

"This is not just a house. I will not be satisfied until I have fully created a true home, with *all* that word embodies. I know that specific strategies, tips, and steps toward order are important, because they are the nails that hold together the boards of this dream."

This book is about defining your dream and setting a pace to pursue it.

What is the allure of marathons? There are many, I'm sure. But for most, I think, it's the challenge of doing something you thought you could never do. When you do it, what a thrill!

This book will help you make a commitment to your dream, challenge yourself to new heights, and upgrade your house and life in a way that may seem impossible now. Take it day by day, slowly and steadily. You will be thrilled when you cross the finish line of your desires.

Do Just a Little Better

I won't bore you with the cliché of a journey beginning with just one step, though I'm tempted to do so, because it's so true—especially in this context. In housekeeping, truly, just a few little changes can make a huge difference.

Often careless or casual habits just need to be upgraded a little bit. Usually the difference between good and great is just a little more effort, just one more step.

If you find yourself being too relaxed about something, simply decide to ratchet up your effort a notch next time. Then make that upgrade a habit.

Below is one example of something we all do—buy a new multipack of toilet paper. The question is, what do we do with it? This is a task we handle at different levels of organization. Take the famous Felton Toilet Paper Test. Which level are you on?

- Leave it in the car until needed (or nearly needed, I trust!).
- Bring in the package and drop it in the kitchen or by the back door.
- Put the still-wrapped package in a bathroom.
- Remove the rolls from the package and put them all in one bathroom.
- Distribute toilet paper to all bathrooms, so it will be easily available when needed.
- Slip them under cute, little decorative covers, stashed close to the toilet.

Wouldn't it be easy to jump up one level at least? The importance of upgrading is this: your needs will be met with greater ease. Certainly having toilet paper readily and consistently available relieves stress, saves time, and keeps the household moving along without unnecessary effort.

> **A year from now you may wish you had started today.**
>
> Karen Lamb, author

Stop, Start, Continue

To put feet to your goals and start moving ahead, you must realize that reaching a goal requires behavior change. Have you thought recently about the behaviors that get in the way of your dreams, or about the habits you must initiate to get where you want to go? It's time to evaluate them, decide how to deal with them, and move forward.

Make three columns on a sheet of paper, labeling them *Stop, Start, Continue.*

In the first column, write three habits you want to stop because they are hindering your journey toward your dream.

> **Conduct is influenced, not by our experience, but by our expectations.**
>
> George Bernard Shaw, British playwright and novelist

Maybe you will write, "Watching late-night TV every night," because you know it zaps your energy the next day, or "Serving as president in my club," because it takes up more time than you have to give.

Under the second heading, list habits you intend to start. They may be things like, "Make lunches every night," or "Do one load of laundry each day," or "Hire help."

Behaviors to continue are those that are useful and successful in your life, like "Continue painting regularly," or "Continue walking each morning."

For this to work, under each heading you'll need to list three or more behaviors. Writing your planned behaviors and reviewing the written goals daily will dramatically increase your chances of sticking to them, research shows.

This is amazingly simple. Will you do it and adjust your life in the direction of your dream by stopping what hinders it, starting what advances it, and continuing the good stuff? I know you can!

day 3

party your way to order and beauty

Constantly zeroing in on the problem of disorder in the house can be a real drag. Focusing on overcoming problems is important, but the best motivator is working for a fun, worthwhile goal like (drumroll, please) throwing a party!

As I See It

As I struggled to gain control of the condition of my house, I realized one day that there's more to this building than just a dwelling, a launching point into the world. It isn't just a laundry, dressing room, snack bar, place to sleep, or place my family and I depend on to launch us into the real world.

I'd gotten it backwards. The outside is not the real world. Our house *is* the real world. The outside world existed to support what happened inside the *house*!

In truth, the home is a womb where relationships between family members and with friends are nurtured. Often the home is the wellspring of ministry and nurturing others. Sometimes it's a place of business. Always it should offer relief to the people who live there—to you and me and the loved ones who share the home with us.

Life outside the home is sometimes difficult. We can't control all that happens there, but we can create a soft place to fall within our four walls.

To invite someone into our home creates a bond like nothing else can.

So Much to Celebrate

Despite chaos in our jobs, on the crowded streets, or in bustling stores, the home is the one place we can create serenity and harmony. And one way we can celebrate this fact is by entertaining there.

We can eat with friends at restaurants, but it's not nearly as personal and meaningful—for them or for us—as when we open our home and share ourselves in our own unique context. To invite someone into our home creates a bond like nothing else can.

Yes, it can be scary! Is the house nice enough? Is it neat enough? Is it clean enough? Is it pretty enough? Am I good enough? Many of us bombard the notion of having people over with a cruel barrage of self-doubt.

The result? We keep other people away—away from our homes and away from our very souls. Why? A relationship that becomes personal may lead to visits from home to home. So to avoid the stress of entertaining or the explanations of why no invitations have been extended, many of us remain just aloof enough to avoid that kind of dilemma.

Maybe, as I once did, you've kept people at arm's length for so long, you can't even think of a friend close enough to invite over. What a shame!

Often people with this problem are loving and outgoing people, but they don't want to risk developing and enjoying friendships because of (say this as if you're in an echo chamber) "THE HOUSE."

If you are one who doesn't want to live with this kind of tension anymore, start by slowly developing deeper friendships. After keeping people out of your home for so long, you'll feel more comfortable if you ease slowly into a more welcoming lifestyle. To begin, try inviting someone in "for just a minute" while you get your coat on or grab your purse.

Though it's hard to break old molds, the rewards are great: Nothing else meets the inner needs of the soul like positive relationships. Your home can express your personality at its best. And knowing that someone will be coming to your home will propel you to maintain it in a way that's more pleasing for you and your family.

Ready to claim these benefits for your own? Face the fear and resolve to just do the following:

- Get the house in "good enough" shape to invite someone in. If the task seems too monumental, just straighten the areas your guest will see.
- Choose your comfort level of entertaining. Maybe it will be a neighbor for coffee and a muffin (maybe even without the muffin).
- Keep inviting one or two people into your home (the same ones or a variety) while you build up to bigger things.
- As your comfort grows and your house is more in order, invite larger groups, like a book club or Bible study. You can still close the doors to the bedrooms, even though more of your house will be exposed.

- Graduate to a real party, free of the worry that guests will get off the beaten path and into every area of your home. Now it all feels "good enough."

Sure, you may be saying, with a furrowed brow, "Easy for you to say. How can I actually do this?"

I'll tell you.

- *Gather serving pieces that make you comfortable.* After years of not having people over, your plates, cups, and flatware may be too shabby to show, and you are simply not prepared to entertain. But that's okay. Even plastic and paper works well too. One lady I know has a hot cider party each Christmas and asks guests to bring their own mugs. It works, and it's charming!
- *Bring guest areas up to par.* Does your guest bathroom need fresh hand towels or a spruced-up soap dispenser? No need to go overboard. Just hit the high spots that need refreshing. The house doesn't have to be a showplace—just comfortable and inviting!
- *Extend an invitation.* Choose someone you feel comfortable with and who has been friendly to you, so you'll feel most at ease.
- *Plan easy-to-serve refreshments.* What you offer your guests doesn't have to be homemade or fancy. You might even allow guests to bring their favorites if they ask what they can bring.
- *Create conversation starters.* If you have one or two friends over, talk about a mutual interest, ask for their advice on a specific issue (like which accessories go with a new outfit), or show a family album (don't overdo this one unless you know your guests like this kind

A messy house invites unexpected guests.

Italian proverb

of thing). For larger groups, you'll have no need to fear a lag in the festivities if you focus your guests' attention on a fun activity, such as asking them to take pictures using disposable cameras or starting a mixer that will encourage them to get to know each other. Find ideas on the Internet by typing "party games" into your favorite search engine.

- *Stop seeking perfection.* Relax and have fun, even if you notice a cobweb hanging from a corner during the gathering. Who cares? Cut yourself some slack. You're a novice at entertaining, and it will get even smoother as you practice having more people over.

I feel sure that you have something special to contribute, and this is your time to do it. Open the door of your life, as far as you are comfortable. Then slowly open it wider as your courage grows and your house seems more acceptable to you.

Friends, fun, and fellowship are important. And in these get-togethers you're about to organize, they're all that matter. Really.

Your house is just the canvas. The masterpiece—a work in progress—is the pleasing mix of relationships you build in it.

You have a special song to sing. Don't go any longer without belting out that melody to the world with gusto.

be annoyed—very, very annoyed

There are two reasons people take the trouble to change how they live. The first is a desire for harmony. These people simply want to live more beautifully and peacefully.

Others, however, seek change as a desperate attempt to relieve the discomfort of disorganization and the pain of clutter. They're powerfully motivated to do what it takes to end the frustration they feel.

Good Reasons to Be Annoyed

That said, go ahead and be annoyed. It's okay. It's even desirable. Be very, very annoyed when

- You can't find your tax information. But you have no choice—you have to search doggedly for the lost papers.

> Failure usually comes in many small steps, not through one giant leap. Success is the same way.

- You need to mail a letter but don't have a stamp. So you put the letter aside, hoping you'll remember where you put it when you finally buy stamps. In the meantime, the letter becomes hopelessly lost.
- The new lightbulb you need is stored high on a shelf behind a precariously balanced pile of stuff. Touch it, and everything will tumble. So you put off replacing the burned-out bulb. In the meantime, you strain to see in the dimness.
- You can't find clothes that match. You do the best you can to put together an outfit quickly so you're not late—again.
- You can't invite people into your house because it's just too messy. You learn to live without the companionship you always hoped you'd enjoy in your home. Making excuses to keep people out has become automatic.
- You forget the birthday of your favorite great-aunt, who may not have many more birthdays left. You planned to send her a sweet card, but you don't have a system for remembering these kinds of occasions. Regret over mistakes like this often clouds days that should have been happy.

Tune In to Annoyance

A disorganized life is, at its core, annoying. Maybe you've learned to live with it and have ignored it so often that you barely notice anymore. Like a shoe that pinches or the noise on a busy street near your home, you've learned to tune it out, to a degree. But it still hurts.

Stop. Don't do this to yourself anymore. Tune in to your negative feelings. Turn up the volume on them. Let them bubble to the surface and stay there. Zoom in on the "little" things that are diminishing the quality of your life.

> A disorganized life is, at its core, annoying.

Simply admitting to yourself how these annoying problems make you feel is the first big step toward solving them. Really.

Let the irritation energize you. Let it propel you toward finding a solution that works—one that sends your old friend *annoyance* packing. Ahhhh, it feels so good to get that rock out of the shoe!

Take Better Care of Yourself

Disorganization is a problem of self-neglect. In short, when we're disorganized, we're failing to treat ourselves with the love and respect we want others to show us.

By becoming more organized, we become more powerful in taking care of ourselves. And here's an important payoff: when we take care of ourselves, we take better care of those around us as well.

But it's challenging to keep modern life organized. These days life runs on so many different tracks that if we're not careful, parts of what's important to our well-being can derail.

Getting dressed in the morning is a hassle when you can't find the right blouse, jewelry, or shoes. Because you're late, you don't have time to fix a proper lunch to take to work. You become so frazzled that you forget to write a note to buy moisturizer. You realize you just incurred a late fee because a bill you've been meaning to pay is now overdue. You can't have friends over because of how the house looks. One small derailment after another adds up to self-neglect.

What's more, when you're so muddled in your own life, you neglect your responsibilities to others. You can't find and sign your child's school papers. Dinner is a last-minute affair—no choice but to order in pizza (again!). Finances unravel, so you hesitate to buy what is necessary.

> Winners make it happen. Losers let it happen.

Being disorganized is a disservice to those you love and to you. Becoming well organized is an important gift you give yourself—and others.

learn the secrets of organizing magic

When it comes right down to it, I think people are divided into two groups. The first is made up of those mystifying folks who are efficient without seeming to work at it. Their living rooms always are ready for unexpected guests—maybe not perfect but acceptable. When they step back into the kitchen to clean up after a meal, very little needs to be done. Their laundry is kept up. All of this seems to be done mysteriously without much effort. Those of us who wrestle with chaos look on with amazement. How do they do it?

Like exposing a magician's secrets, I am now about to reveal how they are so organized.

Taking Few Steps

Organized people automatically keep things neat as they go. That's their goal. For example, your organized friend pours a cup of coffee. She tears open the artificial sweetener package and flips open the trash can lid with her foot while depositing the empty packet. In one motion, she grabs and pours the powdered creamer, and without putting the jar down, returns it to the cabinet—coffee, with no mess to clean up, no work.

Her less-organized friend (I will insert my name here) has only one goal in mind—a cup of hot coffee. She pours the coffee and adds the sweetener, dropping the empty or half-empty packet on the counter. She adds her creamer

Slash the Work by Saving Steps!

You can save steps and beat clutter by building these habits into your daily routine:

- Toss messy spoons into the sink or dishwasher rather than leaving them on the counter.
- Toss clothes directly into the hamper as you take them off.
- Carry cleaning products in a bucket that travels with you from room to room. When you're finished, simply put the bucket away.

and sets the jar on the counter too. Even if she stops now to put things away (highly unlikely!), she's created two extra steps, and those few extra steps during the day really add up. But more likely, she plans to straighten up later. She sits down while the coffee is hot, leaving a trail of clutter, including a few grains of sweetener dribbling from the packet—more mess on the counter, more work.

Make this your family's new motto: If you get it out, put it back quickly.

You'll save so much time and effort if you just make this your family's new motto: If you get it out, put it back quickly.

Fixing It Quickly

The difference between people who maintain order consistently and those who have to go back constantly and straighten up messy areas is this: orderly folks hop quickly to a solution when something needs to be done. Simply put, as soon as there is a job to do, they do it. You'll keep chaos under control too if you get in the habit of tackling jobs quickly.

- Unload the dishwasher when the load is finished.
- Empty the dryer, fold clothes, and put them away immediately.
- Insist that kids put away toys they're no longer using before dragging out new ones.

Pursuing Consistency

The system you choose to use is not as important as how you work it. Any system, no matter how simple or inadequate, that is consistently worked is better than the best system that's used inconsistently. This is a bold statement but true.

> Housework is so tedious. You do the dishes, make the beds, and three weeks later you have to do it all over again.

One of the characteristics that sets organized people apart from those who find themselves slipping into disorder easily (often without the slightest idea of why) is that they work in a routine kind of way. They get in a groove of staying on top of the basics and—voila!—they seem to have an

Stay on Top of the Basics

Slide simple routines like these into your daily activities, and—poof!—your house will suddenly be transformed.

- Make the bed when you get out of it.
- Clean the kitchen before you sit down after a meal.
- Put away your toothbrush, toothpaste, and makeup before you leave the bathroom to start your day.

organized house with little effort. But don't let them fool you into thinking they don't work at it. They just work efficiently because they're consistent, and that's what makes things go more smoothly.

Not Allowing Ooze

"Oozing" is when things don't make it to their designated area. Keys are not hung on their hook by the door. A wallet is left on the kitchen counter. A cup is forgotten in the living room, and a jacket is draped on the back of a kitchen chair. When things ooze out into the open where they don't belong, the peace of your home is compromised.

But we ooze away from home too. In hotel rooms, things start spreading out of suitcases. Clothes ooze into the room if not corralled into the closet, drawers, or suitcase. In the bathroom, toiletries lie scattered across the counter instead of being lined up neatly along the vanity. Neat people value the pleasure and convenience of order wherever they are.

Ousting Ooze

When your house looks junky and you can't find things, you are probably oozing. But you can oust ooze forever if you simply

- Get in the habit of putting things away as soon as you're finished with them.
- Make a pickup sweep of the house before dinner and before bedtime. Hint: Stay-at-home moms need to add regular toy sweeps too.
- Think like a sheepdog. Constantly nudge your wayward "sheep" (belongings) back to where they belong in the sheep pen. Better yet, don't let them stray at all.

Being Visually Alert

An awareness of how things look is a powerful help when keeping things organized. It sounds obvious, but some people can't really "see" the clutter. While some people automatically notice when things are out of place, others seem to tune out the mess. They tune in visually only for short intervals from time to time.

It is much better to *keep up* than to *catch up*.

But the act of being visually alert is powerful. Try it, and, well, you'll "see." Focus on the condition of your surroundings. The more you do it, the neater your house will stay.

Here's a trick that will allow you to view your house, and its condition, with fresh eyes. Just turn on all the lights at night, open the blinds and drapes wide, and stand outside, like a stranger looking in. What do you see?

> Every minute you procrastinate putting something back where it belongs is a cluttered minute.

Inside, hold an empty toilet tissue or paper towel roll to one eye, like a spyglass. Then look at your kitchen counter, dining room table, or any clutter spot. Take note of which areas seem orderly and which don't.

As you sensitize yourself visually, you will begin to be aware of the reward in putting things away quickly and consistently. The more beautiful and orderly your house becomes, the more zealous you'll become to maintain it that way. The big, really big, payoff comes when your friends begin to say how nice your house looks. Whoopee!

cooperate with your personality style

You have a wonderfully unique personality. Part of that uniqueness is your organizational style and how you function.

Organizational Style

Most of us use a combination of several styles, but we lean most heavily on one or two that work best for us. Any style that moves you forward is a good one.

When it comes to getting things done, most of us fit one of these five styles:

The Planner. You have developed a basic strategy to make sure life moves smoothly, and you follow those steps. A master plan and calendar are important tools for you. You've tweaked the basic routine to fit your lifestyle, and that keeps you from having to reevaluate every day and every week to know what to do.

The Delegator. As much as possible, you appoint or hire others to help bear the load. In a way, you are a manager. A good manager is a wonderful thing. Not only do things

> The focuser prioritizes well, handles the important things efficiently, and is not distracted by the unimportant.

get done efficiently, but the team (family) learns to work together and the children are trained for adult life.

The Lister. You make lists that dictate your daily and weekly activities. You may create lists for nearly every facet of your life. I know people who write a list and set about doing the items on the list with an impersonal attitude. Zip, zip, zip, they do one job after another, making steady progress and getting things done.

The Vigilant One. You follow the all-the-time-on-top-of-things approach, rapidly completing a task shortly after it presents itself. People with this style seldom put things on a list, because as soon as they see something that needs doing, they hop to it. They often follow a mental list unconsciously.

The Worker. You put in long hours of hard work—a good quality when balanced with qualities of the other styles. You need to remember to take breaks and rest to "sharpen your ax."

The Focuser. No matter which of the other styles you use, everyone needs to be a focuser first and foremost. The focuser prioritizes well and handles the important things efficiently. A focuser is not distracted by the unimportant.

If you allow the unimportant tasks to swallow up your time, your life will be strangely unproductive, no matter how hard you work. But if you're focused, emphasizing only the few important things in your life and what supports their moving forward, you'll be amazed by your progress. And when you're focused, your basic style—no matter what it is—can be a great tool in organizing your life.

It takes courage to grow up and turn out to be who you really are.

e. e. cummings,
American poet

Determine Which Style Works Best for You

I'm not one to keep on top of everything, nor am I one who follows a list in a mechanical way. I'd best be described as a strong focuser.

My style does involve making lists of things to do so they won't drift off my mental radar screen. So, referring to my list, I gather the materials, information, or whatever is required to move forward. I observe the time. Then suddenly I get the urge to do the job. Using a touch of spontaneity, like a spider that feels an insect hit her web, I jump into action.

Becoming aware of my own style helps me keep my priorities in mind, and I seem to accomplish a lot. If I tried to force myself to use other, "better" methods, which are not my style, I would end up doing very little, I suspect. Then I would berate myself for procrastination and laziness.

So here's the key. Tune in to what works best for you. Use that method as your main approach for getting things done. Sometimes you may switch to one of the other ways of approaching tasks, or you may use a combination. Whichever approach you take, make sure you *just do it*.

Basic *Re*training

Some basic styles siphon the power right out of decision making, throwing us out of focus and truly offtrack. You'll find you're much more productive—and, as a result, more relaxed and able to provide a better environment for yourself and your family—if you ease away from employing these basic styles:

> **Until you make peace with who you are, you'll never be content with what you have.**
>
> Doris Mortman, author

The Free Spirit. Doing what is exciting, interesting, or fun are the primary criteria directing your behavior. As a result, much in your life is left undone, causing a ripple effect of disorder and disharmony. Learn to value the dreaded word *discipline*. It is a part of maturity. You'll actually have more fun if you weave it appropriately into your spontaneous life.

The Rusher. Your life is full of demands, and you move spontaneously from activity to activity, hurriedly trying to accomplish much but often sacrificing quality for speed. For you, the word is *focus*. Do less. Tend only to what is really important and stick with it till done.

The Pleaser. You choose activities based on what pleases others and their needs. As a result, you don't accomplish many of the things that are really important in your life. The word you need to focus on is *self-fulfillment.* At first this may seem uncomfortably selfish. But you don't want to neglect the God-given reason for the unique talents you have.

See a lot of yourself in one of these styles? Don't be afraid to change. Modifying a few characteristics like these will not destroy your unique nature. It will enable you to develop the valuable parts of yourself more fully—benefiting not just you but others too. That is a formula for happiness and fulfillment in life.

battle boredom and lethargy

Often on the Messies Anonymous website, forum participants express that finding the motivation to just get up and do a job that needs to be done is the biggest challenge. After that, the actual tasks seem simple.

Let's face it. For most of us, housekeeping is not an exciting, can't-wait-to-get-started task.

Some people don't seem to mind doing routine tasks. Others, however, can hardly drag themselves to wade through folding a basket of clothes, emptying a dishwasher, or cleaning a toilet. Because these tasks will start coming at us again soon after we accomplish them, for some of us they seem as tedious and pointless as spooning water out of the ocean. Many of us work best only when we're "inspired," and housework rarely rises to that level.

> Nothing is so exhilarating as finishing up a previously uncompleted task.

So one undone task after another piles up. Looking at the magnitude of the job, the uninspired person is more listless than before. A recipe for failure is brewing.

An Exciting Antidote

Blast boredom! Eliminate lethargy! They're stumbling blocks that hinder organizing plans, no matter how well intended we are.

Consider the problem of low adrenaline. Having little adrenaline often makes the difference between someone being a go-getter or a slow-getter. But adrenaline can be boosted!

William James, the famous psychologist, says, "Nothing is so fatiguing as the eternal hanging-on of uncompleted tasks." The reverse is true. Here's what I say: Nothing is so exhilarating as finishing up a previously uncompleted task, or to put it more simply: Wow! I did it! I finally did it!

Tricks for Success

By stimulating ourselves with goals, and the happiness of achieving those goals, the downward spiral turns upward. To start that upward spiral, try the following tricks. They will help you become more interested in doing what needs to be done, boring or not.

> Success comes in cans. Failure comes in can'ts.

Put on stimulating music. Polkas, marches, rock, whatever happy music gets your blood (and adrenaline) flowing. Knowing there is an end to the music also encourages you to get the job done quickly.

Make a commitment to complete the job by telling someone your deadline. Maybe they can join with you in a buddy system. Or start an accountability group with several friends. Put money in a winner-takes-all pot that will be forfeited if you don't get the job done. The pressure of being accountable will stimulate your spirits. Sometimes people call a friend or place a fifteen-minute challenge at an online support group chat room, like the ones at www.messies.com. Promise to get back in touch, either by phone or email, to report how you've done. Then do it!

Change your thinking. Tell yourself that although this part of the job is boring, it's part of a larger and exciting project—transforming your cluttered home into an organized oasis. Still not convinced? Listen to something motivating that will guide you through transforming your thinking. I recommend the audiotape *Create Your Dream and Live It* at www.messies.com.

Reward yourself for finishing the job. Plan to make a special long-distance call, take a friend to lunch, treat yourself to a body splash or piece of costume jewelry, or whatever makes you happy, as a reward for a completed job.

Attach a boring job to something you enjoy. For instance, borrow or buy a book on tape and listen to it only when you're filing, cleaning the kitchen, dusting, or doing whatever boring chore you've been avoiding. You'll be excited to get back to it the next day to see what happens.

Set up an automatic routine that includes the boring job. Commit to a routine of three or four "boring" jobs (like making up the bed, taking out the garbage, handling the

It takes less energy to be successful than to be a failure.

Dennis Waitley,
psychologist, author, and motivational speaker

mail, and folding laundry) first thing every morning. That eliminates the extra energy drain of having to make a daily decision of when, or if, to do tasks you know need to be done. When you make the commitment, habit takes over and gives a boost. It surprises some people to learn that you can be committed to jobs, not because you like the job itself but because you like the result.

Finally, if possible, get help. Consider hiring someone—a professional house cleaner, a teenager, or a family member—to do some jobs you really despise. The energy and time you save may allow you to focus on something that will provide an even bigger benefit to your family. You may even find that when you work alongside someone else, the job is much easier and less boring.

recognize the time realities of modern life

Why are we so rushed and pressed for time? It seems that fifty years ago people had more time for family, hobbies, visiting with friends, even rocking on the porch. They had a general ease of life. Even just decades ago people seemed less stressed and less hurried. What is going wrong?

While we weren't looking at what was slowly happening in society year after year, little time-stealing rascals began sneaking in, ruining our efforts at sensible time management. Now, thanks to a swarm of new inventions and demanding societal changes, no matter how hard we try to simplify, our lives are inexplicably short on time.

But you *can* break free from many of these greedy, modern, time stealers, like:

> **A habit cannot be tossed out the window; it must be coaxed down the stairs a step at a time.**
>
> Mark Twain

- *Hanging on hold.* Sometimes there is just no way around it. You're afraid to hang up the phone for fear of losing your place in the customer service line. You may have a chance to leave a message, but you're concerned that they won't return your call. Besides, you have all that time invested in the waiting already.

No matter how hard we try to simplify, our lives are inexplicably short on time.

Three Ways to Keep Time on Your Side

You can put off your urge to procrastinate if you simply

- ***Post action-urging reminders.*** In areas where you're often tempted to let chores pile up, place notes such as "Do it now" or "Put these away." Need more encouragement? Add to your little sign the positive consequence for your quick action or an empowering Scripture verse.
- ***Commit for a week.*** Choose one area of weakness, like making the bed, emptying the dishwasher, or swooping the toothpaste tube back to its proper place. Then vow to do it quickly for a week. After that trial period, consider whether to continue the commitment until a productive habit is cemented.
- ***Set deadlines for yourself.*** You'll urge yourself to action if you follow through on unpleasant consequences, such as: "If I don't plant this plant this week, I am going to give it away" or "If I don't pay this bill today, I will burn a dollar bill."

Be brave! Leave a message. Better yet, see if the company has a website and send an email to customer service. Then let your email in-box do the waiting for you.

> **We are what we repeatedly do. Excellence then is not an act, but a habit.**
>
> Aristotle, philosopher (384–322 BC)

- *Reading complex owner's manuals.* Most new gizmos come with a quick-start guide that describes all we'll ever need to know. Don't buy into the warning on the box demanding that you must read the entire manual before using your new time-saving gadget. Glance at it for the parts you need and note the safety info. Usually that demand is more for the company's protection than yours. (Ignore this bit of advice if you are skydiving or handling dynamite.) Just be sure to file the complete guide for reference later.
- *Driving long distances unnecessarily.* If you're driving across town for appointments with your hairstylist, dentist, doctor, or other service providers, consider finding professionals closer to home.
- *Ferrying kids to organized activities.* Instead, strive mightily to do the car pool thing, sharing chauffeuring responsibilities with another adult. Get older, responsible siblings to do some of your driving. Or engage the grandparents if you can. Depending on where you live, older kids may even be able to use public transportation.

- *Having to become a technician.* I never dreamed I would find myself fixing the printer on my computer, hooking up the cordless phone, and trying to solve complex computer glitches. In the "old days," professionals hardwired the phone into the wall and you took a broken appliance to the local fix-it shop. Seldom, if ever, was "some assembly required" on things purchased for the house. If you're wasting a lot of time assembling things, stop buying things that need assembly. If you're trying to fix or install mechanical items, consider calling an appropriate professional to do the job for you. The money you spend may actually be a savings in the long run.

A nail is driven out by another nail. Habit is overcome by habit.

Desiderius Erasmus, sixteenth-century philosopher

- *Watching TV or surfing the Internet for hours.* You'll be amazed at the free time created by turning off the television, the mother of all time wasters, and her sleek, even-more-modern sister, the computer.

You leave old habits behind by starting out with the thought, I release the need for this in my life.

Wayne W. Dyer, author of motivational books

Did You Know?

- About 90 percent of children who lived within a mile of their school walked or biked to school in the 1960s. Only 31 percent do so today.
- About 30 percent of morning traffic is caused by parents dropping kids off at school.

Think of your life. What are the time stealers that are carrying away precious minutes from your day? When you added them to your life they seemed so innocent and necessary, but now they're working together to leave you time starved. Kick them out, and start living peacefully again!

Nothing so needs reforming as other people's habits.

Mark Twain

be patient with yourself and the process

When you're trying to upgrade or change your methods, you are truly a work in progress. You may get a great idea for how to organize something, and it may flop badly. Or you may try something for a while and later think of a better way. Sometimes it requires a lot of patience to get through the process of halting and backing up.

Evolving Methods

For example, I decided to keep a record of the paints used in each room of our house. That way, if I wanted to get more paint for repainting or repair, I would have the information I needed. I had several inventive ideas—in the end, none worked well for me.

Don't give up if a method doesn't work. Try others until you find one that fits your style.

My first plan was to tape the brand and color behind the light switch plate. But that made it too troublesome to check.

Then I decided to keep the information on a card in a Rolodex card file under "Paint." That was okay, but later I decided it fit better in the "Household" section of my files.

I also dipped paint-stirring sticks in the paint, labeled them, and stored them in the utility room, as instructed by Martha Stewart. But having so many methods made it hard to remember which method had the most complete record. As it turned out, I recorded some of the paints using one method and some using another.

A friend of mine puts the leftover paint (probably in a smaller container than the large cans) in a closet or storage area of the room in which it was used. This idea is beautiful in its simplicity.

One time I purchased an impressive time-management notebook, then promptly found it too complex for my needs. I was also afraid of losing it. So I abandoned it for a very small notebook and one piece of paper with telephone numbers on it. I tucked both in my purse and hung a large calendar showing the whole year (from an office supply store) on the back of a door.

Obviously it's better to get one great method and stick with it from the beginning. But if you find yourself flip-flopping for a while, be patient as you search for the method that is best for you. Eventually you'll find one you can live with happily. Just don't give up if one particular method doesn't work. Try others until you find one that fits your style.

Perhaps you have the kind of personality that propels you to change systems just because you enjoy a fresh approach. That's okay too. If you get bored with one method and desire to try something new, switch methods without feeling guilty or wasteful. Just try to limit fresh starts to no more than absolutely necessary, so you don't lose valuable information or miss a step in the changeover.

> Do not fear the winds of adversity. Remember, a kite rises against the wind rather than with it.

Toss Destructive Thoughts

Gail was making every effort to improve the condition of her house. Somehow it wasn't working. She worked hard to tidy and clean consistently. But as she looked around, she found she was doing too much work for too little result. There must be a leak in her system somewhere, she told herself.

Gail was right. The leak was at the source of her efforts—in her own mind! She harbored certain destructive thoughts as she moved around the house. They were the source of her continued frustration and failure.

What were the thoughts that slowed her progress? Read on. These probably will sound familiar:

- *I'll get back to that later.*
- *It's not all that important.*
- *Things don't have to be perfect.*
- *I'm too busy right now.*
- *I'll decide on that when I have more time.*

The truth is, Gail is impatient, and her impatience keeps her house disorganized, despite her effort to tidy it. Eager to be on to the next task, she skips details. And she uses the destructive thoughts to give herself permission to move on, leaving jobs unfinished. Along the path of her hurried efforts, she leaves a trail of uncompleted tasks and clutter.

But Gail—and the rest of us like her—can succeed in her quest to get organized. And the key is far simpler than most would ever imagine. We must simply replace destructive thoughts with action-supporting thoughts like:

> The solution will not come in a day, but it must come daily.

- *Do it now!*
- *Never leave it till it's done.*
- *If you get it out, put it back—now, not later!*

True, it's tough to break mental habits. But you can do it. Think about those mechanical gopher heads that are part of the children's arcade game—the ones you bop with a mallet as soon as they pop up. Treat your destructive thoughts the same way. When one pops into your head, bop it as fast as possible with the opposite, action-supporting thought.

With this treatment, those gopher heads will get discouraged and stop appearing. And your home, like Gail's, will take on a new look.

get mad at the mess

Becoming fed up with the junk, the struggle, and the whole insane way of life we have created for ourselves is often what it takes to push us into action.

In my case, when I finally came to the last straw (after many straws that I should not have endured), I was, at last, willing to break old habits, like keeping too many things and procrastinating. It was not until I was angry about what clutter was doing to me that I was able to abandon old traditions and standards that had woven themselves into my identity. It was soul wrenching at first, but it was necessary.

Consider this confession from a self-proclaimed chronic Messie who benefited when she finally decided she'd had enough and wasn't going to take it anymore:

> My room, as a teenager, had a clear path from the door to the bed, and that was about it. This pattern repeated in my adult life, and continued after I got married and had my own office in our apartment.
>
> When we moved to a town house with twice the square footage as our apartment, I knew that unless I got my mess under control (both in the house and in my mind), nothing would change.
>
> I'd rationalized over the years that I would clean up and make a trip to the Salvation Army to donate things that were

> **Do not keep anything in your home that you do not know to be useful or believe to be beautiful.**
>
> William Morris,
> nineteenth-century poet and philosopher

still usable. I had to face reality that I was never going to do that. So I just gritted my teeth and said, I just want this stuff out of my life! So into the trash it went.

I'm sure that in the grand scheme of things nobody starved to death or died of exposure because of my decision. Our new house is much roomier. And because we threw away 75 percent of our possessions when we moved, it's been wonderful having much more open space!

Linda

Good for her! Not only did she discard her possessions, but she surrendered her commitment to donating her things to charity, because it was holding her back. She finally admitted the truth to herself—that donating was never going to happen. Nothing is more freeing than learning to make decisions in the light of cold reality. Linda stepped out of the box of limitations she'd created for herself.

> Nothing is more freeing than learning to make decisions in the light of cold reality.

Is donating to charity good? Absolutely! But when Linda finally faced the reality that it was holding her back, she threw caution to the

Ditch Unnecessary Stuff and Feel Better Instantly!

One visitor to the Messies Anonymous website shared this telling observation about her motivation for—and the instant payoff of—getting rid of not-quite-right garments:

"I've been working on thinning out my closet. One rule I'm using is to get rid of anything I don't like.

"It sounds simple, but I have so many things that are a little too big or too small; or I don't really like the color; or they need to be ironed, and I never do it, so they're always wrinkled; or I don't like the neckline; etc.

"I'm always a little less happy with how I look on the days when I wear one of these not-quite-right things. If there's less in the closet, and I like all of it, it's easier to find something to wear, and I'm always happy with how it looks."

Chris

wind and went against her original plan. So again, good for her! And good for you if you face whatever realities are holding *you* back and make the moves necessary to boldly overcome them.

So get mad at those messes. And become less tolerant too.

Here's what I mean. Most of us tolerate living with things we don't like. Think about one now. Are you picturing it? Chances are it falls into one of these categories:

- A gift someone you love gave you, but, well, you know . . .
- A "mistake" you bought but feel you should keep because you paid good money for it.

- Something you no longer enjoy because your tastes have changed.
- Something that doesn't fit you or the space it's in.
- Something that's broken.
- Something purchased in good faith that turned out to be unsuitable for your lifestyle, like a rice cooker, hot dog steamer, or salad chopper.

If you're willing to move the excess out of your life but find it difficult to actually do it, make your plans specific. Ask an organized friend to help you make decisions about what to keep and what to toss. Set aside things to sell or give away—then give yourself a deadline to do it. If your deadline arrives and they're still sitting, toss them!

> Space is not something to fill with beauty. Space is beauty.

You may find it helpful to take pictures of any items you want to remember but don't want to keep. If actually letting go of the unwanted items proves too difficult, simply place them in storage boxes and set them aside in an out-of-the-way place like the garage. Dip into these boxes as opportunities to give things away arise. On the outside of each box, write a date on which you'll discard what's left.

It's hard to dispose of those things with which we have a love/hate relationship. Our ambivalence keeps us from making firm decisions about what to do with them. But when you finally do what your heart tells you is right, you'll experience a sense of freedom and power.

Start by moving out the things you can part with most easily. As you gain confidence, you'll find the job becomes easier and the pleasure you feel becomes even greater.

always have a backup in the wings

Even the most capable person has times in life when best-laid plans fall through. A natural disaster hits. You become sick or tired (or maybe just sick and tired). Somebody else needs you full-time. You need to work overtime or do a big project. Things get lost. There are conflicts in schedules. Face it. These things happen to everybody.

Save yourself the frustration of trying to solve a problem when you are in the middle of it. You can avoid problems altogether by simply having a backup plan waiting in the wings. Like a Boy Scout, be prepared for the unexpected, so that when it comes—and it will!—you can seamlessly switch over to your backup plan.

Must-Have Backups

To ease the strain when plan A fails, consider setting up for yourself these must-have backups:

- *Old-fashioned "corded" telephone.* Sure, your cell phone and cordless phones are great—when you can find them and the batteries are charged and the signal

Like a Boy Scout, be prepared for the unexpected, so that when it comes—and it will!—you can seamlessly switch over to your backup plan.

is strong. But what about when you've misplaced the handset, or the batteries have run out when the power is off, or the cell-phone towers are out of service? An old-fashioned "corded" phone can save the day! It won't get lost and will still work when the electricity goes off.

- *A battery-backup power strip.* Like any other power strip, this device allows you to plug in multiple electronics, like your answering machine, computer, clock, and the like, all in one spot. But on a battery-backup model, when the electricity flickers off, the battery kicks in and keeps the electronics from turning off. So you won't lose your messages or have your computer crash. Your clock will not have to be reset, and your alarm won't fail to awaken you.
- *Computer files backed up.* "For all the sad words of tongue and pen, the saddest are these: 'It might have been,' " wrote John Greenleaf Whittier. And in no instance are these words more heartfelt than just after a computer crashes, taking your data with it, and you realize how long it's been since you made a backup copy of your work. At the beginning of each

Lack of planning on your part does not necessarily constitute an emergency on my part.

> **I am a great believer in luck. I find that the harder I work, the more I have of it.**
>
> Stephen Leacock,
> Canadian humorist and essayist

month, or preferably much more often, use whatever backup system you have devised, so you can avoid those dreary four words.

- *Fill-ins for you.* It's wise to keep your eyes open for personal and household help that can be your backup should you ever need it. Make a personal backup list that includes a handyman, house cleaner, lawn service, and the like. Watch for a high-school student who may be willing to help with chores around the house on a regular basis. Should you need help in the future, you'll already know whom to call.

Alert! Warning! Having a backup doesn't mean you keep on hand eight staplers, ten glue sticks, or an abundance of any other item, just because you can seldom find what you need when you need it. That is an entirely different problem and is solved by having a sane and usable storage system. Remember, order is maintained by rigidly following the queen of all habits: When you get it out, put it back! Now, not later. ASAP!

More Must-Have Backups

You'll save time and avoid frustration if you simply keep the following backups handy:

- *Nonelectric can opener.*
- *Disposable plates, cups, and utensils.*
- *A spare car key* hidden up under the chassis in a magnetic key container.
- *A spare house key* hidden outside where only you can find it. (No, not above the door!)

> If you've made up your mind that you can do something, you're absolutely right.

- *Your list of often used phone numbers* tucked in your purse for quick-and-easy reference.
- *An extra phone book* in the car for last-minute changes in schedule.
- *A standard plan for where lost children should meet you* if you should get separated. For example, older children meet at a central place, like the entrance; small children go to any adult behind a counter or in a uniform.
- *A photocopy of all the credit cards and important info* in your wallet, in case it's lost or stolen. Keep the copy at home.
- *A flashlight in a central location.*
- *A battery-powered, plugged-in emergency light* that automatically turns on when the electricity goes off. It doesn't illuminate the whole room, but it does give enough immediate light to help you find your way around.

simplify your solutions

If a simple solution can meet your needs, by all means, embrace it! Think KISS—keep it super simple. You'll make moving toward a more organized life easy if you KISS your way to order. Here are some ideas:

- *Do less laundry.* Pass out one towel per person a week. Change bedsheets every two weeks or more. Wear clothes more than once, when you can. (Slacks, skirts, and lightly worn tops often can be worn several times between washings.) Redirect children who want to change clothes (and towels) more than is needed.
- *Wear glasses that darken automatically in the sun.* My path was strewn with lost sunglasses before I changed over to a prescription pair that turn dark in sunlight and become clear again in the shade.
- *Cover your bed with a comforter or thick quilt.* A fluffy topper hides a multitude of wrinkles underneath. Perfectionists, especially, spend too much time trying unnecessarily to straighten the sheets and blankets. The main question is whether it "passes" as a made bed. In bed making, a C grade is good enough.

Think KISS—keep it super simple.

- *Cook with nonstick cookware, and replace it when it starts to stick!* It cleans so easily. Sometimes all you have to do is swipe it with a little soap and water and put it back. It's far easier than putting it in and taking it out of the dishwasher.
- *Avoid complicating your life with "innovations" that don't work for you.* For instance, I tried the rechargeable-battery approach. It promised all good things. I approved of the savings and the ecological benefits. The only problem was that I never was able to use it. Remembering which batteries needed charging and which didn't, and where each group was kept, was just too complicated for me. Undoubtedly many people do it easily and can't understand what my problem is. I don't fully understand it either. The only thing I know is that for me buying already charged batteries is the best way (no, the only way) to go.

There is no greatness where there is not simplicity.

Leo Tolstoy, author of *War and Peace*

Sometimes the simple solution means giving up a complicated organizational trick. I confess that in my pursuit of order I tried keeping my spices alphabetized. I quickly found it more trouble than it was worth. There were numerous occasions when I have overorganized, only to abandon my system for something more effective and easier.

The Miniaturizing Concept

Unless you have a very large house with broad expanses to be filled, whenever you can find a smaller appliance, tool, or anything that takes up limited space, select the smallest one adequate for the job. For most of us, finding enough storage space is serious business. Let a consistent and careful commitment to the concept of miniaturizing come to the rescue!

Become Mini-Wise

You'll simplify—and free up loads of space—if you miniaturize whenever possible. How? To get started, consider downsizing your

- *Christmas tree and ornament stash.* One of the smartest moves I ever made was to buy a two-foot artificial Christmas tree with lights already evenly distributed on the branches. Each year I pull it out of its compact box, fluff the branches, and it's ready for decorating. It needs fewer and smaller ornaments, so they take up less storage space, and I spend far less time trimming the tree. Placed on a pedestal table with gifts rising up from the floor, it makes a very fine Christmas presentation indeed, if I do say so myself.
- *Bakeware.* My muffin tin makes only six muffins. That's plenty for Ivan and me. Previously I used half of a bulky, twelve-muffin tin that took up too much precious space in my cramped kitchen. Eventually I woke up to the fact that there were muffin tins with only six cups. An unexpected advantage is that the smaller tin fits nicely into my economical toaster oven.

- *Appliances.* Speaking of toaster ovens, we need a new one. Ivan wants one big enough to roast a turkey, even though our counter is small, and I haven't roasted a turkey or anything like it in years. But I am holding out for (you guessed it) one just large enough for toast and muffins.

> **Beauty of style**
> **And harmony**
> **And grace**
> **And good rhythm**
> **Depend on**
> **Simplicity.**
>
> Plato, Athenian philosopher (427–347 BC)

Coming Clean about Laundry

Think you're doing a lot of laundry and cluttering up your laundry room with too much stuff? You're probably right. Consider these facts from the Soap and Detergent Association:

- Women do 88 percent of the laundry.
- More than six thousand garments are machine washed each year in the typical home.
- The average consumer has eight laundry products in the laundry room—three types of detergent; one container of bleach; an oxygen-powered, color-safe bleach; two fabric softeners (a liquid and dryer sheets); and a stain remover.

wrestle that email to the ground

You step away for five minutes from your computer, where you've been striving to answer your email. When you return, you have eleven more messages stacked up in your inbox.

Email has the potential of being your biggest time-saver and friend.

Email is often a major source of frustration and wasted time.

Why the paradox? While email can make life easier by bringing you valuable information quickly, most of the time there's just too much of it! And so much of it is unnecessary!

Like a runaway steer, "that thar thing" has got to be controlled. So let's jump on the problem right out of the chute and wrestle it to the ground. Here are some of the ways you can take control:

- *Corral the junk before it gets to your screen!* If you're not using a good antispam software, statistics suggest

While email can make life easier by bringing you valuable information quickly, most of the time there's just too much of it!

that most of the email you receive is the electronic equivalent of junk mail. Your local office supply or electronics store should have a vast selection of software that can easily help you eliminate spam from hitting your inbox. Tip: Don't respond to spammers' messages, even to ask them to remove your name from their lists. That just spurs them to continue spamming you, because they know you're actually looking at the email.

- *Ask friends and family to stop forwarding messages.* It's nice that they want to pass along "cute" or "important" messages. And a lot of the information they send is good, I'm sure. But it's not good for you to have to deal with all of it. So just get up the nerve to send out a polite request to people in your address book. They'll get over it. And you'll be amazed at the time you save when you no longer feel compelled to open and read all of those messages.
- *Delete with enthusiasm.* Spammers are masterful at thinking of ways to make you think they are writing an important personal message to you. But if you don't know who sent a message or can't decipher what the subject line is about, press "delete" in a heartbeat. Whole groups can be deleted with one swipe, if you learn how to do that trick on your computer.
- *Take care of easy responses first.* Go to the email that can be dealt with quickly. If you can respond in just one or two lines, with thirty seconds of typing, do it! Get it off your radar. Get it off your screen. Get it off your plate. Then move on.
- *Write less!* You don't need to make each email your finest example of information sharing, wisdom, and prose. Just keep the conversation moving, writing quick

Email Clutter

Email is a kind of modern clutter prevalent both on home and business computers. A typical business user spends over two hours handling email. In businesses, 53 percent of users check their emails at least six times a day and 4 percent check it constantly all day.

responses. Stop composing the next great novel and burst out of the chute, or that steer will get away from you. If you've been waiting to respond to certain messages until you have enough time to do it properly, grab that bull by the horns, type an adequate response (not the perfect one you'd imagined), and move on—guilt free! By writing shorter messages, you'll save time for those who receive them too. A former agent of mine often responded to information I sent with a one word message—Noted. Now *that* is a quick response.

- *Don't catch the same steer ten times in a row!* You're bound to receive emails that could all be answered with the same response—questions such as, "So how are all of you? Tell me what's been going on!" Don't type the same lengthy responses over and over. Imagine the time you'd save if you kept an up-to-date response for frequently asked questions, ready and just waiting to be sent out. Then you can use it whenever you need to, without having to rewrite the same information over and over again. Just write a good, generic, informative response—a kind of template—and save it in a place where you'll remember to use it. When you need to answer that kind of question again, simply pop open the template you've created, copy the bulk of the message, paste it into the email you're composing, and top it with an appropriate introduction. That will save you from retyping the same information over and over. Whew!

> **We get rid of clutter to make room for fulfillment.**
>
> Sandra Felton, The Organizer Lady

- *Save important messages to specific folders.* If you must save them, at least free up your inbox as a place that's just current information that needs to be handled.
- *Read what came in last, first.* It can save you oodles of time. Here's an example: I recently received a request to send a picture for media purposes. Later in the day, I received a message canceling the request, as the sender had found one. Because I'd started from the bottom of my inbox (where my most recent email waits to be read), I got to the cancellation before the request. That saved me the trouble of having to think of how I was going to solve the problem. Just figure out where your newest email waits for you, and always start working your way through it—newest to oldest.
- *Turn off the "auto-check" feature.* This is the one that checks your email and downloads new mail regularly, as often as you've commanded. Downloading frequently is important for some people who use email in business and have to know as soon as new messages come in. But for some of us, the notification that new email is waiting is too tempting to ignore, even if we don't *need* to check it right away. Computer experts who advise on boosting productivity tell us that if we don't have to have notification every time a new email is

received, turn off the features that download it automatically and notify us instantly. Choose instead to download and check email when it suits *our* schedule.

If you can't move the mountain, move a few stones.

Email will keep coming out of the chute. And that's good—much of it can make our lives easier. Manage it wisely, and you'll turn your computer-time rodeo back into a joyride.

At last count, studies suggest 30 to 62 percent of all email is spam. And though we can easily delete unwanted messages, the trouble is, we can't delete the cost. Experts at the Coalition Against Unsolicited Commercial Email (CAUCE) point out that spam costs businesses and consumers an estimated eight billion dollars a year. That's because all that spam costs Internet Service Providers, who have to buy more bandwidth to handle it all. So their fees go up. And spam overload often causes computer crashes, the CAUCE experts say, resulting in lost business opportunities, time on the job, even valuable information that must be re-created. How much worse could it get? If only 1 percent of the 24 million small businesses in America send you only one piece of spam each year, you'll hit the delete key about 657 times, CAUCE experts say. Try clicking your mouse 657 times as quickly as you can. That shows how much time is wasted by spam, even when we delete it without reading it.

If there is a better solution . . . find it!

Thomas Edison

day 14

make bold judgment calls

Sometimes the only thing that keeps us from making needed changes is one bold decision. What bold decision would make a positive change in your life? You might gain freedom if you'd

- *Drop out of a group or club.* Sure, you love the people there and they'd miss you, but is the commitment still good for you? Or could you gain needed peace by dropping out, at least for a while?
- *Give up leadership positions.* Can't bring yourself to drop out completely? Then just leave behind time-consuming leadership roles. Give somebody else a chance to do the job. You can take it up later if you want to.
- *Schedule one less sport or activity for your children.* Spend your extra time in a stay-at-home family activity, such as a weekly game night or reading-aloud-together time—anything less stressful than running around.

> **Your life becomes better only when you become better.**
>
> John C. Maxwell, leadership guru

- *Give up addressing Christmas cards by hand.* Instead, create a mailing list that will allow you to print sheets of mailing labels or print the addresses directly onto the envelopes. I did that for the first time this year, and I won't go back to the handwritten approach again.
- *Stop sending Christmas cards.* Okay, I know this is controversial. But if you're just too swamped at Christmastime, I think it's perfectly acceptable to send greetings at Thanksgiving, Easter, Valentine's Day, or some other holiday instead. The bonus: your friends and loved ones will have more time to focus on your card at one of these less busy times of the year.
- *Toss all mail with a bulk postmark—unopened!* We have to give up the curiosity that nudges us to spend valuable time on the interests of somebody else (in this case, the company that sent the mail). I have a friend who says, We are not bulky people, so we don't need bulk mail.
- *Keep only one-quarter of your knickknack collection on display.* Knickknacks are dust collectors. Pack away three-quarters to be rotated back out on display later, maybe as the seasons change. Using this system, you'll appreciate them all the more. And you'll be less of a slave to dusting them.

What a Waste!

About 44 percent of all junk mail is thrown in the trash, unopened and unread. About 40 percent of the solids in our landfills are made of paper and paperboard. That's expected to climb to 48 percent by 2010.

Stop Junk Mail

To remove your name from national commercial and nonprofit organizations' lists, write to the Direct Marketing Association (DMA), an organization representing more than three thousand direct-mail firms, service organizations, retailers, publishers, and catalog companies. Your name will stay on a no-junk-mail list for five years.

Just send your name (all the variations you use) and mailing address, with a request to remove your name from all mailing lists, to:

Mail Preference Service
Direct Marketing Association
P.O. Box 643
Carmel, NY 10512

Mail Preference Service
Direct Marketing Association of Canada
1 Concord Gate, Suite 607
Don Mills, ON M3C 3N6

Go to www.dmaconsumers.org/cgi/offmailinglist to register online ($5 charge).

- *Use the potluck system when entertaining.* You make a main dish and dessert. Let the guests fill in with breads, salad, vegetables, appetizers, and whatever else you think you need. This cuts down markedly on preparation and on cleanup afterward. For those who think proper etiquette requires a hostess to do it all, this will definitely be a bold decision.
- *Use paper plates when you need quick cleanup.* To avoid waste, use the smallest-size plates you need for each meal.

Save Time, Money, and Trees

Another great reason to drop your newspaper subscription, if you're not really reading it daily, is that it's good for the planet. Consider this: it takes 75,000 trees each week to produce the Sunday edition of the *New York Times*.

- *Give away unwanted, outgrown, or downright unpleasant items.* Many of these were probably gifts. For the sake of others' feelings, you may want to keep or even use them for a short period. But you did not make a lifelong contract to provide shelter for these things in your home. Bid them a fond adieu and let them bless others.
- *Cancel the newspaper and magazine subscriptions.* I believe strongly in a thriving press. However, we need to think carefully about how we are going to manage the flow of printed information into our homes. Try this: If you see something on the newsstand you'd like to read, buy it. But don't allow great gobs of paper to impose on you on a regular delivery basis. Canceling daily newspaper delivery brought me great relief when I began to seek order and simplicity for my life.

Sometimes the only thing that keeps us from making needed changes is one bold decision.

It may feel strange, at first, to make bold changes. Force yourself to do it anyway. The peace you'll gain will be worth it beyond measure.

day 15

save time and frustration!

Fatigue and time pressure, Mark Twain once astutely observed, have done more damage to families than anything else. It's "the almost universal condition of fatigue and time pressure," he noted, "which leaves every member of the family exhausted and harried. Many of them have nothing left to invest in their marriages or in the nurturing of children."

Wow, what a downer! But Mr. Twain tells it like it is.

Still, there is hope for change. Though we have different pressures than people experienced in his era, we can still make choices that help us manage our time wisely and find ways that are best for our loved ones.

We can make choices that help us manage our time wisely and find ways that are best for our loved ones.

Making the Effort Now

Often we can gain relief from the frustration of wasted time only when we take the time now to put a method in place that will save time later. Here are some ideas:

Set up your phone to use automatic dialing. This is one

of the best time-savers available. Invest fifteen minutes in learning how to program the phone, then enter the numbers you call regularly. You'll be amazed by the time you'll save in the future as you eliminate the need to search for those numbers.

Delete junk faxes. If you have a fax machine, you probably receive lots of faxed messages you don't want. You can easily eliminate junk faxes or ads. (Can you believe companies have the nerve to use your paper and ink to send you their advertisement, in your home, without your permission? I don't want to refinance my house, invest in penny stocks, buy insurance, or do any of the other things those faxers are pushing, and I surely don't want to pay for their unwanted sales pitch! Thanks for letting me vent. I feel better already.) To eliminate junk faxes, scan the fine print for instructions on how to call to be removed from the company's marketing list. This call is usually an automated, toll-free number, and you can complete the process in a jiffy. I have done this many times, and it definitely stops unwanted faxes. As time goes by, however, new faxers, like weeds, will drift in and need to be eliminated as well.

Add yourself to the do-not-call list. You'll save lots of time by heading off calls from telemarketers. To make it illegal for them to call you, log on to www.donotcall.gov or call 888-382-1222. If you register over the telephone, you must call from the phone you're registering. The registration lasts for five years. This won't stop calls from groups like political organizations, survey companies, charities, or companies with which you already do business. When they call, if you'd prefer they didn't call again, ask to be removed from their calling list. If they call again, they could face an eleven-thousand-dollar fine.

Meet with Mrs. Crock-Pot regularly. Take five minutes to plop meat and vegetables into the Crock-Pot in the morning, and by evening you'll have a mouthwatering, time-saving, fragrant meal!

Jot down phone numbers as you dial them. Keep a paper beside the phone, maybe taped to the wall. When you call a number, note it if it's not already stored in your phone's automatic-dialing feature. Why? We often expect to dial a number just once, but often we end up needing to redial. Having the number nearby will keep you from having to go searching for it again.

> Before the reality comes the dream. We create our tomorrow by what we dream today.

Put an end to "quick" fixes. If you find yourself "fixing" something repeatedly, take time to fix it permanently instead. For years, every time I wanted to create a new document on my computer, I had to take the time to change the default font setting to the size and style I wanted to use. Finally I took the time (about one minute) to figure out how to permanently set it to automatically use my preferences. Whew! What a relief.

Look down the road for trouble. For instance, I bought a new front-porch swing, and there was more than a little assembly required. The job entailed fitting slats into a metal frame. Looking back, I see it would have been so smart of me (and not too hard) to have taken the time and energy to weatherproof those pieces before attaching them permanently to the frame. But did I do that? No-o-o-o. In my enthusiasm and, I might also admit, because of a bit of laziness, I put that thing together and hung it proudly. You can guess the rest of the story. Time passed. Now it is weather-beaten, and I will have to go through the time and expense of redoing it or buying another swing. I could have saved myself a lot of aggravation—and time and money—if I'd just taken time to do the job right in the first place.

Snatch the "best" times. Do you habitually schedule wisely? There are good times to accomplish certain tasks efficiently, and there are decidedly not-so-good times. For example, shop when stores are less jammed, avoiding the weekends when students and working people are most likely to be scurrying along the aisles with you. If you live in a big city, it's wise to schedule appointments or errands when it's not rush hour.

> Ideas become real at the point of action.

Scheduling Strategies That Save Time

Consider the time you waste whenever you're forced to stand in a long line or watch the minute hand sweep along the clock while you sit in a waiting area. Now, imagine how much more free your schedule would feel, if you could reclaim those lost, unproductive minutes. How would you spend that "found" time? Relaxing with loved ones? Immersing yourself in a hobby you love? Taking a few moments just to do nothing, with no pressures and no rush? Ahhhhh!

You can prevent your time from being unnecessarily wasted and reclaim those minutes. How? Simply employ these wise scheduling strategies with

> The difference between good and great is a little effort.

Doctors and dentists. Request the earliest appointment of the day, before the office's schedule for the day is out of whack. The first appointment after lunch is a good bet for being on time too, but the doctor may not be as refreshed as in the morning. After school, children mob doctors' and dentists' offices. So if you'd like a short, peaceful wait, that's something to consider too. Tip: If your doctor is a surgeon, request an appointment on a nonsurgery day.

Merchandise returns. Aim to be at the store when it opens. That's when it's more likely to be fully staffed with more-experienced employees—those trained to open the business. If you can't make it that early, at least try to avoid lunch-hour and after-work crowds.

Post office errands. Surprise—don't go to the post office as soon as it opens. Instead, plan to arrive about a half hour later. That way you'll miss the onslaught of early birds who stand in line, waiting for the doors to open. Save even more time by eliminating post office trips altogether. You can order stamps, calculate postage, track packages, and find ZIP codes online at www.USPS.gov.

Hair salons. Again, ask for the coveted first appointment of your stylist's workday. That way you won't be left waiting through unexpected delays and, as with your doctor, you'll get your stylist's attention when he or she is most energetic.

day 16

attend to little things

King Solomon wrote that the little foxes spoil the vines (see Song of Songs 2:15). That wisdom certainly can be applied to the organization of your home. Neglecting one little thing after another insidiously ruins the order you are trying to achieve.

The opposite of Solomon's statement is also true. Doing a lot of small things consistently makes the "vine" of housekeeping flourish and bear a lot of really good fruit. By keeping up with these little things, you'll find an amazing transformation taking place. You will have more time. Your house will be more presentable. You will be able to find things more easily—all because of these small but powerful actions.

You'll begin to enjoy this result when you

- *Keep a list of items that need replacing.* Tally grocery needs on a whiteboard so whoever goes to the grocery store will get everything needed.

  We cannot direct the wind, but we can adjust the sails.
- *Return jewelry to its place as soon as you remove it.* It helps greatly to have enough designated drawers, hooks, or jewelry box space to hold your pieces.
- *Wipe water fixtures right after using them* so they always look good. The bonus: water deposits, soap, and mineral gunk won't build up and take a lot of your time and energy to get them off.

- *Stow empty hangers in a separate part of your closet* as soon as you remove the garments from them. Hang them in a designated spot on the bar or place them on a shelf within easy reach.
- *Serve dinner dishes on the kitchen counter* rather than family style to avoid spills and splatters. You'll save time wiping surface tops, washing tablecloths and place mats, and cleaning up serving pieces.

Neglecting one little thing after another insidiously ruins the order you are trying to achieve.

- *Take an extra moment to clean up quickly when you're in a not-often-cleaned area* of your house. For instance, when you change the times on wall clocks twice a year, take a second to dust the top of the clock. When you retrieve something you dropped on a seldom-cleaned spot on the floor, like behind a heavy bed, make the effort to dust that area.
- *Put a new trash bag in the can* as soon as you take out the filled bag. Otherwise you or others will put trash in the unprotected trash can, or it will begin to back up on the kitchen counter. Ugh! to both of those. Hint: Store a few additional unused trash bags in the bottom of the can for easy access.

List and Save!

About 55 percent of us admit we make a list—but don't stick to it. Simply shopping with a list can mean big savings at checkout.

If you have a history of losing things, take heart. Scurrying to find misplaced objects seems to be built into life these days. In fact, studies show that the average American spends approximately six minutes looking for car keys before going to work each day.

No problem can stand the assault of sustained thinking.

Voltaire

Imagine the time saved by always putting keys in the same place when you enter the house, like on a hook near the door or in a basket "holding area." It would add a half hour of free time to your week and a total of twenty-five free hours to your year!

Not everything you face can be changed, but everything you change must first be faced.

One of the subtle secrets of organized people is that they consistently and somewhat automatically keep on top of such details.

Kick Out the Bag Quickly!

When you pull the full garbage bag from the can, seal it and whisk it right outside without setting it down on the floor or (yuck!) a table or counter. Why? A garbage can is a breeding ground for bacteria. Given the right conditions, researchers say, a single germ can multiply 281 trillion times in 24 hours!

day 17

circumvent predictable problems

Sometimes we ask for organizational trouble by not thinking ahead to avoid problems. We become so used to being insulted and frustrated by the conditions in the house that we begin to think of them as normal and unavoidable.

I used to suffer the same inconveniences over and over again because I never took the time to thoughtfully prepare to make things easier for myself. Finally I admitted that I would not let others do to me what I was doing to myself. This realization propelled me to make changes. Suddenly I could move more effortlessly through every day.

A few proactive steps can save time and work and keep us sailing smoothly in calm organizational waters. For example, you'll head off many predictable problems if you simply:

Sometimes we ask for organizational trouble by not thinking ahead to avoid problems.

- *Buy a manageable bedcover.* You'll avoid having a soiled, messy look to your bed if you buy a duvet with an easy-on-easy-off cover. When your bed needs freshening, you'll be able to pop it in

> **Reflection on a Cleaning Schedule**
>
> I typed out a sheet of what I need to do each day, then a sheet for each room. On these I've put how often I do the jobs for each room, listing "Daily" first and going down to "Seasonal." I am figuring how often I really need to do each job and what cleaning/organizing is needed, making notes to help me remember.

the washing machine effortlessly instead of wrestling with the whole comforter, which may be difficult to wash and dry at home. You'll have the additional advantage of being able to change the mood of your room just by changing the coverlet. Store several for seasonal change.

- *Write storage reminders.* If you split up like items in storage, place a reminder note with each stash reminding you where the other items are stored. For example, you may have sheets in a hall or linen closet and extras in a box in the basement. Tape a note on the edge of the shelf under the sheets, saying, "More sheets in basement on second shelf." And if your stationery drawer won't hold all the envelopes you have, put a note at the bottom of the pile reminding you (or the family member who uses the last one) where the rest of the envelopes are located.
- *Sidestep dirty disasters.* Place soil-catching mats and rugs both outside and inside, so that by the time someone has entered your house, he or she has taken several dirt-shedding steps on floor coverings that catch soil and guard your house from unnecessary dirt. When you pare and clean vegetables, put down a paper towel to catch the parts you discard. When you crop snapshots, sort mail,

Time-Out!

Have trouble keeping track of everyone's appointments, deadlines, and other commitments? You're not alone, but you can prevent scheduling snafus if you simply:

- *Post a family calendar in a spot where everyone can see it frequently.* Use it to record everyone's appointments rather than trying to compare individual calendars. Keeping more than one calendar is like trying to ride two horses at once.
- *Train everyone to record every commitment* on that calendar. Some families use a different color pen for each family member. To keep pens from "walking away," attach them to the calendar with string or Velcro.
- *Block out vacation days* as soon as they're scheduled. This includes time off work, days the kids are out of school, or anything else that can affect your planning.
- *Record final deadlines for projects,* like filing income tax reports or completing a science project. If possible, record interim steps along the way. That will make those deadlines harder to ignore and will make it harder for them to sneak up on you.

or anything else that generates wastepaper, drag a trash can over and drop the paper directly into it.

- *Buy bigger.* When you purchase storage containers for a specific purpose—say for a filing system or gift-wrapping supplies—select larger sizes than you need at this time. You'll probably find you need more space than you expect as you add a little more now and then. And "buy tall" when getting a new step stool for the house. You'll need two or three steps more often than you think. Be careful, though! Don't buy jumbo plastic containers if your only use will be to dump a multitude of unrelated junk into it. In this particular case, smaller is probably better.

- *Be efficient.* Plan proactively by doing things like doubling up on cooking, putting aside some to freeze for a later meal. You'll never be caught again with nothing for dinner.
- *Make and use a workable to-do list.* A long list of unrelated items is unwieldy. I divide a page into quarters, labeling the four parts *Do, Write, Call,* and *Buy.* I learned this from professional organizer Marsha Sims. Then I categorize my tasks, writing each item under the proper heading. Beside each item, I draw a small box, because a box sitting there calls for the action of filling it with a check as the job is completed. Simply crossing the item off the list or putting a lone check mark next to it doesn't have nearly the same power for me as filling an empty space. If I do part of the job but it needs more work, I divide the little box in half, check only the first half, and leave the second half to be filled when the job is totally finished.

You will never change your life until you change something you do daily. The secret of your success is found in your daily routine.

John C. Maxwell, leadership guru

> **It's coming together! I am actually getting much more done. I feel great about being in more control of myself and my life. Things are looking up and are a whole lot more shiny!**
>
> Minnie

- *Call for appointments well ahead of when you need them.* This way you will have a better chance of reserving a time that's convenient for you.
- *Schedule cleaning/organizing time.* It may help to set aside blocks of time or designate "zones" of the house to be done each day. Having a plan helps you stay caught up and helps you avoid the roller coaster of cleaning binges followed by steady decline into disorder. Post a master list stating your plan until it becomes automatic.
- *Set up your house so that cleaning becomes almost effortless.* For a step-by-step guide on making adjustments to your home, check out *Make Your House Do the Housework* and *No Time to Clean: How to Reduce and Prevent Cleaning the Professional Way* by cleaning guru Don Aslett.
- *Set up a meal routine.* Post a list of the week's menus, shopping needs, and mealtime chores for the family, including setup and cleaning afterward. Often the family scatters as soon as the meal is finished because no one has taken time to divide the labor—a serious waste of kid (and husband) power!

abandon extremism

Wanting to do things perfectly, or at least very well, is good. Sometimes. When the desire for perfection becomes a requirement, that's extremism. And that can be a significant hindrance to getting and staying organized. Consider whether you need to abandon the following extremes.

Recycling

My husband and I recycle paper and glass because our city picks it up every week. We also compost our raw fruit and vegetable scraps. But I've learned that it's easy to overdo and try to recycle every stamp-sized scrap and every seed. This puts us constantly on the alert and causes us to make little piles of scraps to be handled later. In the end, it junks up the house and wastes time.

Trying to do a good job of recycling turns into extremism when you save every empty margarine dish for reuse and every pair of old stockings for pillow stuffing. Materials to be recycled pile up in the house, garage, basement, or back porch. This is a problem.

Sometimes friends and family challenge us when we're overdoing something. If yours do, listen to them and change. If you're not that lucky, remind yourself that your house should be a place of order and beauty, not a recycling bin. It is a matter of balance.

When the desire for perfection becomes a requirement, that's extremism.

Regret Avoidance

Don't fall into the trap of being so fearful of regret that you never get rid of anything. Feeling some regret when you get rid of things is an expected, even desirable, part of getting organized. If you never regret getting rid of something, it's a sign you are being too easy on yourself. Avoiding any and all pain interferes with the simplicity of an orderly life.

If you give away or throw away (gasp) some item and start to berate yourself for doing it, say "Yahoo! I'm doing it right!" It's natural to sometimes feel you have made a mistake.

I remember when I discarded an iron skillet—the traditional tool, used by us Southerners, for making corn bread. It had been passed down from my mom. But I had not made corn bread for years, and cast iron is hard to maintain. I didn't want it or need it. Discarding it was a defining moment for me. And would you believe it—the very next day I got a nearly irresistible urge to make corn bread! That's precisely

When we are authentic, when we keep our spaces simple, simply beautiful living takes place.

Alexandra Stoddard, interior designer

> **A man is rich in proportion to the number of things which he can afford to let alone.**
>
> Henry David Thoreau

the destructive game we play with ourselves to keep from getting rid of things we haven't used in years.

My mom, a neat lady who did not struggle with discarding as much as some of us do, once tossed out a watchband from my grandfather's Rolex. Later a jeweler told her the band was valuable. She discarded my brother's BB gun, much to his dismay. But she never seemed to feel regret because she knew that if you don't keep things moving smoothly along on a regular basis, clutter and messes will ensue.

If you play it so safe that you never make a mistake, you are not going to make progress. So accept those thoughts and feelings of sadness as okay, even helpful, on your journey to making your home a better place for you and your family. Your decision making will mature as you progress, and you will eventually learn to make fewer and fewer mistakes.

Niceties

Everybody knows that china dishware is nicer than disposable plates, and cloth napkins are nicer than paper. Everybody knows a handwritten letter is nicer than a printed or (groan) emailed one. We know handwritten addresses on greeting cards are better than computer-generated ones. It's very clear that a well-cooked, homemade meal beats takeout or frozen food. Certainly there are occasions when it's important to go the "nice" way.

Prepare your heart. Pursue your dream.

But don't get stuck in the rut of always defaulting to the "nice" way just because you've always done it that way and have never considered another way. Try shifting to a more casual lifestyle. You just might find it works better for you.

Do You Overdo?

Those who tend to overdo often do it in many areas of life. The result is an unwieldy struggle. It becomes difficult to make decisions, to move ahead on projects, or even to locate things—everything seems to be on hold until the "perfect moment" arrives. You may find yourself holding on to extreme habits like:

- Keeping all receipts—even for the ice cream cone you just ate!
- Saving all schoolwork papers while telling yourself that the children are little for such a short time.
- Holding on to memorabilia and too many toys from the past in an effort to remember the wonderful times.
- Not deleting emails, telling yourself that you will look at them more carefully when you have time.
- Storing all pictures ever taken. As a result, the "keepers" are lost among the bad and just plain ugly.

Wherever you see extremism creeping into your life, take a chance and change. Be bold! Be brave! Be tough on yourself and break out of old ways that feel familiar. Remember, rigidly going to extremes can hinder your progress toward bringing more order to your home and creating a stress-free life.

become your own good mother

Orderliness brings comfort. When the sunlight filters into a clean, beautiful, and organized living room, I feel like a child with a good mother. Someone cares about my well-being and has provided for my needs. Except that now, as an adult, I have become my own good mother.

Perhaps the chief reason that order is so important is that it chases away fear—the fear of being out of control. When I can't manage even the basic daily affairs of my life, my needs are not met and I worry—worry that my finances are in trouble and I may not know it, worry that someone will drop in and I will be ashamed, worry that I will need a receipt or important paper and it will be gone.

The good news? We can whisk away those worries when we simply care for ourselves the way a mother would. If a mother figure were to come to your house today, what

> Today is a gift. That's why it is called the present. Open it carefully, use it wisely, and don't forget to say "Thank you."

> The chief reason that order is so important is that it chases away fear—the fear of being out of control.

would she do for you? Would she clean and organize the kitchen, vacuum and dust the living room, go through the closet and discard old clothes, or reorganize the shed?

Be your own good mother. Go now and do what is needed for yourself. Or hire someone to do it. In one way or another take care of yourself.

You'll be treating yourself as Mom would if you simply

- Buy ahead so you can eat nutritious and tasty meals
- Clean a long-neglected spot
- Organize an annoying area of clutter
- Maintain an adequate wardrobe
- Obtain nice dishes, glassware, and flatware
- Buy what you need to make organizing work

And when the household needs are met so your home supports your needs, follow Mom's advice and indulge in yourself a little. Take the time to

- Soak in a warm bubble bath
- Exercise or take a walk
- Enjoy doing something artistic
- Read a book
- Get a haircut and manicure

> Messiness is a disease of self-neglect.

Warnings of an Organized Mom to Her Daughter

My Dear, whatever you do, don't ever:

- *Put stuff in an unlabeled box or pile "just for now."* That creates a black hole of junk, and you may never see those items again—certainly not when you need them.
- *Bring home things without knowing where they will go.* Think hard about where you are going to put things before you jump for those "good buys" or "cute" items.
- *Save things for undesignated people or events, "just in case."* It's not your responsibility to over-clutter your house to take care of possible future needs of the world.
- *Put unneeded things in needed spaces.* Don't stuff an item in a space just because it fits, like I did when I put old newspapers under the kitchen sink, then had no room for cleaning products.
- *Put off organizing just because you don't feel like it.* Act like an adult and "do the hard thing anyway." You'll be so glad you did.

- Get a massage
- Go to a movie or play
- Visit more with friends
- Get more rest

creep up on tasks

If you find that you are avoiding a job you don't like (I'm GONNA do it! Today I've GOT to do it! Well, maybe tomorrow), you may need to abandon the frontal-attack method. It's not working for you.

Instead, slide slowly sideways into the job. Soften it up, so to speak. Time-management expert Alan Lakein, author of *How to Get Control of Your Time and Your Life*, calls this the Swiss Cheese Method. Punch small holes in the project until it is done rather than attack the whole task at once. Punching small holes in it helps overcome our resistance.

Why We Resist

Sometimes our resistance comes from not being mentally prepared. Perhaps, for example, you want to color your hair with a new product, but you are hesitant because of uncertainties about how to do it. Punch a few holes in the project. You need information. Mostly you need to take a step forward to begin. To prepare mentally

> Punch small holes in the project until it is done rather than attack the whole task at once.

- Buy the product.
- Open the box and read the instructions.
- Call the number listed on the box for advice about how to use the product.
- With this information, estimate the time and tools you'll need to finish the job, once you actually start it.
- Gather the tools.

Do these steps, and then you'll know you can complete the job competently, as soon as you have the time to do it.

Sometimes we're just not emotionally prepared to do a job. For instance, you may need to clean the oven. You know how but hate to do it. To prepare emotionally

- Look in the oven and scope out the dirty spots. Get a lay of the land, so to speak.
- Reread the directions on the cleaning product. Is there enough in the can? How long does it take? Do you need gloves and do you have them?
- Place the cleaning product near the oven. In the near future, when the wind blows right and you have had a good night's sleep, you may find yourself spraying into a dirty oven. Shortly thereafter, with less work than you had dreaded, you will find yourself looking into a sparkling oven.

When we strive for effectiveness and let go of perfectionism, we can achieve excellence.

Beverly Clover

Dread Not!

Shaking the dread that comes with procrastination can make you happier—and healthier—researchers say. It's no surprise that studies show procrastinators feel instantly less anxious and guilt ridden once they get on task. But now studies also suggest that putting an end to procrastination can improve your *physical* health too. College students who procrastinate have higher levels of drinking, smoking, insomnia, stomach problems, colds, and flu, says researcher Tim Pychyl, Ph.D., associate professor of psychology at Carleton University in Ottawa, Canada.

You can use this method with all kinds of projects: making those phone calls you've been putting off, cleaning the rug, straightening a closet, and so on. By getting the information you need, you punch holes in the project, allowing yourself to prepare mentally or emotionally. And suddenly, the task doesn't seem so overwhelming anymore.

Warning: Be careful using this system, or you'll have "project tools" sitting all around the house waiting to be used. Do this with only one task at a time.

Why We Procrastinate

Psychologists and researchers have found procrastinators put off tasks because of one or more of the following:

- *False beliefs.* "I work better under pressure" or "I'll feel better about doing that later." Research suggests the truth is this: last-minute work is often low quality, and procrastinating produces much more negative emotion than just jumping into a job before a dreaded deadline.

- *Fear of failure.* They'd rather be seen as lacking in effort than in skills.
- *Insecurity.* Believing they must be perfect to please others, their forward motion freezes.

Just do it!

Nike slogan

- *Impulsiveness.* Unable to prioritize appropriately, they're often distracted away from necessary tasks to do the unnecessary.
- *Rebellion.* Their refusal to do a job is an angry message to someone else.
- *The pleasure of pressure.* Some enjoy the adrenaline rush of finishing a job, just before it's too late.
- *Depression.* When blue, all options can seem equally difficult and pointless.

day 21

find out where you stand—or fall

You're halfway there! You've finished day twenty of a forty-day program! You've probably made a lot of progress in your quest to become better organized, less stressed, and more at peace with the condition of your home. But you may feel that you still have a pretty long way to go. And that's okay. It's a journey. The path you're on is the right one. You just need to stick to it. Push on! Push on!

Maybe you're wondering, like a child in the backseat of the car, *Are we there yet? How much longer till we arrive?*

To get a better idea of where you stand—or fall—take a few minutes to answer the questions below. Knowledge is power. With the clarity you gain, you'll be better equipped to get back on that path and continue toward your goal.

For each question, circle the response that feels right for you—not the answer you think I'd want to hear.

___ **1.** There are parts of my house I won't let nonfamily members see.

a. strongly disagree **b.** disagree **c.** no opinion **d.** agree **e.** strongly agree

___ **2.** There are disorganized areas in my house that I've put off tackling for years.

a. strongly disagree **b.** disagree **c.** no opinion **d.** agree **e.** strongly agree d **3**. I cringe about how the house looks when unexpected guests knock on the door.

a. strongly disagree **b.** disagree **c.** no opinion **d.** agree **e.** strongly agree

b **4**. I have a hard time keeping up with my belongings. They are often misplaced.

a. strongly disagree **b.** disagree **c.** no opinion **d.** agree **e.** strongly agree

d **5**. I don't have a routine. I do things as I have time.

a. strongly disagree **b.** disagree **c.** no opinion **d.** agree **e.** strongly agree

d **6**. I buy groceries as I need them, or as they appeal to me in the aisle.

a. strongly disagree **b.** disagree **c.** no opinion **d.** agree **e.** strongly agree

d **7**. When I try to organize things, my brain seems to get muddled.

a. strongly disagree **b.** disagree **c.** no opinion **d.** agree **e.** strongly agree

d **8**. Getting rid of things is very hard for me.

a. strongly disagree **b.** disagree **c.** no opinion **d.** agree **e.** strongly agree

d **9**. I have piles of paper sitting around waiting to be dealt with.

a. strongly disagree **b.** disagree **c.** no opinion **d.** agree **e.** strongly agree

e **10**. If I could, I'd like to move out of this house and start all over in another one.

a. strongly disagree **b.** disagree **c.** no opinion **d.** agree **e.** strongly agree

Add up the points as follows: **a** answers, **1** point; **b** answers, **2** points; **c** answers, **3** points; **d** answers, **4** points; **e** answers, **5** points.

10–17 Wow! I'm impressed! Can you come over to my house and give me a hand? Come to think about it, if you are too rigid about keeping order, maybe you need to relax a little, instead.

18–25 You're on a good road and your house works pretty well for you. You have been doing a lot of things right. Keep on making plans and carrying out those plans. Concentrate on the statements that got the highest number and vow to get better in those areas. Upcoming chapters will help you a lot.

26–33 You're pretty average, and that's not bad. Use this test as a chance to improve and help you move your house forward in the specific areas you identified. Upcoming chapters will help you create order and beauty. Pump up your enthusiasm by visiting model homes, carefully designed to have a "lived-in" look that's immediately pleasing to the eye. Be inspired! You can have a home like that too! Keep reading to find out how.

34–41 You have a lot of unresolved anxiety about the condition of your house. You need to take better care of yourself. Address your needs by putting the tips in this book into practice. Check out other books that give a comprehensive plan, like my books, *The Messies Manual* and *Smart Organizing*, or whatever else rings your organizing bell. Commit to a plan and follow it. Any plan consistently followed is better than no plan at all. Tweak your routine to meet your needs as you go along. Keep reading. Keep working. You're getting there!

42–50 You are living a hard life because things are not working for you organizationally. You deserve better. A better way of life is out there waiting for you. As well as keeping up with your reading of this book, it would be wise for you to

- Get outside help from a professional organizer or an organized friend. Google "professional organizer" for personal and online help suggestions.
- List the problem areas you identified in the test, in order of importance to you. Begin working on solutions to those problems right away. Check the contents page of this book and skip ahead, if you need to, or go back and reread chapters that apply most to your current concerns.
- Spend a few moments now in thought about this fact: you may need to make major changes in your circumstances and behavior. If you keep doing the same thing in the same way, you will keep getting the same unpleasant result.
- Investigate further why you are having so much difficulty. Read my book *Messie No More* for enlightenment about why some people struggle with getting organized and others don't. You may find that now you are aware, you will notice help all around you that you overlooked before.

watch those four-letter words

We should bring things into our houses only because we planned for them and because we need them. Sometimes, though, we act impulsively (and therefore contribute to our struggle to create an organized, beautiful home!) because of these alluring four-letter words: *free, sale, cute, good,* and *nice.*

- *Free.* If we don't need something but take it only because we don't have to pay for it, it just becomes clutter.
- *Sale.* No matter how good the buy, if that's the main reason we buy something, we've simply spent money on new clutter.
- *Cute.* Perhaps this is the most appealing of all because it tickles our emotions in a very feminine way. But if it's just cute and not useful, it's still clutter.
- *Good.* Yes, it's a four-letter word too. There are many things at a garage sale, for example, that are "good" for somebody or

> Life is one long obstacle course, and I am often the chief obstacle.

something—Mason canning jars, for example, or a lovely, child-size, velvet dress. But if I don't can, and if I don't know any little girls who wear that size, those "good" items aren't good for me. Bottom line: if they're not "good" for you, don't bring "good" things into the house.

> If you find yourself admiring something that you haven't already determined you need, walk away.

- *Nice.* "Oh, that's nice" is not a good enough reason for bringing more stuff into an already overstuffed home.

Beware of these four-letter words. They'll tempt you and pull your home in a direction you don't want it to go.

If you find yourself admiring something that you haven't already determined you need, walk away. And if one of these

Steal the Power from Four-Letter Words

If you struggle to resist bringing home things that are free, on sale, cute, good, or nice, you're not alone. Trust me! But you can diminish the power these words have over you by practicing resistance to them. So go ahead. Shop! (Another four-letter word, by the way.) And when you see something you love, pick it up, admire it aloud, enjoy it. Then walk away. The more you do, the more you'll be able to resist these four-letter words—and their intoxicating allure—in the future.

> **There is no defeat except in no longer trying. There is no defeat save within, no really insurmountable barrier, save our own inherent weakness of purpose.**
>
> Elbert Hubbard,
> author and publisher

four-letter words pops into your mind, run! Maybe it really is free, on sale, cute, good, or nice. But when you get it home, it will become another four-letter word—**junk**.

More Four-Letter Words to Avoid

- *eBay.* A world of possible clutter—and expense—at your fingertips.
- *Deal.* It stirs up the thrifty side of you. Walk away until it subsides.
- *Want.* Wants come and go. If you really desire an orderly house, ignore those frequent and fleeting wants that add little more than clutter to your home.
- *Need.* Just because you might use it sometime doesn't mean you need it enough to take it home.
- *Give.* Fight that kindly instinct to take things home just because you want to give them away later.
- *Love.* You love many things. Remember, you'd love a serene life more—one that's free of junk and clutter.

do it the easy way

As you move through life, try moving in a continuous sweep, smooth and purposeful, like a dancer on the dance floor. Actually, make it a continuous swoop.

One of the things that sets apart people who seem to be organized all the time, so organized that they seldom, if ever, have to "get this place cleaned up," is this habit. They "swoop" everything quickly back into order, before it gets a chance to become clutter.

Here's a simple example: When you break an egg, swoop the shell directly into the trash, without putting it down on the counter to be moved later. By doing so, you eliminate living with an eggshell on the counter and also save the step of wiping up egg goop! This is the one-step method.

Dancing the One-Step

Not everyone dances the one-step. Some do the two- (or more) step dance. Here's what I mean. I'll use the coffee example again in more detail. When making a cup, some of us

- reach for the creamer
- pour it in the coffee
- set the creamer container on the counter

> One of the things that sets apart people who seem to be organized is that they "swoop" everything quickly back into order, before it gets a chance to become clutter.

- reach for the sugar
- pour it in the coffee
- set the sugar container on the counter
- reach for a spoon
- stir
- set the spoon on the counter
- put away the creamer
- put away the sugar
- put the spoon in the sink
- wipe the counter
- put the spoon in the dishwasher

Whew! What a workout!

It's far easier and quicker to do the one-step, returning the sugar and creamer to their places immediately, in one graceful swoop, without ever setting them down.

I've found that if you put sugar and cream into the cup first, the act of pouring in the coffee stirs it all together, saving the steps of getting, using, and cleaning a spoon. Another step saved!

If you still want to use a spoon, try rinsing and drying it immediately and returning it to the drawer. You'll be amazed by the amount of time that simple one-step process can save.

> There are two kinds of pain in the world, the pain of discipline and the pain of regret. The pain of discipline weighs ounces. The pain of regret weighs tons.

It eliminates the clutter cleanup! You'll never have to go back and "get this place picked up."

I don't know much about dancing, but when it comes to doing the one-step, will you have this dance with me?

More Ways to One-Step

One-stepping things right back where they belong saves time and effort and creates valuable peace of mind. But to put things away quickly, you need to designate a place for everything. After you do that, you'll find jobs are accomplished more easily and won't pile up when, instead of dragging your feet, you

- *Put tools back* in the toolbox or on their spot on the wall, instead of just laying them near the door of the garage or shed. Next time you need them, you'll know right where to look!
- *File papers* in their proper place, rather than piling them on top of the filing cabinet.
- *Shelve videos, DVDs, or compact discs,* instead of laying them on top of the player.
- *Unpack and return your suitcase to storage* when you come in from a trip, instead of wondering, until your next trip, if someone stole your clothes.

> **The bitterness of living in a mess remains long after the sweetness of resting is forgotten.**
>
> Sandra Felton, The Organizer Lady

- *Remove clothes from the washer* before they "sour." Forgive me for suggesting this might happen. I speak here from personal experience.
- *Remove dry clothes from the dryer*—ASAP! It will save you from having to iron so much. Notice *iron* is a four-letter word.
- *Handle all groceries quickly.* This not only helps clear clutter, it's the safe thing to do. You never know when a cold item may have been put in with the canned and boxed goods.
- *Take purchases from the bag,* and put them where they should go. Leaving items in bags is a serious sign that your organizational abilities are grinding to a gummy halt.
- *Wipe the stove* quickly after use. It cleans more easily before the grease and drippings get cold and harden.
- *Slip sandwich ingredients right back* into the refrigerator or cabinet, after you use them.
- *Carry things in from the car* as soon as you get home, rather than making an extra trip out to get them later.
- *Drop junk mail into the trash* (or recycle bin) before sitting down. Some people even put a receptacle for that purpose right by the door, so junk mail never gets any farther into the house.

avoid the quagmire of passivity

In today's world, where most women don't have servants in the home, choosing to do nothing, when work is required, causes significant problems. We could all wish for a time and place when the house was kept orderly and clean by full-time maids, supervised by the lady of the house (that's us!). But it would be a fruitless wish. For most people those days are long gone.

Today housekeeping is a do-it-yourself job. Keeping the house in order is like running on a steep treadmill that never pauses. As soon as the kitchen is tidied, another meal begins. It seems we walk out of a neat living room, only to return to a messy one a few hours later. Bedrooms drift ceaselessly toward disorder with unmade beds and misplaced brushes, clothes, and shoes. Living is a process of progressive deterioration. Or so it sometimes seems.

Some choose a passive way to meet this relentless challenge of keeping an orderly home. But passivity just won't cut it in a world of burgeoning possessions and activities. However, aggressively changing a few activities will make a tremendous difference in the condition of the house.

Whence Cometh This Problem?

> You can't go in your everyday life where you haven't gone in your dreams.

The Bible tells us that "by much slothfulness the building decayeth; and through idleness of the hands the house droppeth through" (Eccles. 10:18 KJV). Adopting a passive approach, with its resulting messes, carries a sense of personal and spiritual failure.

For our purposes, though, let's look at the problem of passivity dispassionately, without moral or emotional overtones. There may be several reasons for taking a passive approach to chores that need to be done. They include:

- *Physical*. People with low-grade physical illnesses, such as low thyroid or anemia, find it hard to get the work done. Often these physical reasons are undetected. These people appear just not to care, but they do.
- *Emotional*. Depression saps energy from and interest in many activities, especially those that are repetitive and unstimulating. And some women who were pressured into work when they were very young may try to show their independence by refusing to work as adults.

> **The chief cause of unhappiness is giving up what you want most for what you want at the moment.**
>
> Zig Ziglar, motivational speaker

> **God, give us the grace to accept with serenity the things that cannot be changed, courage to change the things which should be changed, and the wisdom to distinguish the one from the other.**
>
> Reinhold Niebuhr, twentieth-century theologian

- *Educational.* A child who lived in a messy home or who was never taught how to keep house is at a disadvantage. A child who tried but never did it well enough for the one teaching her learned early on that she is "incapable" of keeping house. As an adult, she may cease to try.
- *Cultural.* Some cultures put neatness at a high priority; others have a high tolerance for disorder. A person from an easygoing society where messiness is no big deal struggles in a neater society where she is considered indolent.
- *Circumstantial.* Some situations make working so difficult that it's hard to overcome the discouragement. It may be a house that's too small, too large, or poorly designed with too few closets. Perhaps someone died and left you a lot of belongings—and you can't bear to part with any of them. It may be the work you do—for instance, farmwork that brings in dirt or a teaching job that requires a lot of papers and supplies. You may be renovating or cleaning up after a flood, hurricane, or some other disaster that makes it all just too much.

- *Familial.* Yours may be an uncooperative family, creating many messes but failing to help with cleanup.
- *Entertainment interests.* Very few people prefer emptying the dishwasher to reading an exciting book. It takes an atomic bomb to blast a child away from the television or electronic game to feed the dog. With the entertainment opportunities in today's world, it takes a lot of maturity and training to develop the kind of habits that we need for an orderly life.

> **Take charge of your life. You are the only one who can—or should.**
>
> Sandra Felton, The Organizer Lady

- *Personal characteristics.* Some people are visually alert and see things out of place. Some just move faster than others. Some naturally have more energy. These characteristics can help a person overcome the temptation to let things slide. But a person who lacks these characteristics will find it harder to build up enthusiasm for work.
- *Mental outlook.* People who stay on top of things organizationally say they would rather do the work than have it preying on their mind. They love to check items off their lists, mental or otherwise. It gives them a feeling of power or happiness. But those who don't keep on top of messes seem willing to bear the burden of fatigue or don't seem to be suffering enough to make change worthwhile.
- *Relationship manipulation.* Sometimes people act passively to annoy someone else by not working. No one

can *make* the person clean up, so he or she has the final "weapon" to use in an ongoing conflict.

> The best way to change is to recognize and tackle the cause of your lackadaisical attitude.

Those who have fallen into a passive lifestyle find it hard to turn the tide and change their behavior toward a more productive way of life. Although they may be convinced, from a logical standpoint, that it would be beneficial to themselves and their families for them to behave differently, when all things are considered, they choose not to make the necessary effort. It takes a great deal of mental energy

"Behave" Yourself to Success!

You choose your behavior. So you choose the consequences.

The condition of your house today is the result of your daily repeated choices. If it's a mess, it's because you've chosen for it to be that way. If your house isn't beginning to change and become the tidy home you desire, it's because you are not changing enough.

I've got good news for you. You *can* "behave" yourself to success. You don't have to wait to *feel* differently or *think* differently. All you need to do is act right and the house will *be* right. And the more you choose to do the right thing, the less it will be a choice in the future—and the more it will become just an automatic part of life.

and positive motivation to alter any habit, especially one as pervasive as this.

But the effort is truly worth it. I promise.

Find Solutions

The best way to change is to recognize and tackle the cause of your lackadaisical attitude. Start by listing the problems that contribute to this pattern of life, and your turnaround will begin.

For instance, if you suspect your health is the root of the problem, see a doctor, get a diagnosis, and begin treatment. If chronic depression is the cause, it's time to face it and seek help. Even natural characteristics, such as a slow way of moving or visual inaptitude (the problem of not really "seeing" the mess), can be overcome, once they are recognized.

Once you are enlightened about what's causing your problem, you can do what's necessary to move into a life of productive activity, making a giant leap toward an organized life!

Is passivity interfering with *your* success? Start thinking now about what you can do to begin moving toward an uplifting and energizing way of life. Today!

embrace old sayings

I don't know about you, but I tend to find clichés a bit simplistic—and maybe a tad annoying. On the other hand, old sayings wouldn't last from generation to generation if there weren't a lot of truth to be found in them. Actually Grandma knew a thing or two that could help us. Let's look at a few clichés that have survived for many years because they contain a lot of wisdom—wisdom that can help you get and stay organized.

A Stitch in Time

A stitch in time saves nine. Can't argue with that one. I personally don't do much stitching, but it's easy to get the picture that if your seam is coming undone, the earlier you sew it back up (or staple it, as a friend of mine did), the less it will continue to unravel.

In the house, the sooner you wipe up a spill on the floor, the less likely someone will walk through it and track it all over the house. The quicker you clear the counter of clutter, the less likely clutter will continue to collect. (Clutter is magnetic, you know, and will attract more clutter to itself.)

If you wipe a greasy stove while it is still warm, you will do less work than waiting until it cools and hardens into gunk.

A Place for Everything

A place for everything, and everything in its place. Though this is a good statement, it would be great if it contained just one more bit of information: the location of the best place for everything. The fact is, to be truly useful, storage spaces must fit the job they were designed to do. For example:

Organized people make it a habit to avoid procrastination.

- *Keep oft-used items close—within arm's reach or at waist level.* Seldom used items may be stored higher or lower. And rarely used items should be in deep storage, like the garage, attic, or basement, sometimes known as archives.
- *Group like items together to make finding them and putting them away effortless.* For instance, all tools should be together, all hair products, all photos, all craft items, and so on. You get the picture.
- *Store items in just-right containers.* Avoid the temptation to use very large containers, unless you are storing a very large object, such as a heavy comforter. When you use a large container to store a multitude of smaller things, they'll fit, but they're not easily retrieved. Once in, they tend to get "lost" and be unused. Small items need to be grouped in smaller containers.

Your level of success in life is directly proportional to your level of planning for it.

- *Label the outside of every container.* At the very least, identify the category, such as children's art supplies. You may find it's worth the extra effort to list more specifically what's inside, so when you go to the storage closet, you (or someone else) can more easily find what's needed. This is especially important for containers holding items we rarely use. Use pictures as labels if your children are young.

Plan purposefully.
Prepare prayerfully.
Proceed positively.
Pursue persistently.

Don't Procrastinate

Don't put off till tomorrow what you can do today. Okay, the limitation of this saying is that it's impossible to do *everything* today. Just thinking about it wears us out! No doubt we're limited by time, energy, and sometimes interest. The question is, which of those many things that we *could* do, should we do?

Organized people make it a habit to avoid procrastination. Some admit staying on top of everything just to avoid the burden of knowing a task is hanging over their head.

Those who are less committed to doing things expeditiously carry the burden of knowing many, many jobs sit waiting to be done. That's not good for them or for the house.

That said, overdoing this old saying can paralyze us. So to apply it wisely, I suggest making a list of ten things that need doing today. Choose the top one, two, or three and commit to completing those tasks. Tomorrow—even today!—you'll be glad you did. And so will others living in your house.

Bulk Up Evening Tasks—Slim Down Morning Tasks

Want to make mornings less rushed? Try shifting these traditionally early-in-the-day tasks to your nighttime routine:

- *Bathe the night before.* It takes some getting used to, if you're in the habit of a morning shower. But it really frees many precious morning minutes.
- *Fix lunches ahead.* But don't wait till too late in the evening, when you're already exhausted.
- *Lay out clothes for the next day.* This is one of the time-savers you can transfer from the morning crunch time to the more leisurely evening time. Make decisions for yourself, and help other family members do the same. Nothing messes up a perfectly good day more than an unwelcome rush of adrenaline that comes when you can't find one shoe or the blouse you need to complete the outfit you're already wearing.
- *Make your top ten list.* Note the ten things you want to be sure to complete tomorrow, so you won't waste time the next day trying to figure out what you need to do and when you need to do it.

Do It Right

When a task is once begun, never leave it till it's done. Be the task, both great or small, do it right or not at all. Applied wisely, this keeps us from leaving jobs half done, with tools cluttering up the house, waiting for us to get back on task.

But if we take "right" to mean that every job must be done with excruciating perfection and in intricate detail, this pithy

> **Our most valuable asset is time, and successful achievers spend this precious commodity more carefully than money.**
>
> Zig Ziglar,motivational speaker

poem will lead us to work our little heads off unnecessarily. Not every job deserves supremely excellent treatment. This is housekeeping, after all, not brain surgery or atomic research.

When we interpret "right" to mean that it's appropriate to give the tub only a quick-but-thorough wipe after bathing, or pick up a few things as we walk by and return them to their proper place, then this ditty will steer us to develop a habit that will, ultimately, save us time, effort, even cash.

Prefer a more modern take on this advice? Here you go: Just do it!

day 26

don't overdo hobbies

Disorganized people are generally wonderful people with many really admirable qualities. And it's precisely these good qualities that often trip us up and lead us into disorder.

The Good Qualities

We are *mentally active* and excited about life's many opportunities, so we tend to try out a lot of different activities.

Because we're *family-oriented*, we want to produce heirlooms and ways to spotlight the people we love and to preserve memories of them.

We are *effervescent,* and as a result, we tend to lack boundaries. We let our activities take over the house, instead of devising ways to keep them under control. We tend to spend more time than we should on them as well.

Being *perfectionists*, we tend to overdo on the buying of products to support our latest hobby. We reason that it's important to have just what we need.

These good qualities often trip us up and lead us into disorder.

We *love to share,* so we keep producing an abundance of items to distribute to others.

We *live in the moment,* so we often fail to take note of how our actions will affect us in the future. For example, we don't think about how bringing all these products into the house, often without adequate storage preparation, will create clutter and disharmony.

Because we are *interested in a variety of things*, we often have several things going at the same time. When we become overwhelmed by tackling too many projects at once, we push unfinished tasks aside. Sometimes, we don't finish them—ever.

We are *imaginative* and can see possible uses for many different items. So we hoard castoffs and unusual items, planning to use them creatively later.

We are *frugal* and often buy products and equipment just because we believe they are bargains.

Keeping Hobbies in Their Proper Place

Perhaps you relish scrapbooking or quilting. Both activities involve piecing items together and therefore encourage the gathering of many items. This opens the door to excessive tendencies. Our good creative juices can flow out of control, and we can find ourselves drowning in pictures, memorabilia, or fabric scraps.

Maybe you enjoy collecting, painting, knitting, decoupage, needlepoint, embroidery, cooking, or sewing. All have their own special supplies and equipment that need to be controlled and organized.

Here's an example of what happens when we let hobbies get out of control. Martha has seventeen scrapbooks—a cross between a journal and a photo album—for her four-year-old, thoroughly documenting ages two through four. Every movement of every day is recorded. Think of the time required!

"The unexamined life is not worth living," the great philosopher Socrates said. I'm sure he never had *this* in mind. He did not say, "The *unrecorded* life is not worth living."

Nice scrapbooks and photo albums have a place. But if overdone, recording activities can become the purpose of the event instead of enjoying the event itself. Sometimes we just need to let it go and savor the moment, without fretting about how we'll remember it. If you love to chronicle life this way, or if you spend lots of time creating other crafts that are meaningful to you, look at the suggestions below. You'll save time, effort, even money; you'll end up with a better result; and it will be more fun.

- *Enjoy enthusiasm—with focus.* What I mean is, don't get so enthused that you take—and keep—too many pictures, hoard quilting scraps, buy an abundance of materials and patterns just because you happen on a "good sale" or something that's "really, really cute." Some people have more paper, scraps, material, patterns, yarn, or other supplies than any two people could use in a lifetime. Every hobby offers the temptation to overdo, and some of us are more likely to give in to that temptation than others.
- *Create an appropriate area in which to work and store supplies.* You can't always put a work-in-progress away. So beware of turning the dining room into a permanent craft area or the bedroom into a workroom. Sometimes, like the camel who takes over the tent once he gets his nose in the door, what you begin as a small, short-term project turns into a bigger project that will take far more time and effort than you'd planned. When you

see that beginning to happen, think seriously about how you can move the work to an out-of-the-way spot, maybe a spare bedroom or the garage. Hint: When a project needs to be put away temporarily, you might try laying out your work on large pieces of cardboard, then stacking them in order on a closet shelf.

> Beware the barrenness of an overcrowded life.

- *Buy only as you see a need.* If you purchase only a short-term supply of materials, as you see the need developing, you will be more sure of what is necessary. The bonus is you'll be letting the store handle the storage. (Why do you think it is called a "store"?)
- *Decide on your needs—before you shop.* Make a list and stay focused on it. If you do, you won't waste money on impulse buying, and you won't have to deal with the overabundance of stuff in your home.
- *Find and use smart storage solutions for your equipment.* Often hobby store clerks can make suggestions. Not only will appropriate storage protect small children from scissors, needles, paper cutters, and other dangerous equipment, but having a place to store your things safely will protect your project from being destroyed by curious little fingers.
- *Schedule a little time each day to reach your goals.* If you have a project that really needs to be completed, imagine how quickly you could make progress and eventually complete it if you simply set aside as little as fifteen minutes a day to work on it. As in everything

else, you can make significant strides over the long run by just being consistent and doing a little at a time.

- *Remember, this is supposed to be fun.* If you get too caught up, and it turns into work, you've gotten off-track. When the fervor to do a good job overwhelms the fun and you find yourself worrying at night and your way of life during the day is cluttered and unpleasant because of your hobby, you need to back up and get some perspective.

Your creative abilities are one of your wonderful characteristics. Just keep an eye on how they are working for you, and make the necessary adjustments. In the area of hobbies, "Easy does it" should be your motto.

let mr. technology help

Technology can be a wonderful time-saver. I highly recommend using it whenever possible to make your life easier. But before you rush out to buy every electronic gizmo you can find, remember, there's a learning curve for any new technology. Choose only those devices that save more time than they take to use them.

For instance, I've known some people who started out using an electronic address book only to abandon it, because the touted time-saver actually made the chore more difficult. Now they're using a good, ol' little black book again.

That said, let's consider whether Mr. Technology might be able to make your life easier. Consider the following:

- *Computers.* If you're comfortable using a computer, it can serve as a time-management reminder tool to help you keep your calendar, to-do list, and much more. I use mine to remind me of birthdays, even though I also have a list posted on the wall.

> Choose only those devices that save more time than they take to use them.

One of the best uses for me has been addressing Christmas cards quickly and easily. I also enjoy being able to print and include a letter that summarizes the year, bringing my friends up to date with what's been going on in my life. That allows me to spend my time jotting meaningful, short personal notes, rather than the tedious task of copying details and addresses by hand. Handwritten is nice, but not nice enough to spend a lot of time on it.

- *PDAs.* Personal Digital Assistants are often known by their brand names, like Palm Pilot and Blackberry. Sometimes they are called pocket PCs. These little technology genies are getting more and more sophisticated. Available with a range of features, they can become the equivalent of a handheld office, with a phone, computer, radio, camera, video player, recorder, and more—all in one! Technology is moving so fast that by the time you read this, PDAs may even be milking cows or mopping floors!

  A man in an airport told me he can do all his work while he travels. Thanks to the features on his PDA, by the time he gets home, he has his work complete and out

Every worthwhile accomplishment has a price tag attached to it. The question is always whether you are willing to pay the price to attain it—in hard work, sacrifice, patience, faith, and endurance.

John C. Maxwell, leadership guru

of the way. And his PDA allows him to be so efficient and plugged-in, so to speak, clients and associates aren't even aware he's not in his office.

An author friend carries her PDA with a plug-in keyboard in her backpack when she travels. She writes as she travels, then downloads her work into her computer when she gets home.

- *Cell phones.* These have become so common, they're now part of the fabric of the lives of many individuals and families. They help families keep up with plans they have in progress. Some include a calculator and calendar. Some now come with the ability to send written "text" messages, surf the Internet, send and receive email, and shoot and send photos. Some even have global-positioning capability.
- *Smart phones.* Home and cell phones are becoming smarter and smarter. For example, some can be prompted to add the last caller to your speed-dial list of numbers, and some new phones can automatically transfer that list from phone to phone using a movable chip. Learning—and using—all the shortcuts available on your phones can save you valuable time.
- *Hands-free telephone headsets.* Headsets allow you to use your phone without holding it to your ear, leaving your hands free to dust, take care of the children, empty the washer, whatever.
- *Call-screening devices.* You don't have to sprint for the

Fast Fax Facts

There are now more than one hundred million fax machines worldwide, and faxing accounts for 40 percent of total telephone expenses.

phone every time it rings. Try screening callers with an answering machine or your phone's Caller I.D. feature, which displays the caller's name and number. Then you can pick up only the calls that relate to your interests and needs.

- *Fax machines or eFax services.* "Get a fax machine," a man once told me and said I would thank him a hundred times for the advice, if I followed it. I did get one, and he was right—it has been invaluable. Other people choose to use a computer faxing system, like the one that can be downloaded and used for free at www.eFax.com. If you do any business from home, I'm sharing this with you so you can thank me a hundred times too. By the way, thanks again, Pete.
- *Navigational systems for your car.* Though it can be pricey, this technology can simplify your life by guiding you smoothly to destinations without getting lost.
- *Digital music players.* Storing your music in an iPod or similar device allows you to carry up to, literally, ten thousand songs in a portable player that's smaller than a deck of cards. And because iPod and other players can be remotely played through any home or car stereo, they eliminate the need to cart around CDs you want to enjoy. If your computer system has enough memory, you can even store (and instantly organize) your entire collection on it.
- *Digital cameras.* Shooting digital photos simplifies

If you work with Mr. Technology on a regular basis, you know how powerful he really is.

your life by allowing you to know, right away, whether you got the shot you wanted. And the camera allows you to delete right away the shots you don't want to keep. There are no negatives to keep up with, and you don't have to go to a store to have them printed if you'd rather print them at home.

- *Scanners.* Using a scanner, you can store snapshots, documents, children's artwork, and much more on your computer, compact disc, or DVD, rather than fill filing cabinets with the hard copies. This will take up less room for sure, and it's useful in some situations. But consider that technology changes quickly. Will you still

Can Your Phone Do This?

Using cell phones to take digital pictures is becoming so popular, 56 percent of people think camera phones will replace digital and film cameras in the next ten to twenty years. A poll of thirty-five hundred women in the U.K. who use camera phones revealed that:

- 20 percent take photos of themselves in new clothing to send to friends
- 18 percent take photos of clothes and shoes in shops
- 15 percent take photos of the sides and back of their hair
- 10 percent use the phone as a mirror to check their makeup
- 5 percent take photos of well-dressed people to copy their look
- 4 percent use their phone as a mirror in a restaurant to check their teeth

have hardware to access those pictures in fifty years? Maybe not. Printed pictures, well-preserved in an acid-free environment, may have a better chance of being available for posterity. Warning: This technology also may seduce you into keeping more snapshots than you should, just because you can. Don't use it to avoid getting rid of poor-quality snapshots that you know in your heart should go.

- *Automatic toll-paying stickers.* If you use toll roads regularly and your state offers an automatic toll-payment device, invest a few minutes in getting that set up in your car. It will allow you to zip through toll plazas, without having to stop and fumble for change.
- *Online bill-paying programs.* If it's available through your bank, this service can organize your bill paying instantly. You'll spend a little time entering basic information. But after that, sending payments for bills becomes practically effortless—and you could easily save forty dollars or more on postage each year.

If you work with Mr. Technology on a regular basis, you know how powerful he really is. Even those of us who are technologically challenged will find we must make him part of our lives, like it or not. So get on very good terms with our friend Mr. Technology, and let him help you make life easier.

focus intently on laundry

Of all housekeeping tasks, two top the list of being difficult to manage when we are disorganized—handling paper and keeping up with laundry.

When it comes to laundry (I'll talk about paper later), it's not the washing and drying that are the problems. With today's modern machinery those tasks are easy. In fact, the ease with which laundry can be washed and dried actually precipitates many of the other problems. Because it's so easy to wash, we

- *Accumulate too many garments*—often because we want to avoid frequent washings. If we had fewer clothes, we'd certainly be more efficient in moving them through the pipeline. But having a lot of clothing ends up being counterproductive and makes a bigger problem because it allows us to go longer without doing the laundry. Pareto's Principle suggests that we usually wear 20 percent of our outfits most of the time. The other 80

> Tell yourself the job is not done until the clean laundry is safely home in drawers or closets.

percent just gum up the laundry process and crowd the closet.

- *Change linens too frequently.* For example, instead of being hung on the towel rack to dry, once-used towels often land on the floor or in the hamper.
- *Change outfits too often.* People in today's world change clothes far more often than in the past when washing was done by hand. A historic school documentary on hygiene suggests students change their underwear twice a week. (Yipes!) We certainly don't want to go *that* far to conserve clothing use, but even fastidious adults should be willing to wear some garments two or three times between washings. And kids may be able to stretch use by changing into "play clothes" when they come in and hanging up dress clothes for another wearing. Kids (even husbands) will often throw clothes and towels, sometimes perfectly clean ones, in the laundry just to keep from making the effort to hang them up. But you can train them—and yourself—to minimize laundry by maximizing wearing time.

And there are more savvy solutions. To cut down your laundry burden, make a point to

- *Sort it out.* Sorting is an annoying task that causes many of us to avoid laundry chores. When we sort clothes that have been in a large hamper, they end up in unsightly piles on the floor waiting their turn in the washing machine.

  But there are easy solutions. One is to wash most of the clothes together in cold water. Some newer products clean even heavily soiled loads well using cold water. If you don't sort, it's important to use a dye-absorbing product to keep lighter clothes from being ruined. These products are available at the grocery store. I use Dye Magnet, but there are several other brands as well.

Another way to end sorting woes is to presort colors as you take them off by tossing them into color-designated hampers—one for bleachable whites, one for light and bright colors, one for darks, and one for delicates. Training your family to toss their clothes into the right hampers could save an hour or more of sorting each week!

- *Be on hold till you fold.* Dread folding, especially when you're facing a mountain of clean clothes? You're not alone—this is, by far, the most common stumbling block to laundry success. But you can make life easier—and more pleasant—if you simply limit the number of loads you do. If that's not possible, vow not to wash a new load of clothes until the one before it is folded. The task will seem far less overwhelming that way.
- *Put clean clothes in their place.* Sometimes, we get the clothes washed, dried, and folded, then heave a sigh

Self-Cleaning Clothes!

Scientists have discovered a way to keep dirt from adhering to fabric, while warding off body odor as well. Garments made with fabric treated with this new substance won't feel any different but can be cleaned with a simple rinse. Dirt—and the water too—will slip right off! The method they're developing was inspired by the perpetually clean, white lotus plant, found in the swamps of Asia.

> Plan the work and work the plan.

of relief that the job is done. Piles sit folded in the basket, on the living room floor, wherever. Items on hangers grace our décor. Say it isn't so at your house!

Try changing your mind-set. Tell yourself the job is not done until the clean laundry is safely home in drawers or closets. Following that rule will save you from loads of unnecessary washing. Why? When clean clothes are put away quickly, they can't be carelessly mixed with dirty clothes in need of washing—a common occurrence in kids' rooms.

- *Stick to a system.* Find a pace that keeps things moving. Decide on a plan that moves you forward consistently. One working mom puts a load in every day as she heads for work. Her husband, who gets home from work before she does, puts them in the dryer when he gets home. Later that evening, they fold and put away together.
- *Recruit 'em young.* With training, your children should be able to do their own laundry by age eight. They'll get into the groove the first time a favorite outfit isn't clean and ready to go when they want to wear it.
- *Attack stains early.* There are two basic kinds of stains—protein and grease. Read the labels of stain treaters in your grocery store and buy one that can wipe out both kinds. Keep it close to the hampers where you toss just-worn clothes. If your stain-treating product doesn't forbid it, treat the stains as soon as you remove the clothes. Not only will this practice make the stains more likely to disappear on the first wash, it will save you from having to search for the stains later—if you even remember they're there.

- *Tame the inside-out monster.* Some clothes come out of the wash inside out because they were tossed into the hamper that way. You'll save time by teaching your family to help you by simply having them turn clothes right side out before tossing them into hampers. If they resist, hang clothes or fold them just as they come out of the wash. The person who wears them can turn them properly and will quickly learn to do so *before* washing. (Note: Some clothes wash best inside out.)
- *Bag delicates.* Tuck stockings and other gentle-care garments in an inexpensive, mesh laundry bag designed for that purpose, then toss them into the appropriate load. That way lace and other delicates will be protected from tearing and twisting. Remember to close bra hooks so they won't snag other items.
- *Get the skinny on towel control.* To cut down on too frequent towel washing, select thinner (and less expensive!) bath towels, especially if you live in a humid climate. The thinner they are, the faster they'll dry. Or use hand towels for drying after bathing because they wash more easily and dry faster.

One Person's Reflection on Training Kids and Reducing Wardrobes

I fold the clothes every evening (when the kids are asleep, and I'm watching the news), then in the morning, they put them all away. I also teach them to put them in their drawers in sets, so everything matches. I'm working on getting rid of a lot of clothes. The less they have, the easier it is.

Blanca

Sound strange? Not really—just smart. You may have seen competitive swimmers and divers in televised sporting events dry themselves using funky looking, small, thin towels. Why? They dry the body very quickly, wring out well, and wash and dry easily. Sold in sporting goods stores, these "swim towels" or "sports towels"—about nine to thirteen dollars—are not luxurious, but used in the home, they can take serious pressure off towel washing.

Some people go to great lengths to avoid excess towel washing. One woman told me she uses a washcloth to dry herself after bathing. I'm not making this up. That certainly would cut down on stuffing the hamper. I tried it, but found I ran out of dry cloth before I ran out of wet body.

Another woman told me that when she was a child, her family used one fresh towel every day. (I recommend one per week, per person.) She has no children but still wants to conserve towel use. So now she drips-dry, she told me. Perhaps she was kidding.

I think you'll find a more satisfactory result by putting the rest of these tips to use. The payoff will be a less cluttered home, cleaner clothes that last longer, and a big savings of time, energy and, in some cases, even cash!

free yourself from the burden of options

One of the reasons we tend to keep so many things and plan so many activities is because, as I have heard people say, "we want to keep our options open." I've also heard this: "I have a hard time making decisions because I see so many possibilities." That's the danger of having too much—too many things, too many clothes, too many activities. We suffer when

- *We pack too much for a trip* because we want to make spur-of-the-moment decisions. We don't know how we will feel like dressing or how others will be dressed or what the weather will be. So we have to drag the heavy case, spend additional time to pack, and take more time to unpack.
- *We keep coupons for things we seldom or never buy* because we might decide later that we want an item. That creates clutter—and for many, guilt, because the stacks of unused and expired coupons suggest to them that they're not being thrifty enough.
- *We collect materials for hobbies and activities* that we will likely never use, but we store them away, just in case we get the urge. We spend money for things we

Do yourself a favor. Set boundaries in your thinking ahead of time, so you won't have to deal with so many choices.

don't use. Meanwhile, the paints and glue dry out, and the supplies clutter the house. By "keeping our options open," we waste money and create the discomfort that comes from disarray.

- *We have too many lipsticks and blushes.* We paw through our makeup drawer trying to find the good among what has become bad. We have colors that don't match our complexion, our clothes, or the current style. Who knows what has dried out or grown bacteria over time? But whether good or bad, we certainly have made sure that we have many choices!
- *We have clothes and shoes in our closets that we never wear*, but we want them in the closets so we can have—you guessed it—options.

Do yourself a favor. Set boundaries in your thinking ahead of time, so you won't have to deal with so many choices. Jettison superfluous stuff. Make your life more "lean and mean." It will be a relief.

At first, as you clear out your "options," the process will make you uncomfortable. But remember, you do not have to gather an

There is no greatness where there is not simplicity.

Leo Tolstoy,
Russian author

abundance of items about you in an effort to be covered, "just in case." If you are doing this, you are carrying an unnecessary burden.

So bite that decision-making bullet. It may help to say to yourself: This item is good, but it is not good for *me* at this time.

From time to time, you will undoubtedly be sorry you got rid of a particular item. That is part of the process and is to be expected. It's even desirable. It means you're doing it right. Take heart in that!

Always follow the Rule of Three: Don't buy a piece of clothing unless you have at least three other pieces to wear with it.

Simplify Your Wardrobe

"I have a lot of clothes, but I can never find anything to wear. Nothing matches!" How many times have you said it? If you're like most of us, you've said it or thought it often.

How does our wardrobe get so full of stuff we don't like and don't wear, leaving us lots of options but none we really like? Most of us fall into the trap of buying clothing only because it's "cute," on sale, or simply fits. But there's a better way—one that will help you get dressed easily for every occasion. Streamline your options!

Stock your closet with items in a few basic colors. Then you'll easily mix and match basic pieces. And you'll always feel pulled together. Black, beige, red, and navy are good choices for most basic pieces. Other colors become popular, then fade in popularity, and can make a once-fashionable outfit look dated.

I choose lots of black and burgundy pieces, adding white for accent pieces, and other colors, like lime green, as they're in style. Your color choices don't have to be the same as mine. But you get the idea.

> No amount of things can fill a hole in the heart.

Allow only a few colors through your closet door. If you strongly desire other colors from time to time, work them in with accessories. Always follow the Rule of Three: Don't buy a piece of clothing unless you have at least three other pieces to wear with it.

The moral of the story is this: Don't cause yourself stress by having too many color choices and patterns in your wardrobe. Buy mostly things that go together—in many different ways.

Don't let renegade pieces invade your color-coordinated kingdom of clothes. Get a plan and work the plan, adding only useful pieces to your wardrobe.

simplify your paperwork

Papers cause the number one problem in organizing because it's so easy to keep them and so hard to manage them. Papers are small and take up little room individually, so we lose sight of how much room they'll take up when they're piled on top of each other. And it's so easy for important papers to become mixed in with unimportant ones—and lost!

The chief problem with paper is there's so much of it. Rather than diminishing the amount of paper, the computer has increased it. Then, of course, there are school papers, newspapers and magazines, receipts, mail . . . well, you know better than I do what you have in your house, piled on the dining room table, desk, or bedside table. How should you handle all this paper? The following four basic steps of organizing are more crucial when dealing with paper than with anything else.

- *Simplify.* Keep only the papers you'll need later. If they can be easily replaced, throw them away.
- *Sort.* Group like papers, such as bills, receipts, bank statements.
- *Store.* Plan a paper pathway, so each has a definite home. Boldly label the spot, file, or container where each kind

of paper will live. Avoid tossing any into the organizationally disastrous "miscellaneous" pile.

- *Systematize.* Develop a routine for handling the papers that enter your home. Set aside a place, time, and method for working with each one quickly and efficiently.

Let's talk about simplifying now. We'll deal with the other *S*s in the next two chapters.

Simplifying, when applied to paper, means guarding against excess. Don't let unnecessary papers into your house. Period.

Because we are curious people who love new ideas, we may be tempted to pick up a pamphlet, for example, on hydroponic gardening techniques in China, even if we never garden, don't plan to, and are not Chinese.

One woman told me she collected information simply so she could be sure to have interesting things to say in conversations. This is a society saturated by electronic, as well as printed, news. Trust me—it's highly unlikely you will ever be information hungry.

Fear of an IRS inquiry makes many of us keep too many papers. And if you're concerned that you're throwing out information you may need later, by all means, give a quick call to your accountant or tax preparer. But otherwise, as often as you can

Paper Clutter

Paper is the biggest source of clutter. Even with computers, the volume of paper has more than doubled since 1995. Although we use only 20 percent of the paper we keep, 90 percent of information is on paper. U.S. businesses spend $25 billion a year filing and retrieving paper.

Discard Papers Expeditiously

Though not all financial experts agree on how long you should hold on to "important" papers, this is a general guide. If you have a special reason for keeping them longer, these may not apply specifically to your case:

Tax returns and records—six years
Real estate records—as long as you own the property
Insurance policies—as long as they are in effect
Bank and investment statements—until tax time
Pay stubs—until tax time
Utility bills—until the next statement comes
Credit card bills—until the next statement comes

Copy, clip, and tape this list to your filing cabinet or wherever your records are kept.

- Avoid bringing home interesting-but-unnecessary papers.
- Toss junk mail in the trash or recycle bin as you sort the mail.
- Cancel magazine and newspaper subscriptions, get your refunds, and buy only the issues that really interest you on the newsstand.
- Toss unnecessary receipts before leaving the store. After all, you are not going to return the hamburger and fries you just bought and ate. Hint: If there's personal information on the receipt, marking through that part with a pen or tearing the receipt into small pieces is a good idea.
- Cancel catalogs.

> **There are many things that will interest you, but only a few things that will excite you. Pursue those.**
>
> Sandra Felton, The Organizer Lady

- Stop the avalanche of "preapproved" credit card and insurance offers by calling 1-888-567-8688.

Follow these tips, and you will immediately reduce the anxiety that excess paper causes in your home.

sort and store your paperwork

Incoming papers can usually be sorted into four categories rather easily. And each category needs its own separate container. Those containers are:

- *Trash can.* The bigger it is, the more likely you are to use it. Have it handy, and fill it with joyful abandon.
- *Read-me file.* Here's where you put things you want to read at your leisure, such as letters from your college alumni association or your favorite ministry.
- *Act-on-it file.* The note from the dentist saying it is time for your annual checkup goes here, along with bills that need to be paid, and other documents that should be dealt with quickly.
- *Save-me file.* Some paper you'll need to keep handy temporarily, like the list of dates for your child's soccer games. Other papers, like the latest car insurance policy, need to be put into long-term storage, as in a file box or filing cabinet.

Commit to dealing with papers immediately, as they come into your home, slipping them right away into their proper spot.

Keeping Them All Straight

How do you sort all the papers? First, determine where you need to do it, then choose an organization tool to keep there, such as a set of inexpensive stacking trays or a file box that's open at the top, so things can be slipped in easily. Then commit to dealing with papers immediately, as they come into your home, slipping them right away into their proper spot.

For long-term storage, a four-drawer filing cabinet usually has plenty of space. My friend Marsha Sims, a professional organizer, divides the files of her clients into People, Places, Things, Money, and—for those who bring home tasks from the office—Work. File your papers this way, and you'll never wonder where to look for them when you need them again.

One Person's Reflection on Handling Mail and Bills

I used to have a very difficult time finding my bills. I finally got a very nice basket that sits on my computer and holds them all. Nothing else goes in there. When I get my mail, I open it in front of the shredder. Things I don't want are shredded immediately. Bills go in the basket immediately.

Leslie

> **You will never change your life until you change something you do daily. The secret of your success is found in your daily routine.**
>
> John C. Maxwell, leadership guru

Sometimes, however, when you come in with mail in hand, you have to stop immediately to do something else—answer the telephone, feed the baby, give older children a snack, and so on. Soon the mail (wherever it has been put down) is forgotten. To prepare for these times when you can't jump right into your quick, four-category sorting, simply create a "holding area" for incoming papers. A basket, kept near the door you usually use, works well for this. You can place mail in it as soon as you enter. Just be sure to get back to it regularly. And if you usually enter through a side or back door, put a trash can nearby for obvious junk mail. Just no trash cans in the living room, please.

Some items will need to be handled at a future time. For them, set up a "pending" area, maybe in a file or another small basket. Limit the height of it, though, so you'll be sure to attend to it before it becomes the Leaning Tower of Paper.

Did You Know?

Studies suggest 23 percent of us pay bills late—and incur fees—because we lose them!

According to a recent study, the average U.S. executive wastes about one hour a day—for a total of six weeks each year—searching for documents lost in clutter.

day 32

work your paperwork system

Consistency! Consistency! Consistency! That's the key to making any organizational system work, especially when it comes to handling paper. Consistency is so important that the mere act of using a system, day in and day out, is far more important than having a good system. Whether your system is a brilliant idea or one that still needs some refining, the key to making it work is to work it consistently. There's just no substitute for that.

The worst thing you can do when handling paper is to drop a piece on a table and put off a decision of what to do with it. Misplaced perfectionism fuels a dangerous desire to do the best possible thing with that piece of paper, so you put it down until you decide how to handle it properly. That is a very imperfect decision, one that causes clutter, chaos, and unnecessary angst.

You've taken the first steps in handling paperwork properly by learning to simplify. That keeps unnecessary paper from coming into the house. You've set up (I hope!) appropriate storage containers for each kind of paper. Now you must commit to following your plan each time you

> Done is better than perfect.

> Consistency is so important that the mere act of using a system, day in and day out, is far more important than having a good system.

have a paper in hand—right away. If the containers for papers are clearly labeled, easily accessible, and simple to use, you can move forward easily.

Your filing cabinet is your best friend for long-term storage. Make an "Important Papers" section for mortgages, insurance policies, wills, and the like. Then place those papers alphabetically in that section. Make a master list of the section and put it in the front of the drawer or on the side of the cabinet so you can easily determine what's in there.

Sometimes kindly insurance salesmen will give you a folder for your policies. If this happens, discard the pretty

The Cost of Filing Too Much

It's important to make sure you don't let perfectionist tendencies lead you to file too many papers. Not only does this waste your time, space, and effort, it's pricey too.

Researchers studying the way we handle paperwork have determined that it costs a business about twenty-five thousand dollars (in employee time, materials, and so on) to fill a four-drawer filing cabinet, and more than twenty-one hundred dollars a year to maintain it!

Your time is valuable too, even though you're not paid for your around-the-house chores like filing. Protect your time by filing only what you really *must* keep.

folder. It's not part of your system. Instead, quickly tuck the policy into the "Important Papers" section of the file under Insurance. If you consistently use the system like that, you'll always know where to look for your most important papers. Follow through, and you'll thank yourself for doing so for the rest of your life.

> **Genius is 99 percent perspiration and 1 percent inspiration.**
>
> Thomas Edison, inventor

zap hidden hindrances

Feel like you're sometimes stumbling when it comes to implementing your newfound organizational skills? Can't quite figure out what's tripping you up? Still feel like you just can't quite get everything under control? That's okay. Really!

Sometimes, in our pursuit of a saner and more organized lifestyle, we're the last to see what's snagging us and pulling us back. I remember my amazement when I conducted a survey on how many drawers people had in their living space. To my amazement they would start mentally counting and saying as they counted, "Twenty, twenty-one, twenty-two . . ."

I had twelve! Twelve measly little drawers, including the ones in the kitchen! No wonder stuff was left out! There just weren't enough places to put all of it.

You would think I would have awakened to that fact without taking a survey, wouldn't you? But that is the way of hidden hindrances. They are not obvious to us until, somehow, we have an "aha" moment.

You'll move forward more efficiently, too, if you zap these hidden hindrances that probably have been slowing you down:

- *Inconvenient work spaces.* Subconsciously, you may put off tasks like paying bills or filling out important forms because you haven't set up a good place to do

> **We shape our dwellings, and afterwards our dwellings shape us.**
>
> Winston Churchill

the job. Make sure you have enough light and the supplies you need are within reach. For instance, if you're paying bills the old-fashioned way, you need stamps, envelopes, pens, and a specific place to stash bills in an organized way.

- *Dressing late in the day.* If late in the day you're still in nightclothes or house slippers, you can't zip the garbage out, take a load to the compost pile, or even step out and soak up some sunshine to brighten your mood. Being fully dressed and wearing street shoes will give you the power to move forward with jobs when they need doing. You'll feel more energized too. Hint: Dressing well and making up the bed are the first two "power actions" of the day.
- *Inadequate storage spaces.* No wonder stuff is sitting around the house! There's no place to put it. But you can solve this problem—either obtain more storage containers or get rid of things you don't need or use. Better yet, do a combination of both! I can assure you, I bought furniture with drawers to make up for *my* deficit.
- *Ugly house.* A beautiful home makes housework meaningful. Few people are enthusiastic about cleaning and organizing an unattractive house. Making your house look more pleasing will add the spark plug you need to your organizational engine. Hint: If you resist spending money on your home, consider the value of investing

> Being fully dressed and wearing street shoes will give you the power to move forward with jobs when they need doing.

in a charming place to live. The payoff will be that you are inspired to maintain the loveliness, and inspiration is a powerful motivator.

- *Saboteurs.* Are others making a mess of your home and leaving the work of cleaning up to you? If you're tolerating their bad behavior, yours needs to change too. Retraining them will be easier than you think. My books *When You Live with a Messie* and *Neat Mom, Messie Kids* can help. For details, log on to www.messies.com.
- *Reluctance to accept help.* In some parts of the country, it seems an adult woman would no more think of having someone help with housework than ask for help cutting up the food on her plate. In other areas, hiring household help is common. But even there, some women don't get help because they're perfection driven, embarrassed, or fearful of theft or breakage.

You Don't Have to Go It Alone

It is my contention that women try to "go it alone" too much of the time. Historically, women have lived and worked in bonding groups. In today's world we no longer gather around the well to get water or at the river to pound our clothes clean, while we talk together, sing, share our needs, and, in general, form a community in which women care about each other

Say What?

One man questioned my advice about getting help, scornfully saying, "Isn't that cheating?" He missed the point. When it comes to getting control of our lives, we're not playing a game; we're accomplishing a goal.

and know each other well enough to know how to offer support. Air-conditioning, washing machines and dryers, and the moving cage called a car keep us well isolated from others, unless we take the initiative and set up networks, both social and practical. Start making a list of outside help you may wish to call on for assistance.

My friend Marion, a single working mom, has a bank of "helpers" in her mind and phone book. She considers it one of her gifts to find out what people do well and what they enjoy doing, whether as a business or personal favor. She has a floating mental bank of possibilities if she needs something.

- Frank has a truck and picks up or delivers large objects. He's happy to help her when needed.
- Fashion-plate friend Jenny, at Marion's request, comes over and advises her on how to match her clothes

Cut the Stress!

Psychologists have done studies that indicate that having a companion reduces stress. So just making an appointment to get together with someone to do a cleanup job can cement your resolve to actually tackle it—and make you feel better immediately.

fashionably. Marion shares one of her talents with Jenny to return the favor.

- Household help comes to her house from time to time to clean.
- So-and-so paints and another is good at laying tile. She calls on them when necessary.

The point is, Marion knows that even the Lone Ranger needed Tonto—and he didn't lead a very complex life, like we do.

When I talk to people who are struggling alone with an organizational issue, I find that, although they may not have considered it before, with thought, they can recall a friend, family member, or service person who might be just right to hire or ask for help. With my "permission" to go that route, they move forward to success.

day 34

upgrade your house

Without our realizing it, things drift into shabbiness, or at least cease to look their best. Look around. Are there areas in your house that need upgrading so that they contribute to a more gracious way of life?

Consider whether you would be more enthusiastic about your house if you simply spruced up your

- *Flatware.* Are you using bits and pieces of sets in a myriad of styles? Buy a new matching set and enjoy the benefits of being proud of how your table looks. Over the years pieces get nicked in the electric disposal, become dulled with use, and look generally dingy. Certainly, if you are going to entertain, you will do so more happily with a presentable table.

  I'd been shopping for a new set of flatware for a while, and I stumbled upon a set at a discount store for a good price. I said, "Enough with using junky flatware!" and snapped it up. I don't know of any purchase I have enjoyed using quite so much. I hadn't realized how ready for retirement my old set was, until I employed the new one.
- *Shoe area.* Are your shoes lying around in a jumbled pile, kicking at each other in the bottom of your closet? You'll feel better about the entire area if you buy a shoe holder

> Without our realizing it, things drift into shabbiness, or at least cease to look their best.

and vacuum the bottom of your closet. Then, and this is very important, get rid of shoes you don't wear. Can't stand throwing them out? Move them into the lives of other people who can happily wear them, while you happily stop storing them. Or throw them away. It's okay. Really. I promise.

- *Towels and sheets.* Are many of yours frayed and grungy? Discard them or use them for rags, and get new ones. But choose towels wisely, depending on your climate and your laundry equipment. I live in hot, humid south Florida, and we use air-conditioning—but only in the middle of summer. I also use a solar dryer (translation: a clothesline), so for me, thin, inexpensive towels are best because they dry faster, both after use and on the line. Also they take up less room in the hamper and on the shelf. Besides, I happen to like them better than heavy towels. For guests, I have a nicer set.

  You may love heavy towels and have no problem with washing, drying, and storing big ones. As we all use towels every day, it's important to buy the kind that works for us. In this decision, cost should take a backseat.

Add a Plant!

Not only can houseplants be a pretty upgrade, they're good for you too! Scientists have found them to be surprisingly efficient at absorbing potentially harmful gases and cleaning the air inside buildings.

It's the same with sheets. You use them nightly, and they meet a very personal need for comfort. So buy what you really like and need. Because sheets last a long time, it helps if you consider that their cost can be spread over an extended period.

- *Kitchen cabinets and drawers.* New handles and knobs are inexpensive but will spruce up your kitchen and give lots of bang for the buck. Your local variety store, hardware store, and home store probably have them. Right now give your kitchen hardware an unbiased exam. They may be whispering, "Change me!" If you're not sure, bring home a couple of samples you can return later and hold them up to the cabinet. That should give you a good idea about what you should do.
- *Front door.* It creates a powerful first impression about your house. What does yours say? Does it need

Choose a Shoes Solution

If your shoes are jumbled or hard to get to, they are telling you that *you* need to take control. Of the many options, consider which solution fits your needs and your pocketbook: stacking wire racks, shelves, pocketed holders on the backs of closet doors, under-the-bed shoe storage, stacking shoe boxes. You have to decide which method works for you.

I was once surprised when someone asked, "Of course, you keep your shoes on the upper shelves of your closet, don't you?" I didn't, but when I tried it, I found it was an excellent solution for me. My four-year-old granddaughter, on the other hand, keeps hers in the bottom drawer of her dresser. And that's the perfect solution for her.

repainting? Cleaning? New hardware, such as an updated knob? Would a new seasonal wreath, kick plate, knocker, or some other decoration give it some needed oomph? Do your street numbers and front porch light need refreshing?

- *Storage spaces.* Are you storing things you no longer need or want? Are you storing your grown children's belongings or other people's things? Free up your house by sending these back to their rightful owners. Invest in adequate storage containers for your own things.

> Live your life so you will never have to say, if only.

- *Rooms.* Has the dining room become a home office? Has the guest room become a storage room? With thought, you may be able to reclaim them for their original purpose, so you can enjoy them more.
- *Flower arrangements and plants.* Are your artificial ones dusty and droopy? Clean them with an air blower or silk flower-cleaning spray. Are your live plants straggly? Repot them or replace them. In the beautiful rooms of decoration magazines, flowers and plants play an important part in making the room come alive. If you imagine those pictures without plants, you will notice the rooms lose a lot of sparkle.
- *Decorations.* Have too many unplanned items somehow crept onto your shelves? Maybe they're from another era of your life. Maybe they were gifts that no longer "fit" (maybe never did!). Give away, pack away, throw away those that are there because you sort of forgot about them. Try to concentrate on each area where you have decorations with the eyes of a stranger. I'll say it again—use an

> The home should be an island of sanity in a crazy world.

empty toilet roll or make your hand into a spyglass to see with "new" eyes the areas you suspect might not look their best anymore.

If all this seems like too much to tackle at once, take a deep breath. Instead of getting overwhelmed, start a list of the areas in your house you've been tolerating but not really enjoying. Then commit to taking steps to upgrade them, one at a time, checking them off your list as you go.

Pretend you're moving and want to make a great impression on the new buyer. Better yet, pretend *you're* the buyer. How does it look? What would make you fall in love with the house? Then upgrade your house for the deserving new owner—you! You'll feel more confident when having people in. And that, in turn, will improve your relationships with others. You'll also find that your energy level and (may I say it) joy will spike as you upgrade what some people call "your larger self"—your home.

> **Twenty years from now, you will be more disappointed by the things you didn't do than by the ones you did do. So throw off bow lines. Sail away from the safe harbor. Catch the trade winds in your sails. Explore, dream, discover!**
>
> Mark Twain

empty the area to be organized

Want to know a trick to organizing efficiently? Totally clear the area before you begin. Use this method for small jobs, like straightening a closet or bathroom cabinet. Try it for a larger area, like a room or storage area. It's a powerful method.

This method can be time-consuming, however, if the area is large. So budget time to do the job right. It helps to be sure you have enough time, helpers, and storage equipment before you begin. Then thoroughly organize a

- *Room.* First, remove everything from the room. They do that on organizing makeover programs, because it can help you visualize the possibilities of the space with a fresh perspective.

  As you empty the room, possibly out into the yard (assuming you are not doing this in December in Minnesota), deposit each item into one of four zones: *throw away, give away, store elsewhere, return to the room.* Deciding what to return to the room, once it's already out, is much, much easier than deciding what to discard while it's still in place. Tip: If you'd like to paint the room or give it a thorough cleaning, now is the time!

- *Clothes closet.* Once you've removed all of the clothes and things kept on the shelves of your closet, surely you won't put back things you have not worn in a year (or is that years?), things that don't match anything, things that don't fit, and things you don't like. Consider painting the closet white, before you fill it again, so it won't need to be painted each time the color of the room is changed. What a future time-saver!

Procrastination is the thief of time.

Edward Young,
eighteenth-century
English poet

- *Car trunk.* Whether you clean it yourself or have the job done by a professional, while the items are out, evaluate what you want to discard, store elsewhere, or return to the trunk. Get rid of the excess. And consider adding some appropriately sized storage containers to keep organized the things you plan to return to the trunk.
- *China cabinet.* Without your careful design, a lot of knickknacks tend to find a home here. Someone's gift, a family picture, an impulse buy of something "cute." They all stand side by side, full of memories but lacking style.

Far and away, the best that life offers is the chance to work hard at work worth doing.

Theodore Roosevelt, twenty-sixth
president of the United States

> Deciding what to return to the room, once it's already out, is much, much easier than deciding what to discard while it's still in place.

To remedy the situation, totally empty the cabinet. Then return only the items you really like—and the ones that look good there. Observe the newly decorated cabinet with an objective eye. Evaluate whether you need to buy anything for the unused spaces, or use those areas to display items you have elsewhere in the house.

Put items you don't return to the china cabinet in storage boxes. Save the boxed excess in an out-of-the-way place. Now, light up your china cabinet with confidence that it will reflect beauty within your home. (If your china cabinet has closed glass doors, they save oodles of time in dusting.)

- *Storage closet, storage room, attic, or garage.* These areas often are stuffed with miscellaneous items and junk, so before you begin, be sure you have time to finish the whole job.

As you empty the storage area, group like items. Put everything that's going back into the area in an appropriate container, and boldly label the outside of each.

Keep the floor of the area as clear as possible by hanging bulky items, such as brooms and large tools, on the wall or from an out-of-the-way beam. Then they will be easier to see and retrieve.

Be sure you're properly prepared with enough storage boxes, garbage containers, shelving, hooks for hanging, even a rented Dumpster, if necessary. Have enough help, either volunteer or hired. And, if needed, rent or borrow a pickup truck. Some people find that renting a portable temporary storage unit, like those from PODS, lessens the stress, because you don't have to finish the job in just one day or weekend.

When you clear any area, and see before you an empty space, you'll probably feel a surge of enthusiasm to do the job—and do it right! When the junk is separated and discarded and the "keepers" are finally stored and clearly labeled, you'll feel like a million bucks. You had to invest a lot of time, energy, and (let's face it) stress in getting it done, but once it's organized, it will be well worth the effort. You've made an investment in a stress-free future.

revamp your family room and kitchen

It's time. You can avoid it no longer. You're now ready to attack your rooms, one by one, giving them your full attention, until they're organized and can be maintained in a smooth-running process that's far easier than you ever imagined.

First, schedule a time to work on each room. Then plan your attack. For each room, you'll need to

- *Take inventory.* How much do you need to store? Buy storage containers only *after* you've determined the groups of like items that will be stored together. That will ensure you buy the right containers for the job. Avoid using very large bins for lots of small items—they're easy to fill, but it's hard to find and retrieve the small items when needed. Large bins can be used to hold a few bulky items.
- *Note places that attract clutter,* such as near the door or by the bed. Rather than try to break the habit of storing things there, go with it. Just find attractive storage containers that can keep items that land there organized and uncluttered.

> **Don't call the police because your house has been vandalized until you are really sure.**
>
> Sandra Felton, The Organizer Lady

- *Identify things that can be hung*—and hang anything you can. Most homes have much more free vertical than horizontal space. And hanging things keeps the floor clear and makes quick cleanups far easier. Revel in brooms and mops neatly suspended in the utility closet; pans aligned on a kitchen wall, rather than in a jumble in the cupboard; tools hung where you can easily find them in the garage; sporting equipment at an easy-to-reach height in a child's room, rather than in a pile on the closet floor.
- *Take lighting seriously,* placing lights (either electric or battery operated) in closets, where you read, and in any murky spots where you find yourself squinting or straining to see.
- *Compress what you can* in plastic storage bags that expel air, squeezing clothes and other items flat. Some of these plastic bags are made to be used with a vacuum to suck the air out. You can use a vacuum hose to do the same with regular trash bags closed tightly with rubber bands. With others, you can displace the air manually. An amazing amount of things take up little space when the air is removed. Hint: Be sure to open the bags after about six months to fluff stored items, if necessary. Schedule it on your calendar, so you don't forget!
- *Stow extra pillows, blankets, or other bulky items* in a tall trash can, covered with a round top and round

tablecloth designed to fit. You have created a decorative table with hidden storage on which you may place a lamp or flowers.

Now it's time to take action. Let's tackle these areas together.

Free the Family Room

If you are cramped for space, as many of us are, it may help to

- *Create space-saving end tables* by placing decorative filing cabinets at each end of the sofa. Inside, stow bills, banking information, craft and office supplies, and other miscellaneous items that you use in that area. You could give plain cabinets a decorative touch by covering them with a tablecloth. When you need to get into one of the drawers, just flip up the cloth.
- *To save space, use swing-arm lamps that mount on the wall,* instead of floor lamps or tabletop models.
- *Use the back of the door for storage.* Organizing stores and catalogs offer an array of hooks, holders, racks, baskets, pockets, and the like for storage overflow. You can find hanging holders for files (I have one on the back of my home office door), for DVDs or cassettes, coats, shoes, children's toys, and many other items. Just be sure these hanging storage areas don't end up being unsightly.
- *Think storage,* when it's time to buy more furniture. For instance, buy an ottoman with a storage compartment inside or a TV stand with drawers or cabinet space.

- *Slide flat items out of sight.* For example, folding chairs you use only occasionally and TV trays may fit nicely behind or under the sofa or bed.

Conquer the Kitchen

An easy-to-use, organized kitchen is within reach. Really! The key is so simple—smart storage. Try these tips:

- *Group like items together* for easy access when working. Keep often used items within arm's reach, tucking away seldom used items in more out-of-the-way locations.
- *Keep things close to where you use them most.* For example, keep pots and pans within easy reach of the stove. Cluster dishes and eating utensils near the dishwasher and sink for easier cleanup. It's a simple principle, but one that's often violated.
- *Have a step stool close by.* Even when you've stored things as conveniently as possible, some things will still be hard to reach. A stool that folds and slides into a narrow space is the best choice. If you are buying one, do yourself a favor and get one with two steps. You will be glad you did—probably sooner than you imagine.
- *Bring the back forward.* The deepest part of cabinets becomes easily accessible with the installation of inexpensive, wire drawers or a lazy Susan. There are even slide-out bins configured to fit around under-sink pipes. And more recently on the market, there are slide-out trays designed for the refrigerator.
- *Don't buy in bulk,* unless you know you have ample convenient places to store what you buy.

- *Install a flip-out storage tray under the panel in front of your kitchen sink.* They're great for holding sponges, vegetable scrubbers and other small, around-the-sink items. I found a kit at my local home store, near the cabinet department. It was about the price of a meal at a midlevel restaurant, which is to say, pretty inexpensive. If you can use a screwdriver, you should be able to install it yourself—at least that's what the salesman said.

The key to an organized kitchen is so simple—smart storage.

- *De-jumble with vinyl-coated wire organizers.* Use them for pot lids, platters, place mats, whatever. There are models that sit on shelves, mount to the wall or cabinet, or install as slide-out drawers.
- *Hang cooking utensils* above the countertop, near the stove. They'll be easier to reach, and you'll free up valuable drawer and cabinet space. This works for pots too!
- *Store seldom used equipment elsewhere.* The turkey roaster you use once a year won't mind being relocated to a storage closet, the garage, or the basement. Worried you won't remember where you put it? Post a note to yourself inside a cabinet door.
- *Add instant shelving.* Put inexpensive wire or plastic shelves on legs into cabinets to double shelf space.
- *Think up, up, up.* In the kitchen too there's usually more vertical space than horizontal. So stack lids and baking dishes. Hang knives and other metal utensils on a magnetic bar attached to the cabinet or wall. Use a Peg-Board for hanging items if drawers are overflowing.

- *Put under-cabinet space to work.* For example, add a narrow shelf between cabinets and countertop to hold small, often used items, such as spices. As you replace worn-out appliances, consider space-saving models that mount under cabinets.
- *Build a shelf about a foot below the ceiling* around the kitchen walls. Store seldom used items there in decorative baskets and containers.
- *Buy a portable dishwasher* that rolls to the sink when you need it if you don't have a built-in model. The top provides additional space for food preparation.
- *Designate zones in the refrigerator.* For example, keep all cheeses in one place, all condiments in another. Place as many things as possible in door shelves, where they're easily accessible. Attach labels to remind you—and others.
- *Meander around display kitchens* at a home store. You'll be inspired to adapt their best ideas to your own spaces.

Now enjoy the fruits of your labor. Your house is really becoming the ultracomfortable, organized retreat of your dreams.

revamp your laundry, closets, bedrooms, and bathrooms

Okay, ready to make progress in other areas of the house? With no further ado, let's get to it.

Lay Out Your Laundry Area

You'll gain valuable space and a decluttered look if you

- *Smartly store your ironing board.* Hang it on an over-the-door ironing board hook, found at home supply stores. Or buy an ironing board that mounts on the wall and folds down. Store the iron within reach. Hint: If you don't do much ironing, or if you do a lot of quick touch-ups, buy a small board. One kind sits on a table or counter. The best kind fits over an extended drawer and hooks under the counter,

> **Obstacles are those things we notice when we take our eyes off our goal.**
>
> Henry Ford

allowing clothes to hang as you iron. Both models are easy to store and retrieve.

- *Keep a trash can close* to the dryer for lint and the debris you find in pockets. Also keep a cup or jar handy for money and other good items left in the pockets.
- *Install a shelf for laundry supplies* above the washer and dryer. Add a space for hanging clothes by installing a tension rod designed for shower curtains.
- *Add a slim storage unit* on wheels, between the washer and dryer. This is available in many catalogs and home stores.

Cure Clothes Closet Blues

Just dive in and

- *Give clothes a deadline.* Those you're not using need to go elsewhere, either into storage, into a bin to be given away, or into the garbage. To determine which clothes aren't getting worn enough to justify the closet space they take, turn all of the hangers so that the end of the hook points toward you. Each time you wear a piece of clothing, hang it with the hook facing the back of the closet. Place a note reminding yourself of when you began this clothes evaluation project. At the end of a year (or sooner) move the clothes on hangers that are still turned outward, because they have not been worn, to a home where they are more needed and appreciated, preferably the nearest charity.
- *Replace wire hangers with good quality plastic—in one color.* Plastic hangers hang more neatly and using just one color makes the closet look more orderly. Buy some

with clamps to hold skirts and slacks. Keep clothespins close by to secure garments that tend to slip off their hangers.

- *Place a shelf just above the closet door, on the inside.* Stow seldom used or seasonal items there.
- *Paint the closet walls white,* if they're not already. White reflects more light, brightening the space and making it easier to see what you need. And when the walls are white, you won't need to repaint every time you change the color of the outer room's walls.

Beautify Your Bedroom

It's important to avoid allowing the bedroom to become an overflow for the home office, sewing room, or any other space. This is your personal sanctuary and should be protected from intrusions that will disturb the peace you find there.

With careful planning, the bedroom can serve many purposes, without disrupting the ambience. The secret is to use maximum wall space and minimal floor space. Ideally the

One Person's Reflection on Organizing Dresser Drawers

I could never keep my (or my husband's) drawers straight. So I came up with this mental plan: undershirts and bras in the top drawers, panties and boxers in the middle, socks and stockings in the bottom! I just have to picture a body and I know where stuff goes! Just a hint! Hope it works for you!

A Reforming Messie

> To have a bathroom that consistently looks well kept, you must commit to two good habits—always returning what is used to the proper spot and always wiping spills immediately.

room should have a floor-to-ceiling storage unit with drawers and shelves to hold a myriad of belongings.

Until you can afford to add a unit like that, take advantage of hidden spaces with storage potential, like under the bed. Long, shallow, plastic containers with wheels are designed for this. You'll gain even more space by slightly elevating the bed with a set of bed-risers. They come in sizes from three to twelve inches. The ones I have are six inches high. You might also consider buying—or building—a bed platform, with built-in drawers.

Better Your Bathroom

To have a bathroom that consistently looks well kept, you must commit to two good habits—always returning what is used to the proper spot and always wiping spills immediately.

To set up a well-organized bathroom, simply

- Create enough hanging space for towels.
- Use the space above the toilet for an added cabinet or shelves.
- Remove medicines from the "medicine" cabinet. Bathrooms are too moist and warm to store them safely.

Instead, put them in sealed plastic containers in a cooler, drier place.

- Store children's bath toys in a caddy that can be mounted to the tub wall with suction cups.
- Install wall-mounted holders for items like toothbrushes, razors, soap dishes, and more. This makes cleaning a snap.
- Add a plastic shoe holder to the back of a door to hold small items.
- Add space for towels by installing swinging towel bars that attach to, and are supported by, the door hinge. A company called Hinge-It makes and sells these unique towel holders that hide behind the bathroom door. Adults hang their towels on the top hinge. Children can reach those mounted on a lower hinge. As always, make it easy for kids to cooperate.
- Install slide-out vinyl-wire drawers on the floor of the sink cabinets so you can pull items forward for easy reach.
- Keep kids' grooming products in a basket or bucket that can be stored in their rooms when they're not being used in the bathroom. This reduces clutter—and prevents squabbles!

By now, half of your house has been transformed. Stick to it! You're almost there!

day 38

revamp your kids' rooms, garage, attic, basement, and home office

Look at the progress you've made! Look around. You're gaining control. I'm proud of you, and happy for you too.

But this is no time to rest on our laurels. Let's just get right back at it.

Conquer Chaos in Kids' Rooms

A few children are naturally predisposed to order. Most are not. Often messy children's rooms trigger family conflict, but it doesn't have to be that way.

Children can learn not only to maintain an organized room but also to enjoy it. If you make it easy for children to keep their rooms neat, you'll decrease conflict in your home while they're living there, and increase the chance they'll be organized adults when they're grown and gone. You'll be on the right path if you

- *Establish zones* for grooming, play, dressing, and study. Then group the items that fit into each zone. Learning to

> If you make it easy for children to keep their rooms neat, you'll decrease conflict in your home.

group like items is an intellectual pursuit that will benefit your children organizationally for the rest of their lives.

- *Label the zones* with words—pictures for nonreaders—to remind them which things should be stored there.
- *Remember, kids are short.* Make sure shelves, drawers, and closet hangers are low enough for them to use. Make sure drawer handles are large enough for them to grasp, and make sure drawers slide easily.
- *Visit a school supply store* for ideas. There are many tools for neatly organizing kid-size things.
- *Shun large toy boxes,* except to contain very large toys. Small toys or toy pieces will get lost at the bottom. Place toys neatly in clear, plastic boxes with labels. Or add a plastic shoe holder with pockets to the back of a door—it's a great tool for storing small things.
- *Decorate in a way that excites children.* They'll be much more enthusiastic about keeping rooms neat and showing them off.
- *Show—don't just tell.* Your children learn by watching your habits. With your consistent guidance, they'll pick up good habits too and will be more likely to make good use of the well-organized rooms you've created for them.
- *Keep short accounts.* Remind children to put items back where they belong on a regular basis.

Groom the Garage

A two-car garage covers about five hundred square feet of floor space. That's about the size of a small apartment!

Two parked cars take up half the space in the garage, when you include room for the car doors to open. This leaves a significant amount of room for storage, and (drumroll, please!) it's the best kind because most is along the walls. To make the most of it

- *Designate zones,* as in other rooms. You may have a building zone for storage of hammers, drills, wrenches, and the like. The garden/lawn zone would include tools hung from hooks on the wall. Sports equipment often fits nicely in a wheeled trash can—labeled, of course—in the sports zone. If you use the garage for general storage for things like games, dog food, decorations, and more, create zones for each category and post signs labeling each zone. That will nudge you—and other family members—to take that extra step and put things away properly after use. Hint: Arrange zones so that items used frequently are near the garage door you use most.
- *Measure spaces carefully* before buying storage containers.
- *Keep things off the floor.* You can hang things for pennies if you hammer large nails into studs around the walls.

> **It never occurred to me until I had this house to take a vacation and stay home.**
>
> Gill Robinson, decorator

Peg-Boards keep smaller items neat. Putting things away is a snap if you trace around them, leaving an outline that shows where they should be returned after use. Anything that can't hang should be in labeled containers, stored neatly on shelves. Lightweight items can go on high shelves; heavy items should stay low. If you can afford them, cabinets with doors create a neater overall look.

- *Put rafters to work.* Exposed rafters can hold a multitude of items. Slide skis and ski poles, long and thin sports equipment, even long gardening tools onto a ladder hung horizontally from the ceiling, above your head but within reach. Suspend large tools and sports equipment—especially bicycles—from hooks screwed into the rafters.
- *Make it shine.* As you organize, give the garage a good cleaning, discarding things you haven't used in years. It doesn't have to be spotless. But the neater it is, the more likely you'll be to keep it that way. Hint: Make oil stains fade by using your foot to grind unused kitty litter into the greasy spot. After a few hours, sweep up the litter with the oil it has absorbed. Prevent future stains

When All Else Fails

In her book *Conquering Chronic Disorganization,* Judith Kolberg describes using pulleys in a client's garage to hoist a fishing net full of clutter up twelve feet to the top. The client simply couldn't categorize those items to organize them, so he settled on lowering the net occasionally and rummaging through it for what he needed. Quirky and a little impractical but interesting and useful in the long run.

> Your home functions like a small business, so develop an office space that will help you manage your home in an organized way.

by taping a piece of cardboard over the spot where you normally park. When you want to spruce up, simply change the cardboard for a new piece.

Warning: Use only the area around the perimeter of the garage for storage. Don't be sucked into using the middle. Just because the space is there doesn't mean it should be used. You'll be far more comfortable and satisfied pulling your car into a well-cleared garage.

Attend to the Attic and Basement

Often attics and basements are untapped resources that can take a lot of clutter-pressure off the rest of the house. If these areas are unfinished, only durable items can be stored there. Moisture can ruin clothing and fragile items, unless they're stored in airtight containers. And even then, temperature extremes can be damaging.

However, if you paint walls and floors with a product that seals and waterproofs, you'll give items stored there more protection, and the area will be more attractive. With a coat of bright paint and plenty of lighting, an attic or basement can be an inviting laundry center, home office, workshop, or craft room. And it will lure you to return items more consistently to their proper places.

In both areas, follow the "rules" of storage. Designate zones, label each zone with a sign, and group like items in labeled containers. Make a master list of the contents of each box, and leave it near the entrance.

Organize a Home Office

Your home functions like a small business, so it's important to develop an office space that will help you manage your home in an organized way. You may need only a small area for record keeping and bill paying. If you conduct outside business from your home, you'll need a larger area.

Your house is your larger self.

Where will this be? you ask. Consider a spare bedroom, a basement, even a closet. Computer armoires that can hold a compact office, when closed, can blend with the décor of nearly any room without looking out of place. And the contents are completely hidden!

Some people don't need a desk. They work fine at a table, when necessary, and can keep everything they need stored in one place in a box or filing system.

For any home office two tools are indispensable in cutting paper clutter—a computer and a wastebasket. A filing system is nearly as important.

Well, you've done it. You've organized your home. Look around. Don't you love it? Congratulations on a job well done!

day 39

control your time

You've gotten your house nicely organized and you've developed habits to keep it that way. Good for you! One more thing is necessary for an organized life—learning to control how you use your time.

It's not hard, once you know how. Organized people understand the two secrets that make it easy and guarantee success. They focus on priorities and divvy up their time wisely to reach them.

That means, you simply must:

- *Say* no *to less-important, C-list priorities.* We have so many opportunities and so many demands on our time in today's busy world. That makes it important to practice saying no to the requests of other people and often to our own desires as well. We don't have the time or the energy to do everything. That means we have to ignore what we may call our C list, in favor of giving our attention to what's essential.
- *Shout a resounding* yes *to a few, well-selected*

> Organized people focus on priorities and divvy up their time.

activities in your life—your A-list priorities. When the yes areas are determined, you can say no more easily to other areas, many of which may be excellent activities, but just are not right for you at this time.

- *Determine the difference.* Not clear about what should be on your A list and what should be delegated to your

Share the Work—Dele-great!

Create more time for the tasks that really matter by becoming a "greater delegator." To help you in your effort to reassign some of your tasks to others, ask yourself these questions:

- Am I doing jobs that would be more appropriate for others to do?
- Am I still treating my older children as though they are small and need me to do everything for them? (This isn't fair to you or to them.)
- Do I fail to hire outside help because I think I should do it all?
- Am I doing it all to prove I'm needed?
- Do I hate to impose on others?
- Am I not sure how to go about delegating to others?
- Do I feel it's easier to do it myself, rather than supervise others?
- Am I neglecting to train my younger children to be independent and helpful?

If you answered yes to any of these questions, it's time to start asking others to share the load. You may be surprised how happily others go along with the new division of labor. Start today! You'll be glad you did.

C list? You're not alone, but it's important to get that straight now.

Your A List

You can start determining your A list by simply listing five areas that are priorities in your life and trying to put them in order of importance. One of the priorities must be keeping up with the trivial, routine tasks of housekeeping, because those tasks fit into the larger important context of organization. These five are your A list.

1. routine housekeeping tasks
2.
3.
4.
5.

When it comes to divvying up your time, ask yourself how much you can give to each of your priority areas. It's an important matter to settle now, because you'll need to make sure you're leaving enough time to give adequate attention to all of your A-list priorities. For example, if church work or some other ministry is in your Top Five, you need to decide

> **Things which matter most must never be at the mercy of things which matter least.**
>
> Johann Wolfgang von Goethe, nineteenth-century poet

how much time and energy you can put into that area and still leave enough time for the other four.

Your B List

Put important tasks that are not your top priority but need to be done on a B list.

1.
2.
3.

Your C List

You have already chosen your A and B lists. Can you determine one or two time-consuming items that are basically unproductive in your life and (gasp!) able to be tossed? Now, commit to tossing them!

1.
2.

bonus maintenance program

You've got disorganization on the run! You're probably eager to keep moving forward in your organizational life without slipping back. Well, you *can* by using this simple and fun six-week maintenance program. (Hint: For maximum effect, enlist your whole family!)

Here's how this maintenance program works.

First, read the following suggestions for each week. Choose two you haven't yet put in place in your organizational plan and commit to them.

Some will be exceedingly simple for you. Others will take more effort. Some require only a little thinking and planning. Others are action-oriented. Some will be onetime tasks. Others will be habits you'll want to put into place for good. Choose what *you* want to tackle.

Like the changes you put in place during the preceding chapters, this maintenance plan is designed as a series of

Like the changes you put in place during the preceding chapters, this maintenance plan is designed as a series of small, manageable steps.

small, manageable steps. Just start poking holes in a project. Enough holes, and the project is done.

With each of the activities listed below, you'll move one step (or hole) closer to developing and maintaining your own organized home. So for each week, check the two activities that appeal to you, then commit. Maybe you'll want to give a copy of the list to each member of your family, so they can choose their own tasks as well. You can download and print copies from www.messies.com. Post the list in a visible place, like on the refrigerator, so you won't forget your commitment.

Now let's begin!

Six Weeks to an (Even More!) Organized Life

Week One

___ Make your bed every day for one week.

___ Try a new cleaning product—for the oven, carpet, bathroom, anywhere.

___ Determine a problem area, either a perpetually disorganized place in your home, such as a jumbled vanity drawer or a child's room; or a habit that causes disarray, like dropping books at the door. Focus on the problem and write it down.

___ Devise a workable solution for a problem area.

___ Straighten up the house for fifteen minutes before bed every evening.

___ Organize a drawer.

___ Discard an unused toy and/or kitchen gadget.

___ Clear and organize the kitchen counter.

___ Write out a simple household-maintenance schedule.

___ Write several motivational mottos and post them where you will see them often.

Week Two

___ Peruse cleaning products at the store, reading their labels to discover new products that can reduce your cleaning time. Also seek new uses for products you're already using.

___ Purchase and put into use a new organizing product, such as a shoe rack, drawer divider, or pot-lid hanger.

___ Keep the sink clear of dishes all day for one day.

___ Write a letter to your house telling it what you intend to do for it.

___ Discard at least one outdated periodical, hopefully more.

___ Donate books and/or videos you're not using to the library, your church, or a charity.

___ Finish—or discard!—an unfinished project.

___ Throw out makeup you're not using anymore.

___ Pull unused clothing out of one closet and donate it to charity.

___ Organize a kitchen cabinet.

___ Repeat your favorite motivational mottos aloud several times.

Week Three

___ Develop an organizational plan for the whole family. Delegate chores.

Eye, Eye!

A patch may be an impressive accessory for a pirate, but to avoid having to wear one because of an eye infection, the experts at the U.S. Food and Drug Administration say you should:

- Discard any eye-area cosmetics you've had longer than three months, especially mascara.
- Toss out cosmetics that have hardened or dried out, even if they're nearly new. Adding water or saliva to moisten them introduces bacteria that could harm your eyes.
- If you've had an eye infection, get rid of all eye-area products you were using at the time, including applicators. They may be contaminated.
- Be wary of products labeled "all natural." They may have substances that encourage microbial growth, and they may increase the risk of contamination.

___ Call a family council meeting to discuss your organizational plans.

___ Talk to a significant family member about your organizational goals.

___ Find and display a magazine picture that represents your dream home.

___ Write out five or more dream statements about your house.

___ List your three greatest frustrations about your house.

___ Recruit a buddy who will hold you accountable for your progress.

___ Write and post a reminder to family members, and/or yourself, to help keep trouble areas in shape.

___ Throw out old food from the refrigerator.

Cool It!

You've had that thawed meat in the refrigerator for only three days, so it's perfectly safe, right? Not necessarily, say experts at the Food Safety and Inspection Service, part of the U.S. Department of Agriculture. Most uncooked meats can be stored safely in the fridge for just one or two days. After that, it could be dangerous to eat it. That is a good reason to organize your eating plan to keep food moving onto the table while it's fresh.

To keep your family safe, it's better to follow the old adage, When in doubt, throw it out. Here are some guidelines. You can refrigerate

- egg salad, chicken salad, or other prepared salad for three to five days
- cooked ham slices for three to four days
- prestuffed cuts of pork, lamb, or chicken for one day
- opened packages of hot dogs for one week
- opened packages of lunch meat for three to five days
- soups and stews for three to four days
- raw sausage for a day or two
- leftover cooked hamburger patties, poultry, or fish for a day or two
- raw chicken, fish, or shellfish for a day or two

For complete guidelines, log on to www.fsis.usda.gov or call the food-safety hotline at 888-674-6854.

___ Peruse cleaning tools in the grocery or hardware store.

___ Write a menu for the week and post it on the refrigerator.

___ Log on to www.messies.com, join an online group there, and read postings about others' successes in getting organized.

Week Four

___ Rearrange furniture in one room.

___ Plan a garage sale.

___ Handle all mail appropriately—the day it arrives.

___ Save or print old email you need. Delete the rest.

___ Buy or make a bill organizer, a container that keeps bills nicely organized and handy on a wall or in a drawer.

___ Set up a system to organize your files.

___ Set up a box or boxes to hold decorations for each holiday.

Week Five

___ Discard one thing from your closet.

___ Organize a sewing box, a hobby kit, or craft material.

___ Locate a professional household organizer in your area by logging on to the website of the National Association of Professional Organizers, at www.napo.net.

___ Talk to a professional organizer about his or her services.

___ Develop a chore list and a system of rewarding your children for their regular help.

___ Skip a TV program and organize something instead.

How Much Do They Really Help?

In a recent survey, about 25 percent of parents admitted to nagging their children "constantly" about cleaning their rooms. However, American children, ages six to eighteen, contribute about 12 percent of all household labor, Arizona State University family sociologist Sampson Lee Blair has found. Blair found that minority children pitch in more around the house. And for all groups, the more housework Mom does, the more kids help.

Chores are good for kids. Not only does pitching in help the family overall, completing chores helps them learn to assume responsibility, gain autonomy, and get practical life skills, including decision making, before they reach adulthood.

In most American homes, children begin helping with chores around age six, with simple tasks, like picking up toys and taking out trash, Blair says. The older the child, the more complex the task he or she is able to accomplish.

Parents of teens won't be surprised that the number of household chores completed by sixteen- to eighteen-year-olds declines sharply. For more information about how you can rally your family to help, read my book *Neat Mom, Messie Kids*.

___ Ask friends to recommend a housekeeper or cleaning service.

___ Pretend you are a stranger entering your front door for the first time. Look around to get a fresh view.

___ Discard games and puzzles that have missing pieces or boxes that are tattered beyond reasonable repair.

___ Interview an organized person you admire and ask for tips. Find out if organization came naturally or was learned.

___ Hire a plumber, electrician, or handyman to do a repair job that's been neglected.

Week Six

___ Choose a home-improvement project—and take steps to do it!

___ Clean the car—the inside, the outside, or both—on your own, or by hiring someone.

___ Invite friends over.

___ Throw out all pens and markers that don't work.

___ Throw out all family members who don't work (a little organizational humor)!

___ Visit an automotive store to consider organizational products for the car.

___ Scout out the organizing section of a variety or hardware store for organizing products.

___ Flip through an interior decorating magazine or book for ideas and styles that appeal to you.

___ Start a home decorating–idea scrapbook or box to keep examples or illustrations of materials and ideas

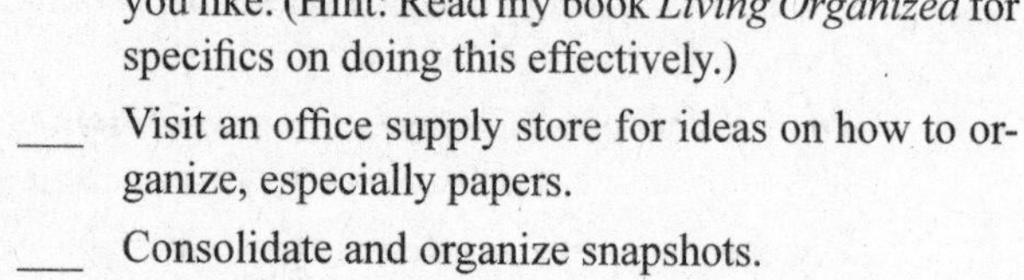

you like. (Hint: Read my book *Living Organized* for specifics on doing this effectively.)

___ Visit an office supply store for ideas on how to organize, especially papers.

___ Consolidate and organize snapshots.

Now keep that progress going! Sign up for my daily email message, "The Organizer Lady," on www.messies.com to receive motivation, reminders, and helpful hints. I'm cheering for you. Let's connect every day, so I can remind you that the secret to success is making very small, yet very consistent, changes—baby steps, baby steps in the right direction!

resources

Books

Books on organizing life fall into several categories. To complement the topics of this book, you may want to look into some of the topics and books below.

If I wanted more information on improving my life organizationally, I would go to my local bookstore and look for books in the household section. The latest books on organizing, including some classics, are nestled among the books on decorating and home repair. Books about taking control of and simplifying one's life are scattered throughout the self-improvement section.

A second place I would look, depending on its proximity, is the local library. It may or may not have the latest books, but it will have books that are no longer on the bookstore shelves. The oldies are often the goodies.

The third place to look is at an online bookstore. Type in the words *household organizing* (if you put in *organizing* alone, you may get information on starting a union) or *simplicity*. Look to see if reviews of books by other readers are available.

I encourage you to refer to my other books, all published by Revell: *The New Messies Manual*—the flagship book for change; *The Messie Motivator*; *Messie No More*; *Neat Mom, Messie Kids*; and *When You Live with a Messie*.

Simplicity

Davidson, Jeff. *Breathing Space: Living and Working at a Comfortable Pace in a Sped-up Society*. New York: MasterMedia Limited, 1991.

Jones, Sheila, ed. *Finding Balance*. Billerica, MA: Discipleship Publications, 2002.

Time Management

Davidson, Jeff. *The Complete Idiot's Guide to Managing Your Time*. New York: Alpha Books, 1995.

Macgee-Cooper, Ann, with Duane Trammell. *Time Management for Unmanageable People*. New York: Bantam, 1994.

Otto, Donna. *Get More Done in Less Time*. Eugene, OR: Harvest House, 1995.

Clutter

Aslett, Don. *Not for Packrats Only: How to Clean Up, Clear Out, and Dejunk Your Life Forever*. New York: Penguin, 1991.

Campbell, Jeff. *Clutter Control: Putting Your Home on a Diet*. New York: Dell, 1992.

Neziroglu, Fugen, Jerome Bubrick, and Tobias Yaryura. *Overcoming Compulsive Hoarding*. Oakland: New Harbinger, 2004.

Organizing

Cilley, Marla. *Sink Reflections*. New York: Bantam, 2002.

Lockwood, Georgene. *The Complete Idiot's Guide to Organizing Your Life*. New York: Alpha Books, 1996.

Mendelson, Cheryl. *Home Comforts: The Art and Science of Keeping House*. New York: Scribner, 1999.

Rich, Jason. *The Everything Organize Your Home Book: Straighten Up the Entire House, from Cleaning Your Closets to Reorganizing Your Kitchen*. Avon, MA: Adams Media, 2002.

Roth, Eileen, with Elizabeth Miles. *Organizing for Dummies*. New York: Hungry Minds, 2002.

Williams, Debbie. *Put Your House in Order: Organizing Strategies Straight from the Word*. Houston: Let's Get It Together, 2002.

Paper Organizing Tips

Barnes, Emilie. *The Fifteen-Minute Organizer*. Eugene, OR: Harvest House, 1991.

Smallin, Donna. *Unclutter Your Home: Seven Simple Steps, Seven Hundred Tips and Ideas*. Pownal, VT: Storey Books, 1999.

Winston, Stephanie. *Best Organizing Tips*. New York: Simon and Schuster, 1996.

Parenting

Elkind, David. *The Hurried Child: Growing Up Too Fast Too Soon*. Cambridge, MA: Perseus, 2001.

Felton, Sandra. *Neat Mom, Messie Kids*. Grand Rapids: Revell, 2002.

Rosenfield, Alvin, and Nicole Wise. *The Over-Scheduled Child: Avoiding the Hyper-Parenting Trap*. New York: St. Martin's, 2000.

Tinglof, Christina Baglivi. *The Organized Parent: Three Hundred Sixty-Five Simple Solutions to Managing Your Home, Your Time, and Your Family's Life*. New York: Contemporary Books, 2002.

Websites about Organizing

Websites have a limited life, but by using a search engine, you will be able to find many that can help.

www.messies.com—The website of Messies Anonymous, founded by Sandra Felton. Contains a lot of information for those who struggle with disorder in their lives. Join online groups for regular support in making changes.

http://groups.yahoo.com/group/The-Organizer-Lady—Sign up for daily encouragement and reminders from Sandra Felton to keep on track and in focus.

www.OnlineOrganizing.com—"A world of organizing solutions." Read excellent articles, join discussion groups, get questions answered by professional organizers.

www.OrganizersWebRing.com—Professional Organizers Web Ring or POWR. Their motto is "You've got the POWR to get organized." Find a professional organizer in your area and read articles on many subjects that affect your everyday organizing life.

www.nsgcd.org—National Study Group on Chronic Disorganization. "The premier online resource for anyone interested (personally or professionally) in Chronic Disorganization."

www.napo.net—National Association of Professional Organizers. Locate a professional organizer in your area or learn how to become one.

www.faithfulorganizers.com—This is a website for Christian Professional Organizers. It is the only place where faith and professional organizing meet. This site helps people all over the country locate professional organizers in their area who also share their values.

They are a resource for churches to find speakers for their women's groups and moms' groups.

Catalogs for Organizing

The Container Store catalog at www.containerstore.com or 800-733-3532. They offer many organizing solutions for the home or office, including closet design, with free personalized planning service in the stores, over the phone, and online.

Get Organized catalog at www.shopgetorganized.com or 800-803-9400. Check out their many "space-saving innovations to unclutter your life."

Hold Everything catalog at www.holdeverything.com is a catalog of storage and household ideas from Williams-Sonoma.

Lillian Vernon catalogs at www.lillianvernon.com or 800-545-5426. Their household organizing catalogs *Neat Ideas* emphasize decorative organizers and tools for every room in the house.

Organize-Everything catalog at www.organize-everything.com has clothing storage items.

Organize It catalog at www.organize-it.com has lots of clothing storage products.

The Storage Store at www.thestoragestore.com has a nice variety of storage boxes.

Catalogs for Cleaning

Clean Report, from Don Aslett, America's Number One Source for Cleaning Information at www.cleanreport.com or 800-451-2402.

Don has available many books and videos on cleaning as well as cleaning tools and products.

Home Improvements: Hundreds of Quick and Clever Problem-Solvers! at www.improvementscatalog.com or 800-642-2112 has lots of interesting things for use around the home, including many unique organizing products.

Home Trends at www.hometrendscatalog.com or 800-810-2340. This catalog emphasizes cleaning products but offers organizing products as well.

High- and Low-Tech Cleaning Schedule Resources

The Flipper is a system of organizing cleaning jobs available from *Messies Anonymous*. For information: www.messies.com or check how you can make your own in *The New Messies Manual* or *The Messies Superguide*.

The Internet has several cleaning schedule lists available online from various groups. A recent search on Google under "household cleaning schedule" turned up 5621 links, several of which looked excellent.

Create your own daily schedule using your computer calendar or online reminders, which may come with your provider service.

Online Cooking Resources

Type *recipes* in your search engine, and your poor little computer will sag with the weight of the responses.

Check out www.30daygourmet.com for cook and freeze suggestions.

Filing Resources

Hemphill, Barbara. *Taming the Paper Tiger at Home.* Washington, D.C.: Kiplinger, 2002.

Sandra Felton, The Organizer Lady™, is a pioneer in the field of organizing. She is the founder of Messies Anonymous, a self-help group dedicated to helping chronically disorganized people who struggle with clutter to find order, dignity, and even beauty in their lives. She is the author of a variety of books on the subject of organizing one's house and life, and applies proven principles to the subject of organizing homes and small offices using the upbeat approach that has become her hallmark. Visit Sandra at www.messies.com.

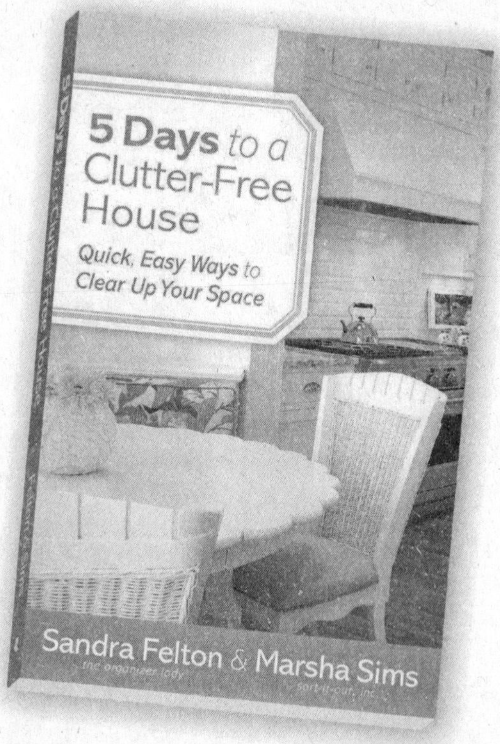

"We might be s
lost on a trans-Pa
famed Count Dra
built Stonehenge

is there really life after death? Do plants speak?

"The quest and the questions presented an unlimited source of adventure.

"More than a hundred people were scattered around the world recording pieces of data, clues, evidence which fulfilled Hamlet's promise that "there are more things on earth than you have dreamed of in your philosophy.' "

—LEONARD NIMOY

Bantam Books by Alan Landsburg
Ask your bookseller for the books you have missed

IN SEARCH OF ANCIENT MYSTERIES
(with Sally Landsburg)
IN SEARCH OF EXTRATERRESTRIALS
IN SEARCH OF LOST CIVILIZATIONS
THE OUTER SPACE CONNECTION
(with Sally Landsburg)

In Search of Extraterrestrials

Alan Landsburg

FOREWORD BY LEONARD NIMOY

To Marilyn, whose sure hand, careful eye and loving support enable me to survive the turmoil of each day's work.

RLI: $\frac{\text{VLM 9 (VLR 8–10)}}{\text{IL 9+}}$

IN SEARCH OF EXTRATERRESTRIALS
A Bantam Book / January 1977

ISBN 0–553–10722–4

Published simultaneously in the United States and Canada

Bantam Books are published by Bantam Books, Inc. Its trademark, consisting of the words "Bantam Books" and the portrayal of a bantam, is registered in the United States Patent Office and in other countries. Marca Registrada, Bantam Books, Inc., 666 Fifth Avenue, New York, New York 10019.

PRINTED IN THE UNITED STATES OF AMERICA

AUTHOR'S NOTE

The chronicle of discovery amassed in this volume is the work of many people. More than 100 researchers, scientists and skilled filmmakers participated in the various quests. For simplicity's sake we have co-mingled our experiences into a single first-person narrative so that we may share with you the essence and excitement of the hunt without a clutter of personal introductions. As author and chief chronicler of the work we have done, I owe an enormous debt of gratitude to those who joined me in the field to explore the world of mystery. To all of those dedicated workers committed to IN SEARCH OF . . . I say thank you. This book is as much yours as mine.

ALAN LANDSBURG

Contents

Foreword

by LEONARD NIMOY

My first working association with the television series "In Search Of . . ." was a narration session in which I was asked to read aloud the major objectives of the various categories—Lost Civilizations, Unexplained Phenomena, Missing Persons, Magic and Witchcraft, Myths and Monsters, and finally Extraterrestrials. The roll call of subjects was mind-bending. I kept on reading the sentences appended to the list but my mind was focused on the prospect of walking the electrifying path between what is scientific fact and what is far out science fiction.

Alan Landsburg is a much honored producer of television documentary films, and his extraordinarily talented staff of directors, writers, cameramen and editors were out in the field collecting some of the most unusual images ever recorded on a television screen. What appealed to me most was the very range of subjects. We might be searching for Amelia Earhart lost on a trans-Pacific flight in 1937, or for the famed Count Dracula of myth and fact. Who built Stonehenge? Where did UFOs land? Is there really life after death? Do plants speak? The quest and the questions presented virtually an unlimited source of adventure. More than a hundred people were scattered around the world recording pieces of data, clues, evidence which fulfilled Hamlet's promise that "there are more things on earth than you have dreamed of in your philosophy."

I liked the sense of butting up against old ideas and demonstrating that new explanations were possible. In pursuit of old baffling mysteries, the programs opened new directions to search for more illuminating answers.

For all of these reasons I immersed myself in the fascinating game. It's good to know that our television series "In Search Of . . ." has now become something of a byword for many viewers.

This book is a chronicle of the efforts that have gone into making the television series. It's a fascinating logbook to me, filled with the excitement of overcoming the impossible and the fulfillment of discovery. I hope you find it as intriguing as I did.

1

The Hunt Begins

"This is an example of a UFO ground effect," he was saying. "It's a soybean field in Iowa where a farmer found that a forty-foot circular patch of soybeans had been destroyed." I stared down at the picture Allen Hynek was describing. A hot white spot had been burned into a large patch of neatly planted rows.

"I went there and examined it," he continued. "The plants were not crushed or broken, but looked as though they had been subjected to intense radiation from the top."

There was a crisp, no-nonsense tone to Dr. Hynek's voice. He was on familiar ground, and warming to his subject. "The circle was discovered in the morning. The night before, the daughter of the man who owned the land reported that she had seen a UFO land."

There was no pause for dramatic effect, nor any particular underlining of the letters UFO. To Allen Hynek, UFOs were commonplace subjects. A former chairman of the Department of Astronomy at Northwestern University, he is director of the Center of UFO Studies at Evanston, Illinois. He had crossed over from academe to what many of his former colleagues might consider the "wild side." I knew him, however, as a dedicated research scientist who pursues the study of UFOs from a hard-nosed nothing-is-accepted-until-it-can-be-verified basis.

I found my attention drifting from the pictures Dr. Hynek was describing, and focusing instead on the man himself. He had come to Los Angeles at my invitation to take part in a television special on *Unsolved Mysteries*. I had surveyed the field of UFO investigators and interviewed almost all the writers who had chronicled UFO events. Among them were many fascinating and reputable individuals, but of the group, Allen Hynek stood out as the dean of UFO-ology.

He had entered the field as a skeptic. Years ago, while he was teaching at Northwestern, he was asked to become a consultant for the U.S. Air Force on Project Blue Book, one of the early studies of UFOs. The conclusion reached in the Blue Book report was that there was insufficient evidence to consider the possibility that UFOs exist. Allen Hynek pursued the study long after the Air Force concluded the program. In the intervening twenty years he has moved from skeptic to expert. Allen Hynek might object to the description. He would prefer, I think, "scientist in search of an answer."

Clearly he enjoyed his labors. Behind his thick-lensed glasses, his eyes gleamed as he detailed the differences between UFOs, IFOs (Identifiable Flying Objects) and Daylight Disks (sparkling circles traveling across daylight skies). After twenty years of research, writing, and analysis, he hadn't tired of his subject, nor apparently had he let any part of his thinking become ritualized dogma. He seemed to accept his role as man-on-the-spot with amazing ease. By the very nature of his efforts he had become the bull's-eye for anyone who wanted to attack the field of UFO study. Allen Hynek was the best spokesman for a rational approach to the question.

I wondered how many times he had stood in a television studio briefing a talk-show host or producer on the subject of UFOs, how many times in the course of his career he had been subjected to the snide grilling of interviewers dedicated to making him look foolish and his subject inane. He certainly had not become shell-shocked by the attacks. He was in total command of his subject matter, and each of his statements was made in a dead-accurate framework. There could be no misunderstanding his point of view or his motives.

I was pleased that Dr. Hynek had agreed to appear on the TV special. His work and the work of his Center helped give a baseline judging of the handful of ongoing UFO studies. It seems incredible that for all the attention given to UFOs, there is little or no government-sponsored research aimed at unraveling the mysteries that surround the subject. Allen Hynek's Center for UFO Studies in Evanston survives by being privately funded, but it's an expensive procedure.

Among its many activities, the Center maintains a field staff and a twenty-four-hour hot line. The telephone ties the Center to such federal agencies as the FAA, the FBI, and virtually every civilian defense unit in the country. Reports of sightings are referred to the Center, where they are checked, cataloged, and —when warranted—investigated. In addition, the Center provides information and facilities for scientists at a number of prominent universities, among them UCLA, Johns Hopkins, and the University of London.

The most critical function of the Center is to collect a data bank, a register of every conceivable type of UFO sighting. Allen Hynek had described the Center's information pool as numbering some seventy thousand entries. For Hynek this extraordinary collection of information represents the most heavily weighted argument in favor of the existence of UFOs.

As he put it during our discussion that day in the studio, "When you ask about real evidence, the one absolutely incontrovertible fact is that UFO reports exist, and not just from the United States, but from all over the world. You may say: 'Well, so what? Reports are cheap.' "

He stopped and leaned back in his chair. He was marshaling the arguments that would point with some conviction toward the fact that UFOs are real.

"One has to examine the caliber of the people that the reports come from, and this is what we do at the Center. The observer is our only fact-gathering instrument. We must know its caliber."

I could sense him trying to detect from the expression on my face whether he was talking to a skeptic or a believer. He remembered, I guess, that he himself made that same pilgrimage. He continued.

"You know, when I first started my work with the Air Force, I was convinced that the stuff was just nonsense, and I thought that, well, we in the USA are peculiarly given to silly things. Then I was surprised to find that the reports were actually coming from all parts of the world, and from credible people. In fact, it was General Sanford who inadvertently gave a very good definition of the UFO. He said, 'It's an incredible tale told by credible persons.' "

Allen Hynek had probably interviewed as many "sighters" as anyone in the world. In the course of cataloging UFO information, he constantly came into contact with policemen, pilots, scientists, and air-traffic controllers—witnesses, as he put it, of unquestionable integrity.

I was particularly interested in the procedures for collecting data used by the UFO Study Center personnel. I was scheduled to produce a television series dealing in part with UFOs. If I were going to successfully mount programs on extraterrestrials, then I would have to evolve a technique for cross-checking information.

Allen Hynek outlined the rules. I would have to be aware that a true UFO must remain unidentified and unexplained, even after severe technical scrutiny of the report and its content by experts. Any practiced UFO investigator who has had several years' experience can weed out almost immediately birds, balloons, aircraft, and searchlights at night.

He then listed forms of corollary evidence that helped convince him that in fact something was seen. "If reports were limited to just the sightings in the sky, I don't think the Center for UFO Studies would exist, and no scientist would be willing to take the time to look at it. But it's because you have radar evidence, photographic evidence, and even evidence of animals."

Dr. Hynek saw the puzzled look on my face at the mention of animals. He explained, "I don't think animals tend to lie, and I don't think cows hallucinate. Often people tell me that what first called their attention to something strange going on was the fact that the horses in the barn were raising a fuss. In one case, when they went out to find out what was disturbing the animals, they saw this glowing craft hovering over the barn. Do you call both the people and cows liars?"

I wanted something more tangible than eyewitness accounts. Dr. Hynek suggested I begin with "trace cases," those times when the UFO encounter actually left a physical trace that could be studied at a later date.

"There are hundreds of cases in the files," he said, "which list real physical evidence, such as burned patches on the ground, landing marks, broken tree branches."

We were coming closer to air time. I escorted Dr. Hynek to the raised podium where the ever-present interview chairs were placed. I thanked him for his help. He had helped set for me the parameters of the task that faced me. In the darkened cavern along the back wall of the television studio I was left to plot the course I would follow. I wanted to seek evidence that extraterrestrials exist, that traces of their presence could be found on earth. I had at my disposal a highly trained staff gathered to produce the television series *In Search of . . .* Six experienced field teams were prepared to record in sound and picture the story of the search for extraterrestrials.

Almost forty people would fan out across the country in order to produce an unbiased and accurate view of the UFO story. I serve as the voice of the teams. For clarity and convenience' sake, all our experiences have been combined in a single first-person narrative form. The actual information in this journal was derived from the dedicated labors of the program's field teams.

One of the first leads to be followed was Allen Hynek's suggestion that I track down "physical traces," those broken tree limbs and burned patches on the ground. Hundreds of hours went into the search for verifiable case histories. As each story came in, it was summarized on a three-by-five index card and put up on a research board. The raw data were then checked by personal contact with on-site witnesses, local police, newspapermen, and city or county officials. The roll call was fascinating.

PLACE: Medford, Minnesota.

DATE: November 2, 1975.

WITNESSES: Richard Kay, wife, and two children. Highway Patrolman Andrew Nesvick.

STORY: The family saw a glowing sphere

touch ground about 400 feet from their house in the Medford football field. It happened at approximately 9:30 P.M. One son followed the object as it ascended over a ridge, but lost it. The next day the family went out to investigate, and there was a dehydrated spot where the UFO had landed. That same night a highway patrolman, Andy Nesvick, reported seeing flashing lights in the sky. Soil analysis shows high radiation trace.

EVALUATION: Kay family seem like credible witnesses. The police department say they are completely reliable.

PLACE: White City, Kansas.

DATE: July 19, 1975.

WITNESSES: Jan Maddox and Richard Gustafson.

STORY: In the early evening Jan and Richard saw four metallic spheres in the sky. They watched as the object began a rapid vertical descent. They followed the UFO in their car, and by the time they reached the spot, the pasture was ablaze. They found three burning rings in a triangular pattern. Nearby farmers also saw the fire. Jan took Polaroid shots of the rings, and she says they are still faintly visible.

EVALUATION: Jan sounds extremely bright and lively over the phone. Strikes me as an *excellent* witness.

PLACE: Coquitlam, British Columbia.

DATE: August 16, 1974.

WITNESSES: David Bates (age 7), Steven Stillie (9), and Henry Stillie (7)

STORY: The three children were playing along the banks of the Coquitlam River. They saw a craft shaped like an inverted disk land in a graveled area. They were terrified and ran home to their parents. One month later the local UFO investigator, R. J. Halishoff, went out to investigate and found two strange black circles on the gravel.

EVALUATION: The UFO investigator says he believes the story and the family are honest. Mr. Stillie has a thick Scottish brogue which is hard to understand, but his children are more intelligible. Halishoff said he'd come out if we wanted to interview the kids. He's a police officer in Coquitlam.

PLACE: Carlyle, New York.

DATE: January 12, 1975.

WITNESS: Leonard Tillapough.

STORY: Leonard Tillapough was plowing his field when a metal object fell from the sky and melted a hole through the thin crust of snow on the ground. He called the local sheriff, Harvey Stoddard, who came out to investigate. NICAP (National Investigation Committee on Aerial Phenomena) investigator Ernest Jahn took the metal and put it through an extensive series of tests (at NASA's Goddard Space Flight Center, Los Alamos Scientific Laboratory, the Chicago Spectro Service Laboratory, and the University of Maryland's Department of Geology). The metal was a cast material not common, and not traceable to any sort of aircraft. Head of NICAP, Jack Acuff, says that the origin of the metal is still a mystery.

EVALUATION: Good story because it provides what may be a piece of concrete evidence.

PLACE: Big Chimney, West Virginia.

DATE: June 12, 1975.

WITNESSES: Carroll Critchfield, wife, and two children.

STORY: UFO landing happened at approximately 10 P.M. Carroll Critchfield saw a bright object in sky, called to his wife and kids. It disappeared down a gravel road. The next morning they investigated and found four landing-gear imprints. The marks were very distinct—the feet had four flat ends with "arcs" in between.

EVALUATION: Story has bonus, because Critchfield wants to take lie-detector test, which I have arranged. Polygraph firm of Elmer Criswell in Wheeling, West Virginia, will do test.

There were literally hundreds of stories. I eliminated those that did not fulfill Hynek's reporting criteria and began to narrow the field.

As I pursued the investigation, one name kept cropping up: Ted Phillips. Subjects would say, "Oh, yes! Well, I told Ted Phillips about that," or, "Ted Phillips was here, and he checked that out." Ted was a field investigator for Allen Hynek's Center for UFO Studies, and I could testify that he had done his work well. No matter what case I was following, Ted Phillips had been there first. Rather than fight, I decided to switch—to join forces with him. I soon found I had an invaluable ally as I tracked down physical traces of UFO landings.

Many of the best stories that turned up came from Ted's suggestions.

We met in Columbia, Missouri, not far from Ted's hometown of Sedalia. We had to make our rendezvous on Saturday, because Ted's full-time occupation is inspector for the Missouri State Highway Department. His avocation is UFOs, an interest that dates back to his involvement in the Vanguard satellite program. He got deeply involved in 1964 when he became so intrigued by a local UFO story that he started his own on-the-spot investigation. Since then he's covered hundreds of cases. His specialty has become physical-trace events. He explained to me how it works.

"The most positive type of report, the most direct avenue of approach to resolving the UFO problem, is through physical traces, because they remain long after the visual observation by the witnesses. We have something that can be photographed, studied, and analyzed for a long period of time. But investigations of physical-trace cases take money. So we are highly selective in cases that we investigate. They have to meet certain standards."

"What kind of standards?" I fired back without a pause.

"Well," he explained, "a high-quality trace case must be seen by two or more credible witnesses within a hundred to two hundred and fifty feet of a UFO. It must be on the ground or extremely near the ground. The duration of observation must be no less than one minute, so the witnesses have a little bit of time to establish that they're seeing something really strange—a physical trace that has no immediate natural explanation.'"

I knew what he meant by immediate natural causes. There have been any number of so-called "fairy rings" that have been misidentified as landing tracks left by UFO craft. They are in fact mushroom or fungus growths in which the spores are released in the soil in a circular configuration. Sometimes, not always, the plant life around that ring will die because of the fungus growth in the soil. Poisons or defoliants occasionally cause a round "bald" spot in an otherwise normal vegetation pattern, but they too are easy to spot. The

UFO trace is generally clear: an irregular burned area or a circular burned, depressed, or dehydrated area with the surrounding environment still standing unchanged. Many times plant life is swirled in a clockwise or counterclockwise position. In other cases the soil is dried, sapped of all moisture, obviously quite dead.

Ted explained his checking process. "After we've done photographic work, then we get the samples. These are generally taken in half-inch increments from the surface down to a considerable depth. These are filed away in separated containers and cataloged, showing the precise spot where they're taken. So if you're sitting five hundred miles away from the site, you know exactly where that sample came from. And then, of course, we take control samples along several given lines. I do it generally in five-foot increments to a distance of up to three hundred feet, to be sure that we're getting a very representative profile of the soil leading away from the landing site."

Then I broke in. "In these laboratory experiments, have any results turned up that are conclusive?"

I was thinking in particular of the Delphos, Kansas, incident. It happened on the Johnson farm at sundown on November 2, 1971. Darrell Johnson and his wife were inside the house. His son was working in the sheep pen. Suddenly flashing lights lit up the yard area. At the same moment, there was a violent reaction among the animals. The family dog went berserk. The sheep began to bellow. Darrell and Irma Johnson came out of the house in time to see the UFO take off. What was left behind was a shiny doughnut ring on the ground. To this day, water will not be absorbed by the ring.

Ted explained that lab analysis had finally determined that the ground was irradiated, that siliconelike particles had been created, which sealed out water. Stranger to me was the information that when Darrell and Irma Johnson touched the ring, their fingers went numb, and the numbing effects have lasted for five years.

When I asked Ted Phillips whether or not he's ever found out exactly what that coating was, he explained that the number of tests needed and the expense of those tests put further examination out of his reach. I was frustrated by Ted's answer. I wanted more. I wanted evidence that a rocket plume had irradiated the soil. As we were talking, I realized that I had lost sight of the goal. What the irradiated ring at Delphos, Kansas, had done was to add credence to Darrell Johnson's story. Hard evidence to back up his claim that on his farm, on November 2, 1971, an object landed.

Still, I wanted to know more about the process of testing. I asked Ted to introduce me to one of the men who had conducted the soil analysis for him. He suggested I contact Dr. Edward Zeller, professor of geology, astronomy, and physics at the University of Kansas. Before I left Ted Phillips, I asked him to put together his notes on a recent case that he felt was the most interesting of the incidents he had been checking.

"That would be Jim Richards' story, up in Columbia, Missouri," Ted said. "That's a real good one."

"Suppose we meet there in one week," I asked.

The date was made, Ted headed back to Sedalia, and I was on my way to the University of Kansas.

2

Beneath the Surface

The Interstate slashed across spring-cold Missouri farmland, still bare of all green life. As I drove, I remembered that this was UFO country. Statistically, an overwhelming number of sightings has been made in rural areas. Heading toward Kansas, I began to understand why there were more UFOs seen in this area than anywhere else. It's not that the people of Kansas, Iowa, Missouri, and southern Illinois, the heartland farmers of America, are given to hallucinating. It's the nature of the landscape in which they live.

The long, rolling, virtually treeless plains and the open fields provide little place for hiding. Open sightlines forty and fifty miles to the horizon give lots of room for tracking lighted objects. UFOs have more room to be seen here. Also, if I were piloting an alien vehicle, I wouldn't want to set it down in New York City. I gave up on that last fancy very quickly. I wasn't ready to enter the "little-green-men" world that exists on the fringes of UFO study.

There was another facet of the "rural" nature of the sightings that intrigued me. Perhaps a large part of the "media hostility" to UFOs was due to the fact that none had turned up in, say, New York. The attitude of most major newspapers and magazines is that UFOs don't exist, and any mention of them must be couched in terms that clearly indicate the invalidity of the report. I wanted to be sure that my background and training in New York media were not overweighted by that seemingly ingrained urban prejudice. I had to be sure I stuck to my search and did not swing into the camp of evangelizing for either side in the UFO controversy. By the time I got to the University of Kansas, I had the focus I felt I needed for the interview with Ed Zeller.

The University of Kansas is a sprawling metropolis of its own. Brand-spanking new. Dr. Zeller's headquarters at the Space Technology Lab is the quintessence of futuristic architecture—a seven-story sandstone building with the chiseled lines and sleekness of a spacecraft. Inside, the high ceilings and marble floors do strange things to the sound of the human voice. When I asked for Dr. Zeller, I could hear my own voice reverberate off the walls.

I was directed to the stark lab where Dr. Zeller carries out his experiments in soil analysis. The lab assistant said Dr. Zeller was en route from his last class of the day. He had just returned from a scientific colloquium in Berlin this same morning and had plunged back into his normal routine.

Most of Dr. Zeller's career has been spent studying the relationship of radiation to solids. His specialty is radiation physics. He was involved in space-program operations, studying the effects of radiation in interplanetary and interstellar space. He had been at

Lawrence, Kansas, for twenty years and seemed to be a likely candidate for my next set of questions.

I had done some preliminary reading about the properties of soil. It seemed to me that a scientist was going to have to look for variability in soil samples that were said to have been affected by the UFO vis-à-vis the control sample. But what is variability in soil? Are we talking about the components of soil or the structure of the soil? After some dry text reading I learned that in order to understand variability I would have to study the thermoluminescence process.

Simply put, if the soil is subjected either to radiation or to heating, a characteristic signature will be left behind in the soil. Most crystalline materials—window glass, sand, normal rocks—will show a certain amount of luminescence if you were, say, to heat them on a hot plate in a dark room. If the materials are strongly irradiated, they show much more of this luminescence than if they're just heated. So when we talk about the differences in the variability of soil samples, we are essentially talking about seeing the differences in the luminescent properties of the soil.

Over the past twenty years Dr. Zeller has run innumerable tests on soil samples taken from UFO sites. I was hoping I could pin down information that would show a high nuclear-radiation level in the samples.

"Dr. Zeller," I asked, "has a Geiger counter ever turned up an inordinate amount of radioactivity?"

"We have never found anything in the samples that I have studied that gave a particularly high radiation account." Luminescence, however, was another story. There had been a lot of unexpected results in luminescence tests.

"Which were the most interesting?" I asked.

"There are a whole bunch of Medford samples, and in the Medford samples the variability is higher than I would expect in material from a normal field. In other words, if you just start across a field and start analyzing soils, you expect a reasonable level of uniformity. In the case of the Medford site, I see such large variability that I find it unexpected."

I dived into my notes on Medford. Medford,

Minnesota. The Kay home. A beautiful two-story brick-and-wood colonial. Neatly manicured lawn. Big circular driveway. Helen Kay, her daughter, Jane, and son, Jerry. Really nice people. Feet on the ground. Solid citizens. Sunday, November 2, 1975. Jane was doing her homework. Jerry and his wife had just left after an evening's visit. They all described an incoming big orange ball alighting on a nearby football field. Jane flashed on the word "UFO." Jerry thought of a huge pyrotechnic display being dropped by parachute. Helen wasn't sure. It was definitely not an airplane, she said, or any helicopter she had ever imagined. She summed up the Kay story this way:

"I've made it very clear that I don't think it's from another planet. I only know what I saw. I'm not trying to tell anyone it has little green men or anything. I have no idea what it was. When you say that you saw something come down, the first thing people think is that you're trying to tell them that you saw something from another planet, that you're trying to sell them a big story, but none of us has done that. We just told the truth about what it was we saw."

The football field on which the Kays saw the UFO set down was the Medford field that had produced the sample for Dr. Zeller. It seemed to me that here was an opportunity to come up with at least tangible evidence of a UFO landing.

"The basic thing at the Medford site," Dr. Zeller went on, "is that some of the samples show almost ten times the amount of luminescence that others do, and that's unusual. We wouldn't expect that level of variability in soil samples that under the microscope look very similar. The Medford-site samples looked to us to be quite uniform initially, and therefore we would have expected them to have similar luminescent properties. We find large-scale variation in the glow curves, but no large-scale variation in the microscopic appearance of the samples. The only thing we can say is that these high variability conditions are unusual. Exactly what they mean, I can't tell you."

Dr. Zeller wasn't willing to commit himself to UFO speculation. He is truly a cautious scientist thoroughly disciplined in scientific method. I forged on. "But what about the strange hydrophobic quality of the Delphos-site soil?"

He retorted, "I cannot account for that by any natural process that I know of. And what we end up with here is a situation in which we generate more questions than can be answered, and that's, I guess, typical of science generally."

I tried once more to get him to speculate what the source of such strange physical traces might be. I asked, "Does the kind of phenomenon that occurs lead you to think of some kind of flying object that exists in our world today? Something that is manmade, I mean."

"Again," Dr. Zeller responded, "I must answer this by saying we're in the dark. First of all, unfortunately we can't reproduce these conditions. We simply can't call down a flying saucer, as it were, and ask it to hover above the soil while we watch the effects."

I interrupted him. "But is there any aircraft that you know of now that would cause the variance in luminescence like that at Medford?"

"Okay, let me say this." He knew I was becoming mildly anxious for something a little more concrete than what he had been describing. "I don't think it would be possible at all for a helicopter to produce this type of effect. There's simply nothing in the down-wash from the blades that could do it. As for other types of vehicles—automobiles, trucks, or aircraft of any other sort—the answer is no, they couldn't produce that type of effect. No possibility at all."

And that was as far as Dr. Zeller would go, on or off the record. The process of wrenching answers from scientists sometimes proves to be very painful. UFOs are the stuff popular journals exploit. They seem to bear a leprous label that puts them beyond the pale of legitimate inquiry. The Viking mission to Mars and the speculation about life on other planets has the federal government's blessings and money. UFOs do not.

Dr. Zeller left me with this thought. He said, "You know, frankly, I've never seen an unidentified flying object. However, I have never seen a meteorite land, and I know they exist." The wall was up. The subject of UFOs could be pressed no further. It was time to search out other investigations in the field. The UFO story abounded with data that had been collected by interested lay people who risked their reputations spending many long hours compiling convincing evidence of UFO sightings.

I wanted to talk to Major Donald Keyhoe, USMC, retired. He was the director of the National Investigation Committee on Aerial Phenomena (NICAP) from 1957 to 1970. Before assuming that post, he had conducted a private investigation on the UFO reports that the Air Force's Project Sign had studied (later called Project Grudge and Project Blue Book).

Major Keyhoe lives in a small town called Luray, Virginia. It's a graceful little community endowed with a sense of southern grace and hospitality. I was on the phone with Major Keyhoe. He was in a quiet mood. He had been through hundreds of interviews before, and I suppose I just numbered one more on his list.

Because of his association with the military, Major Keyhoe was privy to a great deal of classified information. But there was one morsel contained in his book *Aliens from Space* that particularly interested me:

> Since 1947, UFOs have maneuvered over space bases, atomic-energy centers, airports, cities, farms, obviously observing every aspect of our civilization for some highly important purpose. During the long surveillance, the Air Force has made two full-scale evaluations of the verified evidence. In both analyses, detailed and documented later, Air Force scientists and intelligence officers reached this secret conclusion: *the UFOs are spacecraft from a more advanced world engaged in an extensive survey of our world.*

"Major Keyhoe, do you still believe that the UFOs are extraterrestrial?" I asked.

"There isn't any question about it," he exclaimed. "You can go through any alternative there is, and it comes down just to one thing. I mean the idea that everybody's wrong, everybody's made mistakes."

"Is there evidence—?" I began, but he didn't let me finish my sentence.

"There's not only evidence, there's proof. Visual sightings, information—all of them sighting these things, objects flying around the formation. There's radar in two different positions picking up the things and tracking them. Photographs of the radioscopes, all showing exactly what happened. For a while the Air Force refused to release any radarscope, and then they denied there were any radar trackings. Finally they did admit they had trackings, but they said there was none of it that was significant. The only significance was that they were tracking real objects which were under intelligent control."

That brought our conversation to an end. Major Keyhoe was holding steadfast to the accusations he had made in *Aliens from Space*. According to Keyhoe:

> In 1969 the Air Force announced that all UFO reports had been explained. In this same nationwide announcement the Air Force declared its UFO investigation ended. *At that very time, Air Force interceptor pilots were trying to bring down these unknown flying objects by secret orders of the Aerospace Defense Command.*

I wasn't used to such straightforward statements. Major Keyhoe didn't seem to employ disclaimers or qualifiers. It was a refreshing change of pace from the scholarly academic approach, which attempted to remain objective at all times. I decided to contact a few more members of laity working with UFOs. I wondered what kind of speculations NICAP's current chairman, Jack Acuff, would be willing to reveal.

In a telephone conversation, I outlined some of the highlights of my recent interviews and compared them to the latest NICAP findings.

"We have some hard factual data concerning the existence of UFOs," he said. "In many of the better cases that are reported to NICAP, you find that in addition to witness testimony you have hard data associated with the case. Many times the data take the form of radar returns from the object that is being reported."

We discussed the pros and cons of new cases, better

photos that actually depict what witnesses claim to have seen. Lately there are new criteria for determining the credibility of witnesses. Not only must the honesty of the witness be established, but also his ability to evaluate what he is seeing. For example, an airline pilot is probably a better witness than a farmer who has never flown. Overall, there has been a radical increase in the number of highly credible witnesses. At least two to four thousand cases exist that cannot be explained as anything conventional. In addition, there are the radar trackings and some photos. Missing is any clue to the source of UFOs. As Jack Acuff said, "We know UFOs exist, but where they come from and what they are is still theoretical."

As a representative of NICAP, Jack Acuff shies away from discussions of "extraterrestrial origin." He is a businessman with two successful enterprises of his own. He serves as executive director for three scientific associations, in addition to his duties with NICAP. Therefore, some holds remain barred.

Before ending our talk, I asked Jack how he got into the UFO business. "Well, probably like most of the people with a scientific background," he said, "I had a scientific curiosity about UFOs, but in terms of believing in UFOs, I had mixed feelings. So much of the material that had been written was so sensationalized that if it were read from an analytical viewpoint you had to end up doubting the data, but after I became associated with NICAP and had the opportunity to evaluate cases for myself, I became convinced that it's something we just couldn't explain."

"It still is," I muttered, and thanked Mr. Acuff for his time. I was beginning to feel condemned to a limbo of "possibilities" just out of reach, and "discoveries" coming soon. My first excited plunge into the world of UFOs had left me stranded in a chilling never-never land filled with "Stop Here" signs. Cautious understatement was the order of the day. Somewhere there had to be sensible yet daring investigators who were developing lines of inquiry that might produce conclusive evidence that UFOs did or did not exist. So far, each probe has produced a welter of controversy.

I dug back into the history of modern UFO study, and everywhere I looked, the story was the same. It began in the rarefied air near Mount Rainier in 1947. Pilot Kenneth Arnold saw nine saucerlike objects shimmer and fly erratically across the cold, clear sky. His report of the incident did more than add the words "flying saucer" to our vocabulary. It began the modern debate: "UFOs—Yes or No?" After that time, Project Blue Book, the Air Force investigative unit, now discontinued, examined thousands of sightings. Most of the sighted objects were crossed off as birds, atmospheric phenomena, balloons, satellites, the aurora borealis, and assorted planets and stars, but 6 percent remain as absolutely unexplained or "unidentified." Add to this 6 percent the fact that Blue Book falsely attributed sightings to the Orion constellation when it was not visible, to the Goodyear blimp when it was six hundred miles away, and to military activity when none was taking place. Such discrepancies stoke the imagination of every investigator. The Pentagon, some believed, knows something we don't. In the opinion of most of those who follow the UFO problem carefully, the Air Force is guilty of suppression of vital information.

Harassed by such a significant number of Americans continually chafing at what officially was a closed matter, the Air Force in 1966 financed a team of investigators at the University of Colorado in an attempt to unravel some of Blue Book's conclusions. The former director of the National Bureau of Standards, Edward Condon, was to head the team and tackle what could only be considered an intriguing assignment.

Concurrently with this, Allen Hynek addressed *Science* magazine in a letter critical of his colleagues who scoffed at the saucer mystery with "buffoonery and caustic banter." He said that if he had spoken out before the Colorado team had been set up, "I would have been regarded as a nut."

After studying the material from Project Blue Book and other sources, James E. McDonald, a University of Arizona atmospheric physicist, concluded: "UFOs are the number-one problem of world science. I'm afraid that the evidence points to no other acceptable hypothesis than the extraterrestrial. The amount of evidence is overwhelmingly real."

On the other side, a colleague of McDonald's, astronomer Gerard Kuiper, states that the subject is "fanciful," and astronomer Carl Sagan of Harvard says that "at the present time there is no evidence that unambiguously connects the various flying-saucer sightings with extraterrestrial activity."

Debate followed automatically in the wake of any statement made about UFOs. As I picked up the field work, I headed toward Stanford University. I had been told that I might find the first glimmerings of a fine new investigative program at the Palo Alto campus.

My target was Dr. Peter Sturrock. He is a world-renowned astrophysicist who built a very successful pulsar model five years ago. His speech is accented in elegant British tones. He is a member of the American Institute of Aeronautics and Astronautics, and helped establish the UFO subcommittee called the Study Group on Anomalous Phenomena. The group is composed of professional scientists whose purpose is to collect, identify, and evaluate evidence, primarily physical evidence, concerning allegedly anomalous phenomena occurring in the earth's atmosphere.

The informal unit was founded to counteract the general feeling in the scientific community that UFOs must be ignored. Dr. Sturrock's colleagues feel that there isn't sufficient evidence to warrant this kind of wholesale avoidance. They aim to compile some firm empirical data that could clarify the issue.

I started my interview with a question about evidence other than reports. Sturrock smiled and said, "You know, there is no evidence that's as hard as most scientists would like to work with. On the other hand, all evidence is not anecdotal. There are photographs, and a small number of movie films."

I asked him if he could speculate as to the cause of this phenomenon. He quickly responded, "I don't want to speculate. I don't think that's the main problem facing scientists. I think that scientists spending two months looking through the reports might well come to the conclusion that there is a definite pattern to the data, and therefore there is something in the nature of a phenomenon of some kind which needs explanation."

Dr. Sturrock had effectively summed up his position in those few words. He was too new to the field to have chalked up any significant discoveries. Morever, it became clear during the course of our interview that he would move slowly and carefully through any area of investigation. Whatever ideas he decided to pursue, he was confronted by exactly the same problem that plagued Allen Hynek—funding. Regardless of where it was sought, money to pursue the process of identifying heretofore unidentifiable objects was difficult, if not impossible, to come by.

The presence in the general field of UFO study of scientists like Dr. Sturrock heartens old-timers in the game. They have been on the outer fringes of respectability for so long that they welcome newcomers with true warmth. The greeting they are given stuns researchers accustomed to the jeaolusy present in most scientific fields. Despite the fact that Dr. Sturrock is sympathetic with the efforts of UFO-ites, I found little nourishment in our talk. It was discouraging to think that I had all but plumbed the entire roster of "seekers."

In my round of interviewing the investigators, I had one more stop to make. I wanted to visit Dr. Frank Salisbury, a well-known plant physiologist at Utah State University. Utah State is perched on the dust-dry shore of Lake Bonneville in Cache Valley, Utah. From Dr. Salisbury's office window the horizon is etched on mountaintops foamed with snow. The sun was shining, and it seemed a beautiful day to conduct an interview.

Dr. Salisbury started researching UFOs and exobiology, the study of life in outer space, after publishing a paper in 1962 entitled "Martian Biology." In 1968 he participated in the scientific rebuttal of the Condon Report before the House Committee on Science and Astronautics. He helped demonstrate that the report was biased and incomplete. I wondered if his views had since changed. He said, "There are five possible hypotheses sometimes used to explain UFOs, namely, that they're natural phenomena, secret weapons, hoaxes, psychological phenomena, or extraterrestrial machines. I decided that maybe they were indeed extraterrestrial machines. But as the years went on, it became more and more difficult for me to explain them simply as visitors from another world who had just discovered us and were surveying us. From the various sightings listed in history books, it seemed that they've been around for centuries, and it's difficult to imagine that they would survey us that long without some kind of formal contact. Furthermore, they seem to engage in things that just don't make sense. Whatever they were —and at the time, I was thinking of extraterrestrial machines—I thought they were putting on a display for our benefit. Why would they play with us this way? Why would they manipulate us?

He paused. The ideas he was about to articulate were complex matters, and he approached them gingerly. "I think that they really do try to manipulate us. I think there is an intelligence behind it. At least, that's my feeling right now. There is an intelligence of some kind behind it, and they're trying to manipulate us in various ways for reasons that I haven't the faintest idea about. I don't know. I think that we need to broaden our way of thinking about such things; we have to consider not only the idea that they are extraterrestrial machines, but maybe they're something more subtle and more scary in a lot of ways."

I stopped him. "What do you mean?" I asked.

"Well," he said, "maybe you can start talking about devils and angels, if you want to. These are beings in a different dimension that are able at will to manifest themselves for their own purposes, be they good or bad. So how about that?"

Having entered the realm of gross speculation, Dr. Salisbury seemed relieved that he had finally been able to air this growing conviction. He continued. "I think that becomes an extremely unscientific sort of a way to think about things, but I've kind of been forced into it in the last two or three years. And I don't know what to do about it anymore from the standpoint of the objective scientific investigation that I've tried to pursue for these many years."

"It must be quite a dilemma for you, in view of your training," I said.

"Yes," he replied, "I find it a dilemma, except that I must state that I'm an active member of the Mormon Church, and it's becoming easier to think about it in terms of my theology than it is my science."

I ended our meeting and left his office. As I looked back over my notes, I realized that it would be easier for him in view of his religion. Didn't the Mormons believe that they were the descendants of the spirit children of God, that they came from someplace other than the earth? I understood the problem he faced in trying to reconcile his new beliefs with classic scientific methods. I understood all the pauses now. He had begun to stretch far beyond the limits of acceptable scientific speculation—a place which I have often found breathtaking and expansive. Alternative explanations are the launch pads from which old mysteries may be explored and perhaps solved, but they are treacherous swamps to scientists.

I realized now that my search for extraterrestrials would have to turn to the people who had reported encounters with UFOs.

3

To Witness the Fires

The metal fingers scratched an uneven black trail across the paper. The writing was indecipherable, but I kept staring at the marks. I was afraid that if I so much as moved I would break the intense communication that had grown between the interrogator and his subject.

"What was it doing?"

"It was hovering. There wasn't any movement—no rotating movement and no up-and-down movement I could detect at all."

The needles on the polygraph jumped and then returned to their slight wiggling movements. I wondered what the jump meant, but I had to wait until the interview was complete before I would know if Carroll Critchfield was lying.

The examiner went on. "Did you see it land?"

Carroll Critchfield answered, "No, I didn't see it land, but evidently it did, 'cause we didn't see it anymore, and later we went back and found the landing prints."

For a moment the only sound in the room was the hum of the machinery. Elmer Criswell, Jr., an instructor in police science at Harrisburg Area Community College in Pennsylvania, hunched over his work table, noting information along the edge of the printout of the responses of his subject. Carroll Critchfield was hooked up to the polygraph. He had volunteered to take the test almost out of desperation. "Maybe," he had said earlier, "this will convince some of the people I know that I *did* see it."

Carroll claims he witnessed the passing of a UFO. His story of what occurred to him after the sighting is not substantially different from what happened to all of the forty-five people I interviewed as I undertook the search for extraterrestrials. From the moment they reported what they had seen, each was subjected to the hard-bitten skepticism of media reporters, friends, and even family. They were forced to undergo constant questioning, and were bedeviled by what I term the "setup." The "setup" was described to me as beginning with a casual reference to the UFO-sighting incident. It would usually come up in the course of an introduction to a third party.

"This is John—you might have heard about him. He's the one who, uh, saw . . . why don't you tell him, John?"

Prompted to tell his story for the eight hundredth time, John faced the prospect of being "assisted" along the way by his so-called friend. "Tell him, John, about the way the monster looked." There was in fact no monster, but John's friend has created his own version of the event and has come to believe the invented version. When John corrects him, the friend is offended and finally accuses John of changing his report, thus casting a huge shadow over John's honesty and sanity.

I discovered an infinite number of variations on this rather cruel theme as I talked to people who claimed to have seen a UFO land. Their past experiences have made them wary of interviews, and every investigator runs smack up against their reluctance to become involved in investigation of the subject.

Ted Phillips, a field associate of Allen Hynek's Center for UFO Studies, summed up his view of the problem in this way: "The greatest percentage of UFO sightings are being suppressed at the source by the witnesses themselves, for fear of ridicule. When we get reports, if the witnesses so desire, we will not use their names publicly in any way, shape, or form, and only in that way have we received some of the very good cases. And another important thing to point out is that I have found in the very excellent 'trace' cases that the witnesses almost always were absolute skeptics about UFOs. They were simply going about their business. The farmer is going down to milk his cow, and there sits a UFO. Now, the farmer couldn't care less who believes him, you know. He says it was there. I've talked to many farmers in Missouri who had very close encounters, and they frankly say, 'Well, I don't care if anyone believes it or not. I saw it. I know it was there.' These men are very busy trying to provide for themselves and their families and certainly don't have time to be making up stories about UFOs."

As Ted spoke, I remembered the problem I had had in interviewing men like Philip Baker, a millworker from Mellen, Wisconsin. Phil and his family witnessed a UFO landing. As to whether or not he would consent to be questioned, he said, "I don't really want to get involved. I have things in life here that I would consider of much greater interest than UFOs." I finally convinced him to tell his story, but I remember his pained shrugs when he said, "I guess it won't ever die."

I understood clearly what Phil meant and why he and the others were reluctant to tell me their stories. They were afraid "it would just start all over," as Carroll Critchfield said. One of the reasons Critchfield granted the interview was my willingness to set up a lie-detector test. I felt it would be a way to verify his story. Before I set up the polygraph experiment, however, I decided we should have a full "work-up" on the life and world of the Critchfield family.

The Critchfields live in Big Chimney, West Virginia. As the name suggests, Big Chimney is nestled in the heart of the coal-mining country. The terrain is pine-green, rugged, and rocky. The Interstate highway leads into a jagged valley dotted with white frame houses that seem to close in on the road from all sides.

As I arrived, an unseasonable heat wave lay over the valley like a bell jar. The air-conditioner in the rented sedan picked this moment to expire. I desperately wanted to reach the Critchfield house, as much to get out of the heat as to finally hear the story Carroll Critchfield was so reluctant to tell.

There are no street signs in Big Chimney. The town is so small that there's no need for them. The only restaurant, Cook's, is a friendly rough-hewn truck stop. "Sure," the waitress said when I asked her if she knew Carroll Critchfield. "Everyone in town knows each other." And she pointed up a tiny road that led to the Critchfield house.

Carroll Critchfield is a tall, gangling man. His physical movements, like his soft West Virginia drawl, are slow and careful. He works as a foreman in a chemical plant. He's quiet, gentle, and almost shy. He was uncomfortable as he began to recount the events of June 12, 1975. It was probably the most remarkable night in the collective lives of the Critchfield family. Carroll offered only a cryptic version of his astounding story. He preferred to sit back and let his two boys, Jerry, fifteen, and Jeff, twelve, tell the tale. I tried to prod him into opening up, but I soon realized he was a reticent man who eased slowly into a new situation. What's more, he had the lie-detector test looming ahead of him, and he seemed preoccupied.

His younger son, Jeff, was more than willing to relive the events of that harrowing night. Jeff is the loquacious son, whereas his older brother, Jerry, is wrapped up in high-school track and Little League. In fact, it was a Little League game that drew the Critchfield family out on that balmy June night. The way Jeff described it, the overall mood in the car was one of disgruntlement. Jerry's team had suffered a resounding defeat, and Jerry was sulking in the back seat. Their mother, Barbara, was slumped in the seat next to him, wishing that she had never left the house that night. Barbara was eight months' pregnant and starting to feel like a "water balloon ready to burst." She had gone along because the game meant so much to Jerry, but now was of no mind to cajole him out of his sullen mood.

As usual, Jeff had monopolized the conversation. He was asking his father incessant questions about the batting averages of the Cincinnati Reds when Barbara let out a shriek that almost caused Carroll to drive the family's Ford jalopy off the Interstate. His heart dropped, as he now described it, into his stomach, because he was sure Barbara's time had come. Then Jeff noticed it too and started yelling. There were flashing lights in the night sky hovering silently over a grove of thick trees. The family car was directly below the lights, and they could see the underbelly of what appeared to be a spacecraft.

It was at this point in Jeff's monologue that Carroll made a most uncharacteristic gesture and broke into the middle of the story. He began, in an apologetic, almost sheepish way, to say that he "lost himself" for those first few minutes and completely forgot his wife's condition. The only thing he had on his mind was tracking the object in the sky. As if on cue, Jeff made a dash into the adjoining nursery–breakfast room to scoop up his baby sister and bring her into the living room for general inspection. Carroll was beaming with delight. He looks like a man who will spoil his daughter rotten.

As Carroll described the sight, his voice became softer. He squinted slightly behind thick black-rimmed glasses. He wanted to be sure his portrait was accurate. "I looked up, and there was a big diamond-shaped object with big flat ends, sitting right above the treetops. My wife, she yelled out, so then I started trying to get off the road where I could stop to look at it."

"How high above you was it?" I asked.

"It was probably thirty or forty feet over the trees,

and the trees are probably forty feet high. This is just a guess, you know. The lights seemed to be all on top. You could see the form of it just real fine."

"You said the form was diamondlike, right?"

"Yes, looking underneath, it had big flat ends that I'd say were probably six to eight feet across, or maybe even bigger. I thought when I saw it that these were something that had slipped out, that maybe it was a saucer-type object, and these ends just shoved out."

"What was it doing?"

"It was hovering. There wasn't any movement—no rotating movement and no up-and-down movement I could detect at all."

Carroll Critchfield had marked the flight direction of the object and later went back to uncover a scarred landing site. "We found a big burned area and imprints about eighteen to twenty feet apart. They must have been made by an extremely heavy object, because some of them were as much as three inches deep. The imprint was down three inches in the ground."

"What was the condition of the soil?" I asked.

"It was hard. It is kind of a rocky soil," and then Carroll pointed out a strange fact. "The cattle wouldn't eat the grass around the imprints. They had eaten down everywhere else, but not the area where the imprints were."

I was ready to subject Carroll to the polygraph test. Elmer Criswell, Sr., of the Criswell Security Agency in Wheeling, West Virginia, had agreed to administer the test along with his son, Elmer, Jr. We extended the scope of the inquiry to cover the two Critchfield sons, Jeff and Jerry, as well.

The polygraph is only as good at detecting lies as the operator administering the test. In Elmer Criswell, Jr., we had a technician who trains police officers in the use of the machines. He explained that an experienced operator will be 99 percent correct in his subject evaluation.

I watched each step of the procedure that bound Carroll to the polygraph. Elmer described the purpose of each sensor. The readout printed by sensitive styli shows blood pressure, heartbeat, skin sensitivity, perspiration, and breathing rate. Almost invariably the body's unconscious nervous system pumps adrenaline when we lie. The accompanying physical effects can be simply traced. The machine records the reactions so that the examiner can spot the lie the instant it is told.

For almost twenty-five minutes the slow, even tones of Elmer Criswell elicited answers from Carroll Critchfield. Many of the questions zeroed in on what Carroll claimed to have seen. A sprinkling of seemingly unrelated and unimportant questions was added to leaven the mix and provide baselines for evaluating the crucial answers.

When it was over, Elmer Criswell wrote his report. It went as follows:

> I interviewed Mr. Critchfield on April 15 for an hour and a half, and then I interviewed him again April 16 on the morning previous to the polygraph examination. I spent several hours with him giving him the polygraph examination, and after the interview and the polygraph tests, it is my opinion that Mr. Critchfield told the complete truth concerning all events to the best of his knowledge and beliefs concerning this incident with the unidentified flying object.

I hope the Criswell report ends the long harassment of Carroll Critchfield. Perhaps now he will no longer be troubled by those who condemn his story as a fabrication. For the record, both Jeff and Jerry also proved to be telling the truth about their UFO experience.

I had other eyewitnesses to see. I wanted to be convinced that I was basing our quest on solid ground. Whirling lights in the sky, streaming red glow-balls, and iridescent shapes have long been enchanting phenomena. History books are dotted with UFO tales. What did Ezekiel see? What did the people of Fatima observe? In 218 B.C. a UFO was described by Livy. Allied pilots encountered "foo-fighters." Hundreds of tubes and spheres were seen over Nuremberg in 1561. Before Kitty Hawk, our grandfathers sketched mysterious "airships," and one Captain Hooton drew a sketch from memory for the Arkansas *Gazette* in 1897. Waves of UFO sightings have, however, been on a steady increase in recent years, particularly since the detonation of the first atomic device at Alamogordo, New Mexico.

Are they reality or illusion? Just before his death in 1961, Carl Gustav Jung suggested that they are projections of the mind, corresponding to a deep human need. They are the result of a troubled world, an erosion of orthodox religious belief, something new that man has created to fill a deep religious void. Jung wrote that "God in his omniscience, omnipotence, and omnipresence is a totality symbol par excellence, something round, complete, and perfect."

Boston psychiatrist Benjamin Simon tends to agree that the saucers could represent "something for everybody," providing an "oceanic or cosmic feeling of immersion in the total universe, a sort of nirvana."

It was Simon's work with Barney and Betty Hill, an interracial couple from New Hampshire, that prompted author John G. Fuller to write a best-selling chronicle of their adventures in his book *The Interrupted Journey*. Fuller tells us that under hypnosis the Hills were literally abducted by a flying saucer and medically examined by humanoids, who tested Mrs. Hill, among other things, for pregnancy, causing substantial psychological damage. It could be concluded that these fantasies were deeply distorted by the problem of racial criticism and the fact that Betty Hill was childless. Nevertheless, Fuller goes to great lengths to tell a fascinating story that is not simple to reject.

I found a need to see and hear firsthand, minute-by-minute accounts of a UFO landing. I wasn't satisfied with the reports I had read in newspapers and magazines. It seemed to me that they were edited in such a way as to reflect the bias of the reporter.

For those who share my frustration, I have decided to set down a number of stories as I heard them. I have treated each story the way it came to me in the exact words of the individual who lived it.

Phil Baker was one of the interview subjects. His home is in Mellen, Wisconsin, about twenty miles south of Ashland. Mellen brings to life Andrew Wyeth's brown-toned view of rural northern America. Long ribbons of narrow blacktop or just plain dirt roads lived in this country all his life. He works in a wood- link one isolated farmhouse to another. Phil Baker has veneer manufacturing plant, but his heart is with the land. Each spring he anxiously awaits the last frost so that he can get out his harrow, turn his fields, and plant his summer food crop. Surrounded by his family and his land, he feels fulfilled. Fellow townsmen of Phil Baker, like newspaper editor Jasper Landry and Undersheriff George Ree, know him as a solid citizen.

On the night of March 13, 1975, Phil Baker, his wife, and four children—ages ten to seventeen—all participated in a singular event. Here is what happened, in their words, as they told it to me.

"My name is Philip Baker. I live at Mellen, Wisconsin, the northerly part of Wisconsin—that is, I work for Louisiana Pacific, Seaway Division, at Mellen, Wisconsin. I'm a machine operator. We produce high-grade veneer, which is put into the plywood. It's outside skin for the plywood.

"On March 13, 1975, in the evening, right around nine o'clock, I was sitting on the davenport. I had just gotten a box of seed that I had sent for, and opened it, when my daughter came in from outdoors. She was going to put the cats out. She came back in, and she was quite badly frightened. She said there was a UFO sitting on the town road up here. I could tell by the way she said it that she was badly frightened."

Jane Baker: "When I first saw it, I was scared. I felt like running. I didn't know where to go. I was scared. I don't know, when I watch these movies on TV, there's little green men coming out with long arms, getting the people and killing them. I got scared. I didn't know what to do. I really got scared, so I ran into the house. I didn't feel like going out, but when he went out, I went out—but I really felt like going upstairs and going under my blankets and hiding or something. I got scared."

Phil Baker: "By the time I got my shoes on and stepped out the door and stood there on the porch and looked, there it was, sitting big as life.

"What I saw was this object. It was dome-shaped

and had a brilliant halo. Bluish-green lights and red lights were around the outside, and in the center it had a real brilliant yellowish-white light that appeared to be coming from inside. It was really brilliant, and when I looked at it, I kind of had to squint my eyes.

"The object was making a very loud, high-pitched whiny sound. As we watched it, the high-pitched noise died down. It was just like it ran down. The red and green lights—they dimmed, until the colored lights themselves went out completely. The halo that appeared to be over it also dimmed considerably, and then it made a noise. It was like heavy metal hammering. Not like you're hammering tin or something, but a heavy metal. It did not have a rhythm to it.

"I thought I should go a little closer and try to examine it a little. I was frightened. My wife hollered out at me that I shouldn't go no closer, that we should call somebody. And I said, 'Well, who shall we call?' because that was the problem. You read so much about people calling, and everyone thinks they're a little bit odd, or something's wrong. So I hesitated."

Mrs. Baker: "I came downstairs and waited till Jane came running in and saying that Phil's going too close, and I went out and yelled at him to come in, because I didn't know what it was and I wasn't about to leave him get too close to it. It was dark, and all we could see was these lights, and I was ascared of it more than anything, because it was something unknown. I only stood on this porch, so actually I didn't see that much of it, but I knew darn well it wasn't something that had just come out of the sky from around here. That's why I told him not to get close."

Phil Baker: "Finally I called the undersheriff. He just lived down here a couple of miles, and when I was on the telephone speaking to him, the lights on the object completely faded off, and there was a bang, and it disappeared, and that was the end of the object. It was weird. I saw this object on the road, but my mind was telling me: Now, let's not believe it, because people probably'll think you're weird or simply that you're seein' things.

"The undersheriff came, and we went up the road. I

really didn't know what we were going to find. That explosion—I thought maybe we'd find some parts of metal or something, but what we were going to look for, I really didn't know."

George Ree, undersheriff of Mellen, Wisconsin: "Mr. Phil Baker called my residence. He told me there was a strange object north of his house. I could not understand him at first, so I told Mr. Baker to slow down, tell me what his problem was. So I finally got it out of Mr. Baker. I left my home. I went to Mr. Baker's. Mr. Baker and his children were standing out on that road when I came there. Mr. Baker told me, he said, I just missed this object. He said that I was about a minute too late. He was very, very excited. His children were very excited, so I didn't think too much of it. I quieted Mr. Baker down. I talked to his children and Mr. Baker, and I left. Then I came home."

Phil Baker: "I apologized when the undersheriff left me off, because I thought: Now we didn't find anything, he'll think I'm a little off. He says, 'Oh, no, just forget about it.' I said, 'Okay, let's forget about it,' and I said, 'but don't tell anybody about it, then.' Monty, my oldest boy, he was all upset. He says to my other two boys, 'Now, don't say anything, don't say anything to the kids at schools. We don't want any of this to get out.' Janie was in tears. She says, 'Well, I know what I saw. Don't try to tell me I didn't see anything 'cause,' she said, 'I know I saw it.'

"That was all there was to it. I don't think my life has really changed, except shortly afterward I was on the telephone more for two or three weeks after the incident than I was in my entire life before. Otherwise I don't think my life has really changed. Occasionally somebody will mention it to me. I don't think it'll ever die, and I was more concerned like with the kids in school. I mean, my boy intends to go to college next fall down at Stevens Point—it's a branch of the University of Wisconsin—and I certainly don't want him to be on some film on TV that makes fun of him, because that might ruin the rest of his life."

The story might be explained away in many ways. But later that evening, the strange sight on the town road outside the Baker home took another shape in the sky over Ashland County. Undersheriff Ree picks up the narrative.

Ree: "After I arrived at home, in about . . . I would say forty-five minutes, the sheriff called my residence and told me to go down into Iron County and check on these objects in the sky. When I arrived, one of my other deputies was at the scene, and there was two Iron County deputies. I pulled up behind the two squad cars, and I got outside and I asked the fellas what they was looking at. They told me there was a big, large, bright light which would have been on the outside of Highway 77. So we—my one deputy, myself, two Iron County deputies—we were watching this light. As we were watching this one object, one of the deputies says, 'Look to the right!' He said, 'There is another object!' It was about at treetop level, traveling at a high rate of speed toward that big bright light we had seen. The smaller light did not get too close to the large bright light that we were watching.

"In the meantime, there was two deputies working up on U.S. 2, west of Odena, which we call Birch Hill. We were talking back and forth on our police radio, and I told this deputy that if he would go up on the Birch Hill tower that he could probably see what we were looking at. So he drove up to Birch Hill—that's approximately sixteen miles east of Ashland—and him and another deputy got up on the tower, and from the tower he could see what we were looking at. He first saw this one that was very low—I considered it to be much lower than the two other objects. He could see that very plain. It was flashing. I say it was green and white. The deputies claim it was blue and white, so maybe I'm color-blind. I do not know. I still say it was green and white instead of blue and white. The rest of the people said it was blue and white. I'll go along with their story. There's more of them than me. In the meantime, as the deputies were up on the tower, they kept watching the one light. The first light that we saw never moved. It stayed stationary. The second light that came up—that was doing what we later considered was a jig—it was going around in a circle. It was moving from left to right and was just having a good old time up there. In the meantime, this one on the north of Highway 77 just stayed there, but the lights kept on flashing.

"After a period of time of . . . I don't know . . . fifteen, twenty minutes, half an hour—we lost track of time—the one that was north of the highway decided it was going to move. I got on the radio. I was standing by the squad car, I had the mike in my hand at all times talking to the other deputies, and I told him, I said, 'Pete, that one is coming back your way.' He said, 'I'll see.' Then he said, 'I can see it just comin' back.' Pete left the tower and went down to what they call the Madigan Road. He just started onto the Madigan Road when this object came zooming down over his squad car. At the time Pete said, 'The light is going over me!' His radio went out, and later, in about thirty seconds, forty-five seconds, his radio came back on and he told us over the radio that the light was so bright that he could have read a newspaper as this object went over his squad car."

A wild night in Ashland County, Wisconsin. A night with a light show in the sky, witnessed by six policemen.

As for the credibility of the Baker family, George Ree summed up his feeling about their story in these words: "If I would have left the Baker residence and come home and never saw none of this, I would have just thought it was probably a joke or something. But when I got called out the second time, I observed this bright object, and then the second object coming from the right going up to this large object, and then seeing the third object to our left, going north and over another deputy's car and kick out his radio—not just momentarily, but maybe knocked it out maybe for about thirty seconds—and there was two deputies there at the time stating that the light was so bright that they could have read a newspaper. I never saw anything like that before. As far as I'm concerned, they are objects, and I never seen those objects before. I wish I had never investigated the report. If it happens again, I'd go the other way. You don't know the problems this has caused me."

Like the Bakers and the Kay family and the Critchfields, George Ree has been subjected to "that look," to endless interrogations, and worst of all, to the constant questioning of his veracity. Wherever I went, I found similar stories.

There are other eyewitness accounts of UFO landings that I would like to share with the reader. So that I may pursue the main line of the story, I have placed the tales in the Epilogue. Each is reported, as the Baker story is told, in the words of the eyewitnesses as I recorded them for a film episode in the TV series *In Search Of . . .*

I knew now that my next investigations should focus on the reasons why UFO stories become suspect. I wanted to examine the way-out world of the saucer cultists.

4

The Tainting Problem

UFOs came of age in the United States in the year 1976. A national poll found in its opinion sampling that 50 percent of the respondents believed UFOs exist. Despite the cavils of the scientific establishment, despite the evident skepticism of most media sources, half the people of the country apparently consider UFOs a reality. Few topics have been so consistently maligned yet managed to remain part of the public consciousness.

There are obviously liabilities that come along with a subject's tenacious ability to draw followers. The potential for misguided hoaxes is enormous. I suspected that Ted Phillips' work would be plagued by pranksters. "Surprisingly," he told me, "we get very few hoaxes, and when we do, they're very easy to spot." He then told me the story of one attempt to foist a phony UFO sighting.

"A class of high-school students decided they would

conduct an experiment, a UFO landing, to test public reaction and just to study the effects on the people living in the area. And so they got together with a lady living on a farm up there, which really shored up their case. They took some gasoline and burned four kinds of imprinted areas outside of the large burn, and they went back into town and said, 'Hey, we just saw this big egg-shaped glowing orange thing lying in a field.' Some of the townspeople went out, and sure enough, they found the burned area, and when they asked the lady on whose farm this had happened, she said, 'Yeah, I saw it too.' This was all part of their little plot, and with the confirming outside witness it sounded like a really interesting case. Thank goodness, however, before I went up there, the friend of mine who lives in that area went over to the site and in checking around thought he could detect gasoline fumes. When he confronted the boys with this and told them they could be in a great deal of trouble for perpetrating a hoax, they admitted the whole thing. It was quite an elaborate thing, although it would not have stood up under soil analysis. We would have known right away."

It is simple enough to disprove the joker's concoction of a UFO story. It is much more difficult to deal scientifically with a sighting such as Phil Baker's. All available evidence and corroborative witnesses support the tale told by the Bakers.

Researchers approaching the field of UFO study quickly conclude that they have a broad-based puzzle. They have to remold their thoughts on once taken-for-granted facts in physics, astronomy, and geology if the puzzle is to be solved. I remember the short preliminary phone interview I had with Dr. Sturrock before I visited him in Palo Alto. His thoughts captured the essence of the new science's present dilemma. He said, "You know, it's very difficult to study the UFO subject. I have been led to really reconsider the foundations of science and the method of scientific inference. It's all very well to say this study isn't scientific. But then you raise the question: What is scientific? And that really comes down to the question of: What is science? It's very easy to give examples and say that physics is science, and so is chemistry, but that isn't much help when you're facing a subject. And you can't say, 'Study the UFOs the way you study other sciences.' So you're faced with the task of returning to the fundamental ideas of trying to understand the nature of science and the nature of scientific inference."

It's all very well and good to throw away the neat little pocket edition of the universe. Something, however, must replace the old perspective. Drs. Hynek and Sturrock are developing new scientific methods, and I admire them greatly for their conceptual effort. I hope they reach the goal of finding the Rosetta Stone of UFO science. In the meantime, however, we are left with articles that must be taken on faith. There are those in the field of UFO study who have followed their faith down what I consider very creative paths. The cults have helped to taint the study, yet I understand why they have grown up. Through the ages man has woven yarns, myths, and religions to explain the bizarre phenomena he has witnessed. The myths are the result of his frustrations. Man is a great storyteller, assigning fabulous systems of order frameworks from which he can continue to live and function amid a welter of troubling confusions. He lives with and maintains various theories until they no longer make any sense in light of his ever-ongoing experiences. He is the master scenario builder, able both to invent and to document his own comedy or tragedy. I found it no surprise that in the face of the UFO mystery some nonscientists find it fulfilling to establish religions.

One of the first fellowships joining mysticism and interplanetary phenomena in a holy coital union is the Aetherius Society, founded in London on May 29, 1955, according to its followers, "on orders from extraterrestrial intelligences." The Aetherius Society believes the earth has been at the brink of disaster several times in its history. Each time the technologies of previous civilizations (Atlantis and Lemuria included) discovered nuclear energy, water poured over the land, and giant floods devastated the civilization. The Aetherians claim that the flood is man's translation of an axial flip which the earth undergoes in order to save itself from disaster and the impending nuclear threat.

After 1947 the flying-saucer sightings were on the

rise, and the Aetherians claim there was good reason. The Nagasaki bombings threatened our planet's survival, and UFOs were landing in order to assess the situation. They are likened to Peace Corps volunteers coming to aid underdeveloped colonies.

The Aetherians use another example to clarify their credo. Each planet in our system is like a classroom in which people live and learn. We graduate from planet to planet. The length of time spent in "school" varies with each individual lifestream. Earth is the nursery-school planet. Saturn is the oldest and highest planet in the system. Needless to say, reincarnation is a main tenet in this faith. Planetary visitors are considered great cosmic masters who come to earth to guide our less-advanced technology.

The origin of the Aetherius Society can be dated to a Saturday morning in May, 1954. Dr. George King was purportedly given a command to "Prepare yourself! You are to become the Voice of Interplanetary Parliament." Dr. King knew nothing of flying saucers and had not heard of an Interplanetary Parliament, according to Aetherius followers. He had studied Yoga and the art of metaphysical healing ten years prior to this strange visitation. When the command was given, he could therefore appreciate its vital significance even though at that time he couldn't fully understand it. The Aetherian account of the society's founding continues.

Eight days later, in a small apartment in London's West End, King—still bothered by the command—had a visitor. This unexpected guest, a Yogi from northern India, walked straight through the locked door and sat down in front of the startled King. The visitor was aware of the Interplanetary Parliament and described to King the mission on which the cosmic intelligences wished him to embark. He was chosen, it was said, because of his deep and vital interest in truth and his concern for mankind. He had the ability, he was told, to prepare mankind for a new age.

King began the work, throwing aside his own business affairs and personal pleasures, at last attaining telepathic contact with a being living on the planet Venus. The thing from space called himself Aetherius.

In January of the following year, King, following

exactly the instructions from space intelligence, started his long task of convincing the public of the wisdom of the "right path."

From these remarkable beginnings the Aetherius Society, according to their records, has grown into the largest UFO/metaphysical organization on earth. Branches of the society are found in forty-three countries. The latest challenge facing this group is the construction of a gigantic "shape-power" temple on a hundred-thousand-dollar site not far from Sunset and Vine in Hollywood. The temple, the design of which would boggle the mind of the most avid reader of fantasy magazines, consists of enormous "cones and spheres" constructed in such a way as to balance the "natural pranic forces through the stress which they exert upon prevailing lines of magnetic force."

I went to the society's current base in Los Angeles. I wanted to see for myself the universe they populated. Located in the heart of Hollywood, the society's American headquarters consists of three modest stucco buildings, a trinity of one-story tract homes painted pink with pastel borders. Their color was the only feature that distinguished them from the rest of the residential homes in the area. The priest I spoke to seemed totally rational. He was polite, well-read, and quite patient with my questions. He explained that the Aetherius religion was based entirely upon spiritual service in the world, and only coincidentally on personal enlightenment. He cited this as a unique feature in the religion. On the wall in the room of worship was a poster with the words "Operation Prayer Power/3rd Prayer Power Battery Discharge to Cyprus Peacemakers/Cease-Fire Announced Soon Afterwards." I asked what they meant by a "battery." Was this a symbol or an actual physical object like a crucifix in other religions. Quite matter-of-factly he replied, "It's a battery, a box containing certain material which can accept and store a spiritual charge that may be obtained with the right equipment. The energy is created through prayer power."

I realized that in every religion on earth, there are cant and sacred artifacts. The Aetherius Society wasn't very different from any other, except that they explained old-time theology in modern technological jargon. I asked the minister what his interpretation of UFOs was. He showed me a pamphlet that read:

> Flying saucers are interplanetary spacecraft from other Planets in this Solar System. The other planets in our Solar System are inhabited by highly cultured races millions of years ahead of us, spiritually and scientifically. There is no war, disease, old age, earthquakes, violent storms, floods, drought and such on other Planets in this System. The people are peace-loving, compassionate and devote their lives in service to others.

I found the amalgam of religion and UFOs unpalatable, but the Aetherians were on the same side of the scale compared with what I found in northern California.

In the autumn of each year, not far from the Berkeley campus of the University of California, a very special group invades the premises of the gracious old Claremont Hotel. I decided I would join the truth-seekers, and began to prepare myself mentally for my journey to the annual Spacecraft Convention.

The convention was sponsored by Understanding, Inc., Borderline Science, Research Associated, and Source Unlimited. Upon entering the foyer I encountered an endless barrage of booths, display stands, UFO photos, religious symbols, and other curiosities peculiar to that group of people who opted to distinguish themselves from orthodox or establishment UFO investigations. Mounds of books, drawings, and photographs of spacecraft heaped into great imposing stacks lined the stalls and bookracks scattered about the hall. There was an authenticity in the facial expressions of many of the convention-goers. They regarded their business at the convention very seriously. I spoke to some of the exhibitors and found them to be earnest in their beliefs. Many of them honestly feel they have been in either telepathic or physical communication with our planet's intergalactic friends and foes. These people, these truth-seekers, represent the contactees who are beyond the threshold of even the new science. They claim somehow to have tangled with the Master Jesus,

Firkon of Mars, Orthon of Venus, and others. Their speech is peppered and exotically accented with the mention of names like Clarion, Tythan, Korendor, Blaau, Schara, and Foser—the earth's invisible second moon.

I walked over to a booth with a hand-scrawled sign reading "The Reorganized Church of the UFO. Listen to the Words of the Space People." I stared at the spectators around me and noticed a young man in the corner busily signing photographs of himself. He appeared to be a newly recruited celebrity in cosmic society. My neighborly bystander suddenly whispered, "He has made contact with Pollious, the grand coordinator of the Andromeda sector of the Galactic Union."

In the middle of the hall I noticed a fragile silver-haired lady sitting alone in front of an old tape recorder perched on an oak table. She looked at me, eyes twinkling. "Would you like to hear the beautiful message we have?" I nodded. With that, she flicked the button, and a stilted voice began to resound, fading in and out from moment to moment.

"I am Lelan, the head of the government of the planet Nobelia. I speak to you from across the parsecs. We have contacted the president of the United States, the pope, and all the other world leaders, but they have chosen to ignore us, so we are acting through a far wiser man. R. Spencer Jason will be your leader. We must rescue you from the evil influence of vicious inhabitants of the planet Zeno. Let me warn you that the Zenonians will stop at nothing to prevent our saving Earth. They control all government officials on your planet. . . ." The tape was still playing as I quietly slipped away.

Most groups develop because of a strong belief in specific events that have been said to have already happened or that are prophesied to occur in the near future. Doomsday prophets aren't new. However, in the course of my research I discovered a group called the Seekers, which proved to be of significant psychological interest. They had, in fact, committed themselves on record. They stipulated the exact date of their envisioned catastrophic occurrence and invited the press and electronic media to witness this event. Their belief was so strong that it overcame and essentially denied the very outcome. Their prophecy proved false. Yet they were so committed to their belief that no amount of nonevidence could deter them. The following story is a brief account of the Seekers' history.

A number of years ago the Lake City *Herald* of Lake City, Minnesota, headlined this story: PROPHECY FROM PLANET CLARION CALL TO CITY: FLEE THAT FLOOD. IT'LL SWAMP US ON DEC. 21, 1951 OUTER SPACE TELLS SUBURBANITE." "Lake City," it reported, "will be destroyed by a flood from the Great Lake just before dawn, Dec. 21, according to suburban housewife Mrs. Marian Keech of 847 West School St., who said the prophecy is not her own. It is the purport of many messages she has received by automatic writing. The messages, according to Mrs. Keech, are sent to her by superior beings from a planet called 'Clarion.' These beings have been visiting the earth, she says, in what we call flying saucers. During their visits, she says, they have observed fault lines in the earth's crust that foretoken the deluge. Mrs. Keech reports she was told the flood will spread to form an inland sea, stretching from the Arctic Circle to the Gulf of Mexico. At the same time, she says a cataclysm will submerge the West Coast from Seattle, Washington, to Chile in South America."

The book *When Prophecy Fails* details the events leading up to the above article. Marion Keech had become acquainted with the entities of two planets, whom she referred to as the Guardians. She received many messages from the Guardians, instructing her to share her information with only people she could trust. It was soon after this advice that she met Dr. Thomas and Daisy Armstrong, both devotees of the cult and founders of a group called the Seekers, who met weekly to discuss metaphysical subjects. Their friendship seemed to be part of a prescribed destiny. The Armstrongs and Mrs. Keech began to correspond with each other. Mrs. Keech kept them informed of new developments in the Guardians' messages.

During the subsequent months, the Guardians outlined a new philosophy, and their messages assumed a new flavor. The Clarionites, or Guardians, promised they would visit Earth and let themselves be seen. The themes of violence and warfare were repeated, and commands were issued to Mrs. Keech to "instruct the people of Earth . . . that they are rushing toward suicide."

In addition to those general messages, the Guardians also notified Mrs. Keech of an extraterrestrial visit at Lyons Field military base on August 1, and the Armstrongs and Mrs. Keech traveled there to await the visitors. However, with the exception of one "strange visitor," the sojourn to Lyons was uneventful. But later, to her great relief, Mrs. Keech received a message that the visitor was indeed an outer-space-nik disguised as a human. Mrs. Keech considered he was "strange" because he had refused a cold drink and "his eyes looked through my soul and the words sent electric currents to my feet."

Equipped with her new belief, Mrs. Keech, together with the Armstrongs, developed a complex rationale delineating the Seekers' credo while adding momentum to Mrs. Keech's continuing conversations with the Guardians. Their new philosophy surfaced when Dr. Armstrong released a mimeographed "Open Letter to American Editors and Publishers" explaining Mrs. Keech's prophecy. Hence, they embarked on the first voyage of a new movement.

A second dispatch followed: "The place is Lake City, and the country around. The date is December 21. As the scene opens, it is dawn but still dark. The actors are awakened to the sound of a terrible rumbling. The earth shakes, the tall buildings topple. The waters of the Great Lake rise in a terrific wave which covers the city and spreads east and west. A new river forms and flows from the Lake to the Gulf of Mexico."

Having publicly committed themselves to the message, the Seekers began actively to proselytize. Although their effect was minimal, they were able to assemble a group of believers. These followers believed in the legitimacy of the message and were convinced that the Guardians would spare them from the horrible catastrophe about to take place by whisking them away in their flying saucers. One of the Seekers made an interesting comment on her own conviction. She said, "I have to believe the Flood is coming on the twenty-first because I've spent nearly all my money. I quit my job, I quit comptometer school, and my apartment costs me one hundred dollars a month. I *have* to believe." Her comment is a rather astute and perceptive observation when closely analyzed.

The Seekers were evolving in the traditional fashion. They gave lectures. Lessons were mimeographed. Endless discussions were held on the adverse effect of smoking and of eating meat. Their forthcoming voyage from doomed Earth to the planet Clarion was celebrated. Biblical identities were assumed. Séances were held. Ouija boards were dusted, and crystal balls were polished to a gleaming luster.

Time was growing short for the Seekers, and Dr. Armstrong announced that the group was now closed to new members. Thus the group became an exclusive agent.

Publicly committed as the Seekers were, the long wait for the Clarion vessel was pure agony for most of the group. Many went into self-induced trances (one childless woman announced that she was about to give birth to the baby Jesus). As the time grew near, precautions were taken against the group's common enemies—the disbelievers, scoffers, and the unenlightened.

It was now December 17, and Dr. Armstrong explained his position. "I'll say to you that all of you who are interested in saucers are in a special category. Now, you don't know that, but you are—because it seems that the people around the world who have been having a special interest in saucers are people who have had that interest because they had something with themselves that goes back to things they have forgotten. . . . Spacemen have said that they are here for a purpose, and one of those purposes is to remove certain of their own people from the earth. . . ."

Excitement was mounting in Lake City. The newsmen were persistent. The reporting ranged from straightforward news releases to tongue-in-cheek items. Armstrong and Mrs. Keech recorded a tape for national broadcast. The Seekers were readying themselves for takeoff in the spacecraft, and time was drawing near.

But something happened prior to December 21 that

made the subsequent events even more incredible. Mrs. Keech received a call from a Captain Video, informing her that a saucer would land in her backyard before the appointed day. All was ready. The TV station dispatched their mobile unit. Crowds assembled to await the heavenly visitors. But when no glowing disk materialized, the crowds began to shuffle away.

Mrs. Keech told followers that the visitors from space weren't prepared to offer themselves to unfriendly citizenry at that time. She said that another message was received informing her that the previous mishap was simply a "drill" and that the Seekers were to continue to have faith in the men from outer space.

It is difficult to understand how or why this shabby excuse didn't bewilder or discourage even the staunchest believer, but it even seemed, incredibly, to strengthen the faith of the group.

On December 20 Marian Keech received the message they were waiting for: "At the hour of midnight you shall be put into parked cars and taken to a place where ye shall be put aboard a porch [saucer] and ye shall be purposed by the time you are there. At that time you shall have the fortuned ones forget the few who have not come, and at no time are they to be called for. They are but enacting a scene, and not a person who should be there will fail to be there at the time you are to say 'What is your question?' . . . and at no time are you to ask what is what, and not a plan shall go astray and for the time being be glad and be fortuned to be among the favored. And be ye ready for further instructions."

It was signed "Beleis."

The taut line of tension finally slackened, only to be drawn into a knot once again. It was true. Preparations would actually continue!

Calls continued to pour in, and the group handled them with quiet, knowing courtesy. Exhausted by lack of sleep, they carefully explained their doctrine to all who would listen, and many did. In the early afternoon, two wire services informed Mrs. Keech that earthquakes had occurred in California and in Italy. "It all ties in with what I believe," was her comment. Then more instructions came: "Be on your toes and give it to the papers at the time they come to you. . . . Give them the works and put thy furbish in."

And then nothing!

Visitors began to decline. Armstrong's sister tried to have Daisy and him declared legally insane and requested the custody of their children. But Mrs. Keech's belief persisted, although Armstrong began to hedge and in an interview delivered a series of thin, specious denials and excuses. However, the Seekers continued to contend that the invisible spacemen had, in fact, made an appearance!

The followers were satisfied. The world hadn't been destroyed. And despite the cynicism of their enemies, the Seekers—the believers—had fulfilled their need to search for the truth about the unknown. This need to believe proved paramount to the belief itself. It maintained their psychological stability. The Seekers' tale numbers just one more in man's many attempts to order his experiences in the universe in a way in which he can most comfortably comprehend the unknown horizons. But as we will see time and time again, each person's method is unique—and yet perhaps they are essentially the same.

The Bo and Peep story, which filtered out of Oregon in October, 1975, can be added to the list of various attempts to outvie frustration. The following story made the national newswires and was relayed to CBS viewers by Walter Cronkite.

"A score of persons from a small Oregon town have disappeared," said Mr. Cronkite. "It's a mystery whether they've been taken on a so-called trip to eternity . . . or simply been taken. Terry Drinkwater takes a look at that story."

Drinkwater articulated, "Rocket ships from outer space: Buck Rogers fantasy—or is it? Today there is a group of earthlings who believe they're on their way to a rendezvous with such a ship for a trip to the unknown. Here along the cloud-covered coast near Newport, Oregon, a mysterious couple appeared three weeks ago, circulating a flier proclaiming a UFO would follow them to another life, another world. They held meetings . . . to recruit voyagers."

A local newspaperman reported that the vanished

people gave away everything—property, automobiles, boats, and money—and just left. Twenty or more faithful were supposedly headed for the eastern Colorado prairie. Then Bo and Peep were said to have allegedly disappeared. But James S. Phelan tracked the elusive couple down and detailed an account of his interview in the *New York Times Magazine* of February 29, 1976.

Marshall Herff Applewhite, alias Bo, is said to be a highly articulate man aged forty-four. Mrs. Bonnie Lu Trousdale Nettles, alias Peep, is described as a matronly woman of forty-eight. According to Phelan, they do not possess any of the trademarks of fanatics. Phelan states:

> They explained their bizarre project patiently. . . . They talked about their earthly mission for several hours while a bespectacled follower tape-recorded their words in the interest of accuracy. No one has left the planet yet. There have been "misunderstandings" that have caused some defections. But new converts continue to flock in. Their message is now being spread largely by devout followers. The converts engage in something called the Process, which entails seemingly aimless wandering in pairs and small groups, mostly from one public campsite to another. They spend their time in four activities: communing with "those in the next level" or outer space, "overcoming" their human attachments, soliciting small sums of money to live on, and seeking new converts.

They denied that there was anything mysterious to their disappearance and said it was due to the fact that they are busy writing a book.

One of the main bones of contention for some of the more restless devotees concerns the date of their promised departure to the "next level," the term Bo and Peep employ to describe their destination. Because of the muddle about the date, there have been some defections. But Bo and Peep insisted they *never* stated the time. Phelan explains:

> The departure cannot be pinpointed, they explain, because it depends on something called the Demon-

stration, a miracle that they will perform. As they describe it, they are to be assassinated by angry disbelievers and are then to rise from the dead. They base this prediction on the claim that they are not ordinary visitors from outer space but heavenly messengers whose appearance was foretold in the New Testament's Book of Revelation. The Biblical passage tells of "two witnesses" with the power to prophesy, whose message "tormented them that dwelt on the earth." The two are killed, according to Revelation, and their bodies lie in the street for three and a half days. Then the two rise from the dead, and a voice from heaven cries, "Come up hither," and in the sight of their foes they ascend "to heaven in a cloud." Bo and Peep maintain that they are the Biblical Two and that the cloud is actually a spacecraft....

Bo and Peep say that they are heavenly messengers, not outer-space tour guides. And they also claim that the Process's seeking-new-converts clause was in error. They are not interested in talking people into anything. Yet, Phelan reports:

> There are persistent stories that one Oregonian turned in $14,000 in cash in a brown paper bag to demonstrate how thoroughly he had overcome his attachment to money. But since the followers adopt new names and tend to move about a lot when they embark on the Process, it is difficult to locate anyone for questioning about who gave how much money to whom and what happened to it. . . . Successful completion of the Process literally changes the physical structure of the body, the Two declare. And in their reconstituted bodies, the converts will enter a real spacecraft and go physically up to the next level.
>
> "You don't go up to heaven and float around in a spirit form," Bo says firmly. . . . "It is a misguided religious concept that members in the real heaven do not use transportation," added Bo. "The spacecraft are a means for getting from one place to another."

The question is: Why do so many people believe that the Two will take them to heaven in a UFO? A number of followers were interviewed and gave a variety of explanations. According to Phelan, one of the followers explained his reasons thus: "I felt they were sincere, truth-seeking, happy and fulfilled. For the first time in my life I have a firm faith that there is something higher." But Phelan concludes the article:

> There is one common denominator among almost all of the converts. Almost all are seekers who like Moriah [one of the followers interviewed] have been looking for something for a long time. Many have tried Scientology, Yoga, Zen, offbeat cults, hallucinogens, hypnosis, tarot cards and astrology. Almost all believe in psychic phenomena. . . . "Some people," says the former opera singer who claims he will rise from the dead and take his followers to heaven on a UFO, "will try anything."

And that pretty much sums it up. In reviewing the diverse results of man's struggle with the unknown I came away with an inexplicable feeling. Perhaps, way out there, beyond the cold, icy reaches of outer space, these special groups of believers had found their own solution to the unexplained mysteries of man. While the orthodox sector of science and the journalistic truth-seeking buffs still stumbled about in the murky labs of sophisticated science, another sector of society had solved the puzzle in their own way. Perhaps frustration is the true mother of invention.

5

History Visits in the Deep Past

I wanted to see a UFO. So does everyone else who has spent time studying the reports of sightings. The closest I could come to fulfilling my wish was to ask an artist to faithfully render the objects that had been described by eyewitnesses.

Looking at the drawings, I realized that there was no single form of UFO. They were circular, rectangular, domed, and flat. What was universal was the brightness of their lights and the odd sounds that issued from the objects. In addition, there were patterns that emerged in the way witnesses described what they saw. They seemed to grope for adjectives or nouns that would naturally describe the thing they had seen. At first look, most were sure they were watching a helicopter hovering overhead, but then slowly they would recognize their mistake and realize that this time no comfortable, familiar, or natural object was before them.

I remembered their reluctance to talk, offset by their eagerness to share their experience because it had so deeply affected the sense of order in their lives. The UFO was a real event for them, but an event so devoid of explanation that it was almost certain to be ridiculed by sophisticated science.

We are surrounded by the accomplishments of modern science. We have seen rocket probes, so it is not a jump for us to imagine the existence of objects from other spaces in the heavens. But what of the people in the past who have no way to define what they were seeing?

From the earliest times man has gazed at the heavens and tried to extract some understanding of what lay beyond his reach and his comprehension.

Around 600 B.C. Thales of Miletus, near Turkey, and his pupil Anaximander were proposing the existence of other worlds. Many early Greeks also supported the idea that the earth is but one of many worlds, but inevitably they were harshly refuted by the religious institutions of those times. After all, earth was the center of the universe, all-powerful, the star of God.

But as long as man looked to the stars, he could not help but wonder and question. The Greek philosopher Democritus wrote that "all matter is made of atoms, invisible particles too small to be seen, indestructible and eternal. The earth was formed from a whirling mass of these atoms, and since space and time are infinite and the atoms are forever in motion, there must now be, and always have been, an infinite number of other worlds in various stages of growth and decay."

Democritus was supported by the Roman poet Lucretius, who, 350 years later, wrote, "Nothing in the universe is the only one of its kind, unique and solitary in its birth and growth." Although the theories set forth by Democritus and Lucretius were accepted by many, Greek religious concepts and Plato's perfect universe with only one world at the center became the doctrine of most stargazers.

In the early days, Christianity rejected the idea that God, the earth, and even the universe could possibly be duplicated. And since all visions are generally interpreted as being religious in nature, the Bible serves as a fruitful field to harvest in our search for UFOs.

Many examples of visitations to earth by strange beings from strange worlds are given in the Scriptures. Genesis 28:12 gives a description of an unexplained contact. Regarding a vision he had in the desert, Jacob saw a ladder directly from heaven to earth, certainly a good example of early space transportation. "And he began to dream, and, look! There was a ladder stationed upon the earth and its top reaching up to the heavens; and look! There were God's angels ascending and descending on it." In debating UFOs scientifically, Carl Sagan (*The Cosmic Connection*) uses Jacob's vision as an example of explainable phenomena—a full-scale display of the aurora borealis. However, as convincing as Sagan's explanation is, the aurora borealis is generally confined to arctic and antarctic regions, although a major display of lights was recorded in Rome in 464 B.C. But for some, Jacob's ladder will always be Jacob's ladder.

Various people have suggested that the vision of Ezekiel around 600 B.C. might have been a sighting of a spacecraft landing and some UFO-nauts coming out of it. Now, suppose that Ezekiel really saw an actual event and not just a vision inside his head. Then what was it that he saw?

Arthur Orton produced an interesting analysis in *Analog Science Fact/Fiction* in which he suggested that beings seen by Ezekiel might have been wearing individual helicopter backpacks.

The vision begins, "And I looked, and, behold, a

whirlwind came out of the north, a great cloud, and a fire. . . ." And Ezekiel continues, "Also out of the midst thereof came the likeness of four living creatures. . . . Their wings were joined one to another; they turned not when they went; they went every one straight forward. . . . Whithersoever the spirit was to go, they went, thither was their spirit to go; and the wheels were lifted over against them: for the spirit of the living creatures was in the wheels. . . . And when they went I heard the noise of their wings like the noise of great waters."

There is no room here to analyze Ezekiel's vision in its entirety. Arthur Orton's summary presents the vision of Ezekiel:

> We have a description of four spacesuited and helicopter-equipped men getting off of or out of something that landed in a cloud of dust or smoke. The four men start their helicopters, take off and fly to some height. On returning to the ground, they remove their flying gear and wait. (*Analog Science Fact/ Fiction*)

Orton concludes that the nature of Ezekiel's description reads like a deposition. In fact, it has the same style as Mrs. Kay's testimony: someone who is telling the truth—telling exactly what happened—regardless of whether or not it is to be believed. Orton states, "It [the vision] is the presentation of a tableau that makes no sense to the man who witnessed it or to those to whom he is describing it."

During the Middle Ages there were many recorded incidents of appearances by strange beings. At a time when the European power of reasoning seems to be in infancy, there was an aura of ambiguity concerning what man thought was real and what man imagined. Although detailed and abundant chronicles emerge with a history of the Dark Ages, that era was also prolific with sorcery, witches, and the wrath of an unbenevolent God. It may be conceded that the average serf had not the intellect or reasoning to be curious about these appearances by strange beings, no matter how real his beliefs were to him. St. Gregory of Tours, a historian, wrote in his *Historia Francorum* of an incident noted by a follower of Charlemagne:

> Alcuin, the secretary and biographer of Charlemagne, and author of the *Vita Karoli,* states in the thirty-second chapter of his work that in 810 when he was on his way from Aachen, he saw a large sphere descend like lightning from the sky. It traveled from east to west and was so bright it made the monarch's horse rear up so that Charlemagne fell and injured himself severely.

This ancient UFO sighting was taken as a sign of a visit by something wishing to challenge the champion—a prevalent theme in those days.

On our own continent we find an eighteenth-century Indian legend that mentions luminous humanoid beings who paralyzed people with a small tube. The touch was described as being like a bombardment of cactus needles. Most Indian legends have been passed down from generation to generation and tribe to tribe, with little success on the part of folklorists to pin down dates and sources. However, the popular Star Husband Tale indicates a strong belief on the part of early Indians that extraterrestrials did exist and were able to transcend to earth. In this particular tale, two Indian girls sleeping in the open at night gaze at two stars—one bright, the other dim. They both wish to be married to these stars, and upon awakening, find that each is married to a star, one to a young man (the bright star), and the other to an old man (the dim one). They live with these men in the upper world, above the sky that can be seen from earth.

Although many Indian legends, like Greek myths, personified the sun, moon, and visible stars and looked to them as gods of sorts, there is an underlying theme to the tales that indicates a knowledge and willingness on the part of the Indians to accept the concept of life outside of what they could see and communicate with. A Paiute chief, Mezzaluma, recounted an ancient tale for a Canadian journal, *Topside*. When asked where the North American Indians came from, Chief Mezzaluma answered, "The Indians were created in the sky by

Gitchie Manitou, the Great Spirit, who sent down here a big thunderbird to find a place for his children to live. He discovered this land . . . and brought Indians to settle on it. They were taught to use the land wisely and never abuse its natural resources."

Frank Edwards has recorded a more recent story in *Flying Saucers—Serious Business*. It took place at 10:30 P.M. on April 19, 1897, at Alexander Hamilton's farm in LeRoy, Kansas. In a sworn statement dated April 21, 1897, he says, "Last Monday night about 10:30 we were awakened by a noise among the cattle. I arose, thinking that perhaps my bulldog was performing his pranks, but upon going to the door saw to my utter astonishment that an airship was slowly descending upon my cow lot, about forty rods [660 feet] from the house." Hamilton called his son and tenant out, and they grabbed some axes and ran to the corral. They eventually came within fifty yards of the craft.

Hamilton described it as consisting of a "great cigar-shaped portion, possibly three hundred feet long, with a carriage underneath. The carriage was made of glass or some other transparent substance alternating with a narrow strip of some material. It was brightly lighted within, and everything was plainly visible. It was occupied by six of the strangest beings I ever saw. . . . Every part of the vessel which wasn't transparent was of a dark reddish color." Then, according to Hamilton, the huge beam was turned directly on the three men. A few seconds later the "great turbine wheel, about thirty feet in diameter, slowly revolving below the craft, began to buzz, sounding like the cylinder of a separator, and the vessel rose as lightly as a bird." His statement goes on: "When about three hundred feet above us, it seemed to pause and to hover directly above a two-year-old heifer, which was bawling and jumping, apparently fast in the fence. Going to her, we found a cable about half an inch in thickness made of some red material fastened in a slip knot around her neck and going up to the vessel from the heifer tangled in the wire fence. We tried to get it off but could not, so we cut the wire loose to see the ship, heifer and all, rise slowly, disappearing in the northwest.

"We went home, but I was so frightened I could not

sleep. Rising early Tuesday, I started out on my horse, hoping to find some trace of my cow. This I failed to do, but coming back in the evening, found that Link Thomas, about three or four miles west of LeRoy, had found the hide, legs and head in his field that day. He, thinking that someone had butchered a stolen beast, had brought the hide to town for identification but was greatly mystified in not being able to find tracks in the soft ground. After identifying the hide by my brand, I went home. But every time I would drop to sleep I would see the cursed thing, with its big lights and hideous people. I don't know whether they were devils or angels or what; but we all saw them, and my whole family saw the ship, and I don't want any more to do with them."

An affidavit signed by the leaders of the town council accompanied Hamilton's testimony, vouching for his competence and esteemed standing in the town. He was a member of the House of Representatives and had served the county well in positions of distinct trust and responsibility.

Hamilton's account preceded by many years the sighting of the Kay family. I was amazed when I looked at the drawing based on Mrs. Kay's description and matched it to Hamilton's. The object was a glowing red color, using some sort of revolving wheellike thing for part of its propulsion system. The interior was brightly lit. It carried a brilliant spotlight device that could be flashed on the area or on individuals to be examined. It appeared to be under intelligent control.

Gordon Lore and Harold Deneault, Jr., have cited an interesting piece of testimony offered in the late summer of 1917 by John Boback, a storekeeper in Youngstown, Pennsylvania. While he was walking on the railroad ties, an eerie "swishing sound" on his left jolted him. On the north side of the tracks he noticed an elliptical object as large as an automobile sitting in a pasture about a hundred feet away. The outer shell was smooth; it had no fins or propellers. The structure lay flat on its underside. An interior light from portholes on the upper portion of the object reminded Boback of automobile headlights. Moments later it lifted off into a smooth, gradual climb. The altitude and acceleration seemed to make the interior become increasingly brighter. It seems that one aspect of the sighting puzzled Boback. At takeoff the UFO had not nosed upward, as he had expected. It had risen from the ground and remained parallel with the surface. At no time did it hover, spin, or revolve during the two minutes he observed it.

The movement and physical description are consistent with reports gathered by NICAP, APRO, and the Center for UFO Studies. Granted, many accounts drawn from ancient sources could probably be explained as other than UFOs, but the number of explainable phenomena cited in the past is constant with the number of explainable phenomena cited today. Most investigators agree that at least 20 percent of today's reported cases are totally unexplained. Strange aerial objects have been seen and recorded frequently prior to recent times, by people from all walks of life, including a substantial number of reputable astronomers and other scientists. These reports preceded the era of heavier-than-air flight. The very antiquity of the sightings makes it hard to write them off as a by-product of imaginations enriched by twentieth-century technology.

So what were they? How do we explain away all the ancient records? What happened in the dim past to inspire the accounts?

Finds in Africa indicate that a form of man existed in Tanzania perhaps as long ago as two million years. A wall or windbreak, possibly built by human hands, has been identified as belonging to this incredibly early period. We must date the remains of early man by his artificially chipped tools. For example, chopping tools have been found in the Vallonet caves of France dating back one million years. The Olduvai Gorge in Africa has yielded special caches of bones, chipped stone axes, and other tools.

Fire was discovered some 700,000 to 500,000 years ago, possibly the most significant step up the ladder of evolution. Early evidences that man made fires have been found throughout the world: Africa, Asia, Europe. Was early man truly a brutish, apelike figure, as satirized in the comic strip *B.C.*? He has been cartooned as clubbing wives and enemies, gnawing on raw flesh, hunting down animals to eat. But some artifacts that have been uncovered show a true artistic refinement. Knives and arrowheads have been fashioned in such a way that they most certainly were used for ceremonial purposes and not hunting. Early man could also express himself visually. Solutrean bone needles used for sewing have tiny, carefully drilled eyes. Cave paintings have been discovered which reveal a great empathy toward sophisticated subjects. Did primitive man have an intelligence that transcends an image of a gorilla-like caveman? And when did man receive his brain?

There is really nothing in the theory of evolution to explain the mighty leap by which Homo sapiens set himself apart from his family of hominids. Is it possible that the leap from animal to man took place over a much shorter period than we ever believed possible? One finds in material on the subject a villain—the missing link. Without him we can only assume that the brain suddenly underwent a radical evolution, a throw-forward, so to speak. Many believe that man made the leap by artificial mutation introduced by extraterrestrial visitors. Beings that simply bred and made tools have existed for a million years, but when did man first acquire artistic sensitivity, paint pictures, sing songs, love, hate, communicate with others? When did he undergo this cosmic and psychic leap? And who was responsible for it?

Jacob's ladder, Ezekiel's vision, Alexander Hamilton's airship testimony constitute tantalizing, mysterious fragments of a larger story—they are evidential hints of past landings. Each tale suggests the presence of extraterrestrials on earth, yet alone none is conclusive. One further problem assailed me. There seemed to be a great deal of resistance in the scientific community arrayed against acceptance of the eyewitness sightings as proof of UFO landings.

Typical of the reactions to the accounts I had was a passage from the Shklovskii/Sagan book, *Intelligent Life in the Universe*. "What guise may we expect such a contact myth to wear? A simple account of the apparition of a strange being who performs marvelous works and resides in the heavens is not quite adequate. All people have a need to understand their environment, and the attribution of the incompletely understood to non-human deities is at least mildly satisfying. When interaction occurs among peoples supporting different deities, it is inevitable that each group will claim extraordinary powers for its god. Residence of the gods in the sky is not even approximately suggestive of extraterrestrial origin. . . . Accordingly, we require more of a legend than the apparition of a strange being who does extraordinary works and lives in the sky. It would certainly add credibility if no obvious supernatural adumbration were attached to the story. A description of the morphology of an intelligent non-human, a clear account of astronomical realities which a primitive people could not acquire by their own efforts or a transparent presentation of the purpose of the contact would increase the credibility of the legend."

Sagan had clearly outlined criteria which might guide researchers excavating the mythic mines for evidence of past extraterrestrial visits. The trail he plotted led me to a second look at the wonderful world of Sumer.

Sumer was founded in the fourth millennium B.C. No one knows where the Sumerians came from. Their language has no common derivational roots with any other, and were it not for a Sumerian-Akkadian dictionary, the writing would have remained indecipherable. The creation myth of Sumer describes a contact with a superior being (not a supernatural god), amphibious in nature, named Oannes, who imparted to the Sumerians, according to Alexander Polyhistor, "an insight into letters and sciences and art." He taught the people of Sumer to construct houses, to found temples, to compile laws, and explained to them the principles of geometrical knowledge. He made them distinguish the seeds of the earth and showed them how to collect fruits.

In all the history of civilizations that floundered after Sumer, the presence of an Oannes-like figure emerges. Christ, Mohammed, Kukulcan, Quetzalcoatl. All share the qualities of teacher and bringer of knowledge. Further, each returned to the heavenly firmament with a promise to return. However intriguing the possibility that each parallel tale was derived from one or more extraterrestrial sightings, I wanted more than surmise with which to work. My first glimmering came from Walon Green, Academy Award winning producer of "The Hellstrom Chronicle."

"You ought to look into the Dogon Tribe and its origin in myth," he said. The Dogon are an African tribe now living in Mali. The Dogons believe that the origins of civilization came from the star Sirius. Moreover, they frame their belief in a context of astronomical knowledge which is dependent on modern nuclear physics and astrophysics. How they produced the information about Sirius is admitted by all to be a genuine mystery. Robert Temple, a Fellow of the R.A.S., has succeeded in tracing the secret Dogon traditions and beliefs back to the Egyptian and Sumerian cultures.

The Dogon traditions and their supposed ancient Egyptian/Sumerian origin meet all the criteria Sagan has outlined. Furthermore, Temple weaves the most comprehensive tapestry of evidence I have seen so far to prove the extraterrestrial visit theory. However, I shall present only a small sampling of the clues he used in order to patch together that rich fabric of historical evidence that for so long has eluded cultural anthropologists.

Temple began by researching the Dogon tribe's secret belief systems. He used as his reference point the seminal paper on the Dogon written by anthropologists Marcel Griaule and Germaine Dieterlen. He lists the following passage as his take-off point:

"The starting point of creation is the star which revolved round Sirius and is actually named The Digitaria star; it is regarded by the Dogon as the smallest and heaviest of all the stars; it contains the germs of all things. Its movement on its own axis and around Sirius upholds all creation in space."

It was not until 1970 that modern astronomers were able to see that Sirius does in fact consist of two stars: Sirius A and Sirius B, a white dwarf curiously smaller and heavier than Sirius A.

Anthropologists Griaule and Dieterlen recorded that the Dogon believe Digitaria revolved around Sirius every fifty years. Temple confirms that the Dogon were also correct about this figure. Perhaps the most surprising facts of all are derived from Dogon drawings of the universe. In crude detail their creation myth shows Sirius B revolving around Sirius A in an elliptical orbit. Temple asks, "How did they even get the idea in the first place that elliptical orbits existed, rather than circular—much less apply this idea to some invisible star way out in space?" The Dogon had seemed to peer into space. Temple further asks how did they get it right by saying that Sirius A was at one of the foci rather than just somewhere in the ellipse? And not at the center? Wouldn't the natural primitive idea seem to be, even if you wanted to say the orbit was elliptical, still to have Sirius itself at the center?

The Dogon also believe that Sirius B rotates on its axis, another illusion of their general knowledge about stars minus the aid of telescopes. How did they know all of this?

Two further observations have been extracted from the strange creation myth of the relatively primitive Dogon tribe. First, the dwarf star is said to complete a full turn on its own axis once each year. At this time we have no technology capable of checking that Dogon assertion. It should be noted that until 1970 we did not have photographic evidence of Sirius B. The correlation of knowledge about Dogon creation myths and Sirius B did not occur until 1975.

Secondly, the Dogon claim that yet another star exists in the Sirius system. Astronomers agree that a third star might in fact be found but we will have to advance our technology considerably in order to confirm the possibility.

What the Dogon tale evokes for me is a question of enormous magnitude: where did the Dogon acquire their knowledge?

Robert Temple, an anthropological detective of incredible fortitude, tracks a labyrinthian path from the Dogon back to Sumer, and there he leaves his quarry. He adds one other intriguing note to his study. In Sumer they called him Oannes and his bearers of civilization Annedoti, which translates as "repulsive ones." Temple writes, "If ever anything argued the authenticity of their account, it was this tradition that the amphibians to whom they owed everything were disgusting, horrible and loathsome to look upon." There is a parallel in the tales of the Dogon.

The Dogons call their founder of civilization Nommo. The vehicle in which Nommo landed is represented in Dogon drawings unmistakably as a rocketship.

The Sirius puzzle is more than intriguing; it is compelling. It presents almost incontrovertible evidence that extraterrestrials have been here. Egyptians and Sumerians possessed an inordinate amount of accurate scientific data which the Dogons have preserved until today. Only recently, because of advancements in telescopes and photographic techniques, have we ourselves been able to detect any of this ancient knowledge. How did the ancients know things which we have only lately been aware of? I think that it's time for the extraterrestrial visitation theory to move from a scientific possibility to an historical inevitability.

The Sirius puzzle allows us to make some rather well-founded speculations on what these Siriusians looked like and what they might have landed in. However, what they landed in and how they looked in the past takes a back seat to the UFO question now facing us. Might they just be making their appearances once more in the form of UFOs? My search for extraterrestrials was becoming more and more tantalizing.

If advanced extraterrestrials have given us civilization, then wouldn't they have mastered interstellar travel? That last extrapolation doesn't seem unreasonable. And furthermore, if they have visited us in the past, would they continue to visit us into the present? I don't know the answer to the last question, but it is exactly what I want to find out.

There are drawings found throughout the world—in France, North America, southern Rhodesia, the Sahara Desert, Peru, Mexico, and Chile—that all add grist to this mill. An animal of unknown species with gigantic upright horns on its head appears on a pottery vessel found at Siyak in Iran. Why not? But both horns display five spirals to left and right. If you imagine two large rods with large porcelain insulators, that is roughly what this drawing looks like. What should we say about the spirals on the rods? Do they really represent some sort of antennae, just as primitive people have seen them on unfamiliar creatures? Do things which ought not to exist, exist?

What was the influence on the primitive man who created the White Lady of Brandenberg in South Africa? She is shown dressed in a short pullover. She wears gloves, garters, and slippers. The White Lady is a primitive wall drawing, and behind her is a figure with the familiar pipe in his hand. He wears a helmet. He is unlike anything a primitive man could imagine.

There are wall drawings, found at Lussac, France, that show figures dressed in modern clothes. They are drawn in an interweaving style that encompasses realism and impressionistic manners. These are now under study at the Musée de l'Homme in Paris.

Who painted these figures? Who had enough imagination to conceive of a caveman dressed in skins who drew figures from the twentieth century on stone walls?

No one knows how these paintings were executed. The caves were dark, and yet there are no signs of carbon deposits on the walls and roofs. How, then, did the artist see to mix his pigments and create the works? Were lenses and mirrors used to direct sunlight into the interiors of the caves? And why were they painted in the incredibly difficult caves of Lussac? Some of these caves are now underground.

In attempting to trace the vestiges of prehistoric civilizations down through time, we get the impression that we receive or hear only their echoes. But is there something else? Are there any buildings or vestiges of buildings that would indicate techniques clearly differentiating them from other, more easily explainable ancient ruins?

Iron or steel, if such peoples had any, would have disappeared. Wood structures would have vanished. Brick buildings, however large, would have fallen into rubble and would be indistinguishable from hills and small mountains. After all, that has been the case in Mesopotamia, where enormous metropolitan areas—even Babylon itself—were "lost" until the fairly recent past, simply because their soil or sand covered the ruins that were no longer recognizable.

In all probability there will be more mysteries unearthed. With new underwater-research equipment now being developed, the seas and oceans may yield their answers. Over the aeons, perhaps whole continents have been engulfed, and we may look there for our clues. Is it possible that unusual accomplishments are indications of some extraterrestrial interference? Did they, "out there," come here?

The earth abounds wih prehistoric exotica. We could cite Stonehenge, for example, that circle of megalithic monuments on England's Salisbury Plain. It has been proved to be a gigantic time computer in stone. There are others, such as the aligned menhirs at Karnak, or the Zimbabwe ruins in Rhodesia. All of these posed problems that seem to defy the perspicacity of orthodox investigations.

It certainly does not tax the imagination to believe that somewhere there exists a race more intelligent than man, and this is the simple hypothesis of extraterrestrial intelligence (ETI). If the UFO phenomena can be explained as evidence of visitors from another planet or galaxy, we must assume (for the best, it is hoped) that man is not the most developed being in the universe. But why are these beings interested in earth? Of the one hundred billion stars in the spiral galaxy we call the Milky Way, earth is a minor planet orbiting a minor star. Our galaxy, in addition, is a minor one in a universe of billions upon billions of galaxies. Confronted by these figures, astronomers and astrophysicists often rule out UFOs from space as unlikely possibilities. The experts tend to seek more comfortable explanations, provable within the limits of current knowledge. I tend to agree, however, with Allen Hynek, who says, "There is a tendency in twentieth-century science to forget that there will be a twenty-first-century science, and indeed a thirtieth-century science, from which vantage points our knowledge of the universe may appear quite different. We suffer, perhaps, from temporal provincialism, a form of arrogance that has always irritated posterity."

Recently the House Committee on Science and Astronautics agreed that it is time to stop scoffing at the UFO mystery and begin a long-term, government-backed program to solve it. Appearing before a symposium, Arizona physicist Dr. James McDonald said,

"Far too many [UFO sightings] defy our best analysis. It would be terrible if this was surveillance and our technology was represented by the Eveready flashlight."

McDonald went on to point out that the real cause of the pulse which precipitated the great East Coast blackout of 1965 has never been identified. He also said that there were many UFO sightings up and down the eastern seaboard in late 1965, around the time of the blackout. "There is a puzzling and slightly disturbing coincidence here," he added. He went on to say that if indeed our planet was being reconnoitered from space, it was being done by a society so advanced in its technology that ours "would be indistinguishable from magic."

The UFO mystery has long ago developed into a sort of crusade or "religious war," with the believers lined up against the nonbelievers. Agnostic answers provided by many objective investigators to the questions will please nobody.

Carl Sagan comments that overtones of a para-religious nature are particularly strong with those who actually believe they have been in contact with creatures from a UFO. "The saucerians [to believers] are wise and gentle and loving . . . all-powerful, all-knowing, and concerned with the plight of mankind as a parent would be for his children. The saucer myths represent a neat compromise between the need to believe in a traditional paternal God and the contemporary pressures to accept the pronouncements of science."

Perhaps we are unable to accept the possibility of superior forms of life. Perhaps this accounts for our past refusal to analyze the mystery in the skies. Yet, isn't it quite a paradox that we have mounted an intense search for extraterrestrial life but chosen to ignore the influence of UFOs? While science concedes statistically that thousands of planets may be populated and that some of the cultures may be more technically advanced than ours, it still denies the idea that intelligent life may be surveying the earth, even though we on earth have already mastered space travel.

I could not help but wonder why so many knowledgeable people dismiss extraterrestrial UFO origins as impossible. I find a parallel in what they say to what equally knowledgeable folks were saying about one hundred years ago. While the Civil War in the United States was drawing to a close, a French experimenter and storyteller, who must certainly be classed as a scientist and not a clairvoyant, published "From Earth to the Moon." It was what we would now call science fiction. The Krupps had not yet perfected the art of cannonry far enough to send a projectile more than a few miles across the countryside. The steam engine was the chief method of propulsion for vehicles. The internal-combustion engine, one of the few modern devices not attributed to a sketch of Da Vinci's, was as inconceivable to that age as the creation of life in a test tube.

Jules Verne leaped across these pedestrian encumbrances and postulated a moon shot based on the astronomical knowledge of his day. In his imaginary voyage into space, three men boarded a projectile-shaped ship somewhere on the west coast of Florida, possibly near Tampa. Their ship was made of cast iron, with an aluminum lining. It measured twelve feet in height and about fifteen feet in diameter at the base. It weighed 12,230 pounds. This capsule streaked to the moon at 25,000 miles an hour, circled it within twenty-five miles, and returned to the surface of the earth on December 29.

One hundred and four years later, three Americans boarded a cone-shaped projectile on the east coast of Florida. Their ship was made of stainless steel, lined with an aluminum alloy. It measured twelve feet in height and thirteen feet in diameter at the base. It weighed 12,392 pounds. This capsule streaked to the moon at 24,200 miles an hour, circled it within seventy miles, and returned to the surface of the earth on December 27.

The tendency to debunk anything foreign to us—in thought or geography—is so strong that newspapers and periodicals constantly bend over backward in an attempt to be objective. At the other extreme, as we have seen, the devotees of UFO occult theories usually avoid any pretense of coming to terms with conventional science.

For my part, I view the question with a desire to find investigative trails that are challenging. And if they prove absurd, I will at least have had the satisfaction and excitement of the hunt.

6

Out There

I have found a pervasive myth in the annals of UFO diarists. It has long been whispered that the U.S. Air Force has a secret hangar at Wright-Patterson Air Force Base in which a captured UFO is kept. I will not go so far as to say that it is impossible, but I tend to believe that the Air Force does not have a secret hangar or a captured UFO. The inclination of government agencies associated with flight and space exploration is not so much to cover up evidence of UFO existence as to ignore any possibilities. The story of Orbiter-2 and its pictures is typical.

In 1966, America's Orbiter-2 and Russia's Luna-9 took photographs of some monoliths at widely separate locations on the moon's surface. The lunar objects seem to be "constructed" in a definite geometrical relationship and appear to be artificial. Space officials have not chosen to make their conclusions public.

The Soviet probe, on February 4, landed in the Ocean of Storms and relayed photos of straight lines of stones—all identical—that under certain solar conditions produce a pattern that resembles an airport runway. They would be visible only to descending aircraft. Dr. S. Ivanov, a Soviet scientist who has won the Laureate of the State prize, has examined these photographs and discovered that an accidental displacement of the Luna-9 craft caused pictures to be taken from two slightly different angles. Dr. Ivanov, who was also responsible for three-dimensional motion-picture experiments in Russia, applied stereo techniques from these two photographs and was able to develop a stereoscopic display of these "runways."

It is not known why Luna-9 displaced itself. The Russian explanation was "deformation of the lunar surface." The ground may have settled at the spot where the station landed, or perhaps a small stone caused the initial instability. However, it was a fortunate accident, and Dr. Ivanov and engineer Dr. A. Bruenko reported, "With the stereoscopic effect, we can affirm that the distance between stones one, two, three, and four is equal. The stones are identical in measurement. There does not seem to be any height or elevation nearby from which the stones could have been rolled and scattered into this geometric form. The objects as seen in three-D seem to be arranged according to definite geometric laws."

Twenty-nine miles above the Sea of Tranquility, America's Orbiter-2 on November 20, 1966, photographed another monument some two thousand miles from the Soviet discovery. These seem to be eight pointed spires—obelisks, if you will—photographed by Orbiter-2 straight down. Only shadows are visible in these pictures, but NASA scientists who estimated that the sun was eleven degrees above the horizon can estimate that the largest obelisk is fifty feet wide at the base and from forty to seventy-five feet tall.

The Russians disagreed. Their examination reported the smallest obelisk to be "similar to an extremely large fir tree" and the largest to be as tall as a fifteen-story building!

Soviet space engineer Alexander Abramov calculated the angles and asserts they represent a definite configuration known in ancient Egypt as an *abaka,* or Egyptian triangle. Abramov says that "the distribution of these lunar objects is similar to the plan of the Egyptian pyramids constructed by the pharaohs . . . at Giza, near Cairo. The centers of the spires in this lunar *abaka* are arranged in precisely the same way as the apexes of the three great pyramids."

What does the United States say about these monuments? NASA is quiet; when queried, a spokesman said that, "Yes, we know of these photographs, and they were very clear, but there has been no speculation on them, and they have been filed for now."

Thus, little attention has been given these monuments in the American press. That, however, is not the case in the Soviet Union. The photographs taken by Orbiter-2 and Luna-9 have been widely published. In fact, a detailed analysis of the geometry of these lunar obelisks was a cover story in the Russian publication *Technology for Youth.* Soviet scientists, long interested in ETI, have postulated that intelligent beings not only have visited earth but also have constructed these monuments on our moon as some sort of beacon for their spacecraft.

If there is in fact evidence on the moon that extraterrestrials have come our way, then the next logical question is: Where did they come from? I had to go back to the very beginning to devise a scenario for the manner in which UFO visitations have occurred. It was a fascinating excursion that led me back fifteen billion years, to a time when there was nothing. No planets, stars, or galaxies existed. There was no life.

Then something happened. Perhaps it was an explosion. The universe, it is now believed, was hydrogen and helium. Hydrogen and helium weren't evenly distributed. Here and there in the empty caverns of space, unusual pockets of gas began to grow. Gravity caused these so-called "clumps" to attract larger amounts of neighboring gas. As these gaseous pockets grew in mass, their denser interiors, apparently governed by laws of physics, contracted and began whirling around and around at increasing speeds. The spinning motion caused smaller fragments within the gas clumps to break off into billions of smaller shrinking gas pinwheels. Because of the continuing contraction, the atoms in the center of the gas balls began to collide. Temperatures rose, and electrons broke away from protons in the hydrogen atoms. Protons have positive charges, which ordinarily repel each other, but in this case temperatures in the interior of the balls rose enormously, causing the protons to collide with so much energy that the electrical repulsion barrier normally surrounding the proton was penetrated. Suddenly, then, the forces that held the nuclei of atoms together were activated, creating the next atom in complexity—helium. In the process of deriving one helium atom from four hydrogen atoms, a small amount of excess energy remained. This energy, filtering out through the gas globule, traveled to the surface and was radiated into space. And then there was light. A star was born.

Slowly converting hydrogen into helium within their cavernous interiors, and turning the small mass difference into energy, the stars evolved over billions of years, illuminating the skies. But since planets didn't yet exist, there was nothing around to receive that light. The hydrogen-into-helium conversion could not last forever. Eventually all the hydrogen within the star centers was consumed. And some star fires were kindled. Their centers contracted. The higher temperatures were so intense that the helium atoms could now be used as stellar fuel. Within the stars, now swollen red giant stars, more complex reactions occurred. Helium was converted to carbon, carbon to oxygen and magnesium, oxygen to neon, magnesium to silicon, silicon to sulfur. This wide range of nuclear reactions built up simple and complex nuclei.

The gravity is minimal on the surface of red giant stars; their surfaces expand outward from their interiors. These outer layers break off into space and enrich and nourish the interstellar space with carbon and oxygen and any elements heavier than hydrogen or helium.

Later generations of stars were beginning to form. But these second- and third-generation stars were enriched with the heavy elements, a legacy they inherited from their stellar ancestors. As these newer stars were formed, smaller condensations formed near them. These condensations were too small and too cold to produce light on their own. They did not become stars. These cold chunks of thick matter, forming slowly out of the rotating cloud, could only reflect star light. They would be illuminated by the fires that they couldn't produce. These were the planets. Some—very large and gaseous, consisting of mostly hydrogen and helium—were far away from their parent star. Others (like earth)—smaller and warmer, with a rocky, metallic surface—were nearer to their parent star.

The smaller planets released hydrogen-rich gases, some of which condensed to form the oceans; other gases remained above the surface to form the first atmospheres composed of methane, ammonia, hydrogen sulfide, and water.

Storms began. Volcanoes erupted, and their lava heated the atmosphere. Boiling waters produced more complicated molecular structures. The ocean slowly began turning into a complex soup. Among all of the different molecules forming this broth, a subtle, singular organic molecule arose which was able to replicate itself. Inexact copies were produced at first. Soon self-replicating molecules began to multiply. Elaborate systems evolved.

Meanwhile, the energy of the sun—the parent star—produced the building blocks or essential ingredients from which subsequent copies could develop.

The building-block supply was gradually depleted, and a new kind of molecular system arose—again through necessity—which could internally produce molecular building material from air, water, and sunlight. Now the first plants entered the picture. Photosynthesis evolved. Oxygen began to be produced in significant quantities. The increasing amount of oxygen in the atmosphere posed the first great challenge to life, for oxygen was a poison capable of reconverting all the self-replicating molecules into the simple gases from which they came. But life survived by evolving mechanisms which used oxygen to metabolize foodstuffs in a more efficient way.

Then, after billions of years, through progressive stages of evolution, man evolved. His genetic composition was essentially similar to those self-replicating molecules of long ago. But he was able to think about his origins. And he began to question how he got here.

Needless to say, there are other versions of the story. In outlining the fifteen billion years that have elapsed since planet earth was but a gleam in the gaseous world of the universe, I have followed Carl Sagan's version of the tale as he told it in *The Cosmic Connection*. There are other theories that explain the origin of the universe, our solar system, and the planet earth. There are directly conflicting versions of man's arrival, not the least of which considers the possibility that his form took shape on other planets and was transported here in one form or another. What Dr. Sagan's version gives us is a perspective in which to view what we know of our universe.

Space is vast and awesome. Earth is a rather small planet consisting of rock and metal. The sun, our star, is also relatively small, and is one of some two hundred billion suns that make up our Milky Way galaxy. Furthermore, the Milky Way galaxy is only one of billions of galaxies that are also strewn with billions of suns or stars. We aren't even in the center of our galaxy; it takes light traveling at 18,000 miles a second 30,000 years to reach us. Planet earth and the life that arose are products of an endless series of evolutionary events. Therefore, it should come as no surprise that earth is probably not the first, last, or best habitable planet around. Considering that there are approximately 10^{11} (100 billion) stars in our galaxy and 10^{11} other galaxies, there are at least 10^{20} stars in the universe. Most of these stars, according to scientists, may be accompanied by solar systems or planets. Shklovskii and Sagan have computed that a million solar systems are formed in the universe each hour. This fact in itself is a sobering thought for any of us still imagining that we are the only solar system to have evolved life. And indeed, many scientists today think intelligent life exists somewhere out in space. But this isn't just an idea of our day, but one that has emerged over and over again throughout history.

Two thousand years ago, Lucretius, the Roman poet, wrote, "Nature is not unique to the visible world. We must have faith that in other regions of space there exist other earths, inhabited by other people and animals."

Anaxagoras, an early believer in the heliocentric theory, believed the moon to be inhabited. He also proposed that invisible life seeds, from which all living things came, were dispersed throughout the universe. Similar concepts of "panspermia" are still proposed today.

The Epicureans or materialists believed that many worlds, other than our earth, were suitable for life and existed out in space. Metrodoros, a famous Epicurean, wrote: "To consider the earth the only populated world in infinite space is as absurd as to assert that in an entire field sown with millet, only one grain will grow."

After the birth of Jesus Christ, Christianity, influenced by Ptolemaic theories, taught that earth was the center of the universe, making the concept of life elsewhere totally incompatible and incredible.

Nicolaus Copernicus, the Polish astronomer, rejected the Ptolemaic system. He placed earth in its proper perspective as only one planet among many others revolving around the sun. The idea demoted the earth from a central, unique position and suggested the possibility of other inhabited planets. And when Galileo looked through his telescope at the heavens, Copernicus' hypothesis was vindicated.

Galileo's observations opened a new era in astronomy. It was evident that the planets were similar to the earth in many respects. Galileo wrote in his *Sidereus Nuncius:* "I have been led to the opinion and conviction that the surface of the moon is smooth, uniform, and precisely spherical, as a great number of philosophers believe it (and other heavenly bodies) to be, but is uneven, rough, and full of cavities and prominences, being not unlike the face of the earth, relieved by chains of mountains and deep valleys."

Many questions followed this discovery. If mountains exist on the moon, perhaps cities inhabited by intelligent beings might also exist. Perhaps our sun isn't the only star with dark companions known as planets.

Giordano Bruno propagated these ideas. The Italian philosopher wrote: "Innumerable suns exist; innumerable earths revolve about these suns in a manner similar to the way the seven planets revolve around our sun. Living beings inhabit these worlds." In 1600 Bruno was burned at the stake by the Catholic church because of his ideas.

Belief in extraterrestrial life continued to flourish throughout the seventeenth, eighteenth, and nineteenth centuries. Sir Isaac Newton is said to have believed that the sun was inhabited.

Konstantin E. Tsiolkovski, the Russian founder of astronautics, believed in the plurality of works. He states, "All the phases of the development of life may be found on the various planets. Did man exist several thousand years ago, and will he be extinct in several million years? This entire process may be found on other planets. . . ." That extraterrestrial civilizations might exist at various developmental levels has not been proved. The question still remains.

But let's begin to answer the question with a survey of current facts and near-fact speculations about other suns and other planets. What evidence is there that planets similar to ours (a planet that can support life) exist? Since the sun—a star—is our source of life-giving energy, then the first thing we need to know is whether other stars like our sun exist. A few basic mathematical measurements will help us conclude that there are many stars like our sun.

Knowing that there are more than one hundred billion star groups in our galaxy, the next question is whether there are planets around those stars. The guesstimating now begins. But we are still in pretty close range of near-fact speculations. Because of recent findings, most astronomers believe that the majority of stars, except for the hottest ones, will prove to be accompanied by planets. One theory places stars into two basic categories: slow-turning stars like our sun, and those turning rapidly. Scientists now believe that rapidly turning stars could not be stopped by outlying rings of matter, which they presume to be the stuff from which planets are made, and therefore have no dark companions or planets. Slowly turning stars, however, probably owe their lack of angular momentum to the fact that they do possess a planetary system. About 90 percent of the stars observed are of the slow variety. Hence, planets accompanying stars are probably the rule rather than the exception.

In 1964 Peter van de Kamp discovered a dark companion to Barnard's Star, a very close neighbor only six light-years away. It wobbles across the sky, which seems to indicate a planetary companion. If Van de Kamp's hunch is correct, it will be the first planet of another sun discovered with a fair degree of accuracy. It will also serve to reinforce the expectation that at least 10 percent and perhaps more than 50 percent of the stars are accompanied by planets.

Stephen Dole and Isaac Asimov, in *Planets for Man,* classified planets into three types: 1. Planets without a measurable atmosphere. The small gravitational fields on these planets can't hold even those gases with massive molecules. Since there are probably more small planets than larger ones, most solar bodies fall into this class. Mercury and the moon are two examples of this type. 2. Planets with light atmospheres. These gravitational fields here are large enough to retain moderately heavy gases, such as nitrogen, which have been produced by volcanic action. Earth, the one habitable planet in our solar system, and Venus are members of this type. 3. Planets with massive atmospheres composed largely of helium and hydrogen. Jupiter, Saturn, Uranus, and Neptune are members of the third type.

The next question is: What fraction of all these planets are suitable for life? And here I have divided the concept of life in two: life as we know it, and life as we don't know it. First, let's deal with intelligent life as we know it. A habitable planet will be one on which large numbers of earth-grown people can live comfortably and enjoyably without needing extreme protection from the natural environment and without dependence on materials brought in from other planets. In other words, planets which are similar to earth in general, yet different in detail. I have eliminated some life forms by using these criteria. For example, Mars might support carbon-based life. (According to Henry S. F. Cooper, Jr., in *The New Yorker,* some Viking biologists have developed a model for Martian trees, placing them underground to avoid the ultraviolet rays of the sun and the extremes of temperature. According to their model, the trees' taproots descend to a remote water table or permafrost, with perhaps just a flat segment at ground level, like a manhole cover, which can absorb energy.) This group of organic possibilities will be treated in the "life-as-we-don't-know-it" section because of its nonterrestriallike living conditions.

What is life as we on earth know it? Most scientists agree that life arises from the chemical-revolution theory outlined in the creation fable in the beginning of the chapter. But what are the conditions that allowed this carbon-based life to materialize and ultimately led to the emergence of man?

According to Ronald Bracewell in *The Galactic Club,* around each star there exists what he calls a habitable zone, an area containing the most likely planetary candidates. I would agree. Obviously planets too close to a star would be too hot for life to arise, and those too far away would be too cold. The ideal temperature limits are thought to be within that temperature range where water is liquid. Remember, scientists believe that the first organic molecule was created in the oceans. Hence water would be another requirement. The period of rotation should be less than ninety-six hours in order to prevent either extremely high daytime temperatures or excessively low temperatures at night. The planet should be more than three billion years old, the estimated period of time needed both to produce a breathable atmosphere and to allow for the evolution of complex life forms.

After reviewing the requirements necessary to life on planets, I began to understand how every factor played a role in creating the entire environment. The next step would be to speculate on the probability of each of these factors occurring.

I used the computations of Dole and Asimov. They discovered that roughly six hundred million habitable planets might exist on our galaxy alone. Please note that this figure represents only the planets with conditions suitable for human life, places where we on earth could live comfortably, not needing extreme protection from the natural environment and without dependence on material imported from other planets. In our galaxy alone, more than six hundred million planets meet those criteria.

But there's still another field to explore. The second form of life. What about the planets with atmospheric and temperature conditions which spawn "life as we don't know it"? If life on other planets is totally unlike life on earth—not based on carbon—it would prove that life could take multiple forms on the most basic levels. Yet how would we recognize life as we don't know it?

In view of all the possibilities of extraterrestrial life both in the Milky Way galaxy and beyond, a clear definition generalizing all life—carbon-based, silicon-based, or otherwise—seems to be necessary. Carl Sagan in *The Cosmic Connection* states, "A molecular system —capable of replication, mutation and replication of its mutations—can be called alive." So perhaps life is generally defined as something that isn't static. It evolves. But this definition creates problems for present-day explorers. We can't wait around for the slow evolutionary process to take place. Sagan's definition makes it difficult for the space scientists whose cameras can't remain on planets indefinitely, so there is another possible method of detecting "rare" life forms. Motion is an attribute that might signal life. But what if the creature is hibernating and its motion or breathing is invisible? Problems plague the scientist charged with looking for any kind of life form.

In view of these general definitions of life, there is an endless range of possible life forms. I wondered how you could determine which properties of life on our planet are characteristic of life everywhere rather than just mutational accidents. Sagan labels as chauvinism the assumption that life elsewhere has to be, in a major sense, like life here. There are oxygen chauvinists; they ignore the fact that life first arose on earth in the absence of oxygen. In fact, there are many organisms on earth today that live without oxygen and are poisoned by it.

There are ultraviolet chauvinists who believe that life can't exist under ultraviolet rays. But perhaps this is because we on earth developed in the absence of high ultraviolet light. What about life that developed in the presence of ultraviolet light? Couldn't it have built up a tolerance for these rays similar to the tolerance we built up in the face of increasing oxygen from the first plants?

Temperature chauvinists exist too. These people rule out life in the freezing temperatures of Juipter. But according to Sagan, "It is now quite firmly established, both from theory and from radio observations of these planets, that as we penetrate below the visible clouds, the temperatures increase. There is always a region in the atmospheres of Jupiter, Saturn, Uranus, and Neptune that is at quite comfortable temperatures by terrestrial standards."

Carbon chauvinism exists too. Even the most liberal of scientists have trouble ridding themselves of this prejudice. Carbon is abundant and contributes to building a wide variety of complex compounds. However, some scientists admit that there are alternatives. Silicon and germanium can enter into some of the same kinds of chemical bonding that carbon does. What about silicon-based life? Have scientists devoted enough time to silicon or germanium organic chemistry? Or have their prejudices precluded this kind of experimentation?

All of us are at the mercy of our experiences. We have an unconscious bias as to what is possible in the universe. We think that all conceivable life must conform to the preconceptions for which our experiences have programmed us. How much of our present form is due to mutation or accident? The answer is unknown. But I was intrigued by the infinite possibilities. There are perhaps as many possibilities as there are galaxies. Keeping in mind the Dole and Asimov conservative estimate of six hundred million planets suitable for human habitation, I began to marvel at what the other possibilities were. Dole and Asimov restricted themselves to planets that orbited around stars like the sun. But perhaps we are just one possibility—one level of development. Maybe we should realize that there is planetary chauvinism too. Does intelligent life have to develop and reside on planets? Couldn't it inhabit interstellar space in exotic cosmic monuments? Sagan muses, "Just as we are organisms completely at home only on dry land, although we evolved from the sea, the universe may be populated with societies that arose on planets but that are comfortable only in the depths of interstellar space."

I am forever trapped, it seems, by the dictates of so-called "physical laws." As I search for extraterrestrials, however, I find myself tinkering with sophomoric concepts that run counter to currently acceptable scientific thinking. It seems to me that just beyond my learned realm there is another dimension of possibility that has not yet made itself apparent.

In Search of New Answers

Convincing Evidence

MEDFORD, MINNESOTA Artist's interpretation of the UFO that Helen Kay saw near her home: an orange ball alighting on a nearby football field.

A UFO trace is generally clear: an irregular burned, depressed or dehydrated area.

Ted Phillips, a field investigator at the Center for UFO Studies, analyzes physical traces left by UFOs.

Dr. Edward Zellar, professor at University of Kansas, indicated that soil samples taken at the Medford site showed high radiation trace.

BIG CHIMNEY, WEST VIRGINIA Carroll Critchfield saw "a big diamond-shaped object" hovering over a grove of trees. The scarred landing site revealed a burned area and imprints 18 to 20 feet apart.

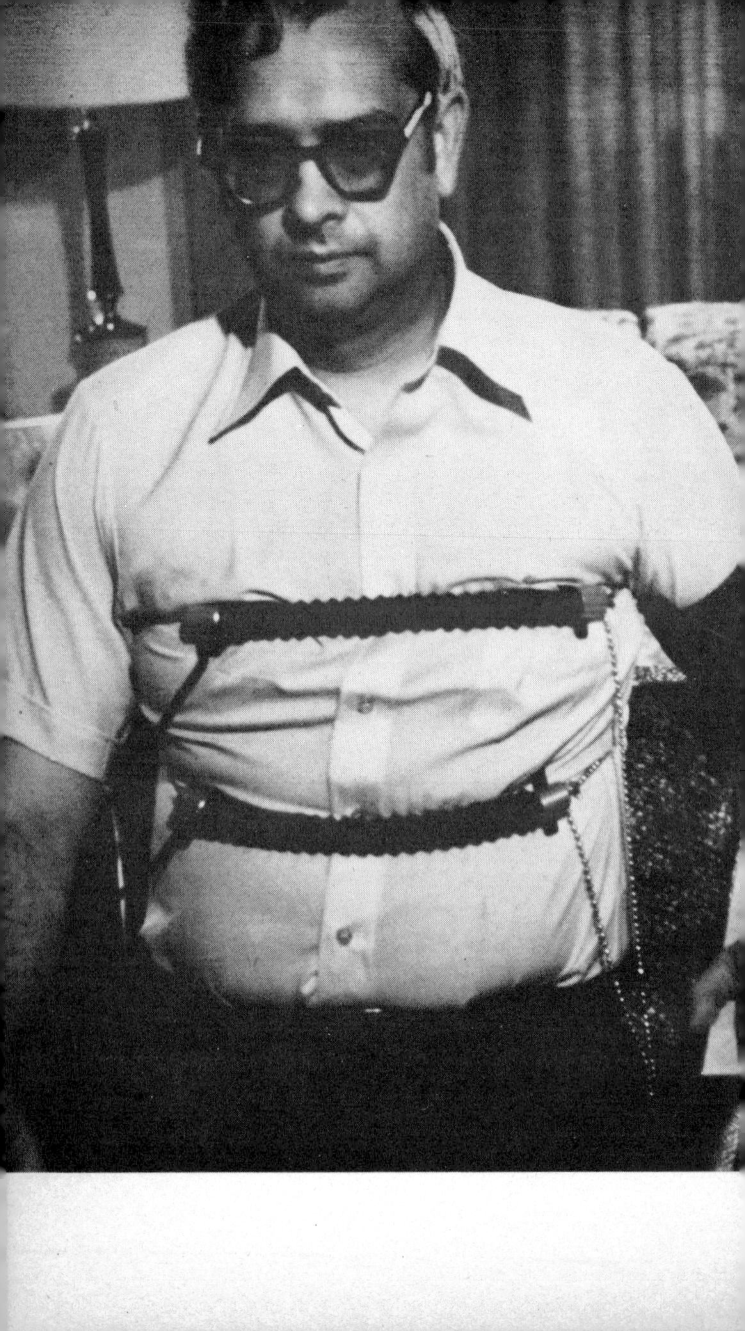

The lie-detector test given to Critchfield by Elmer Criswell, Jr., indicated that he told the complete truth concerning all events to the best of his knowledge.

MELLEN, WISCONSIN Phil Baker saw "a dome-shaped object sitting in the middle of the road. It had a brilliant halo with bluish-green and red lights around the outside. Then the lights faded off; there was a bang and it disappeared."

Aerial view of Mellen. Statistically, an overwhelming number of UFO sightings have been in rural areas.

Interplanetary Communication

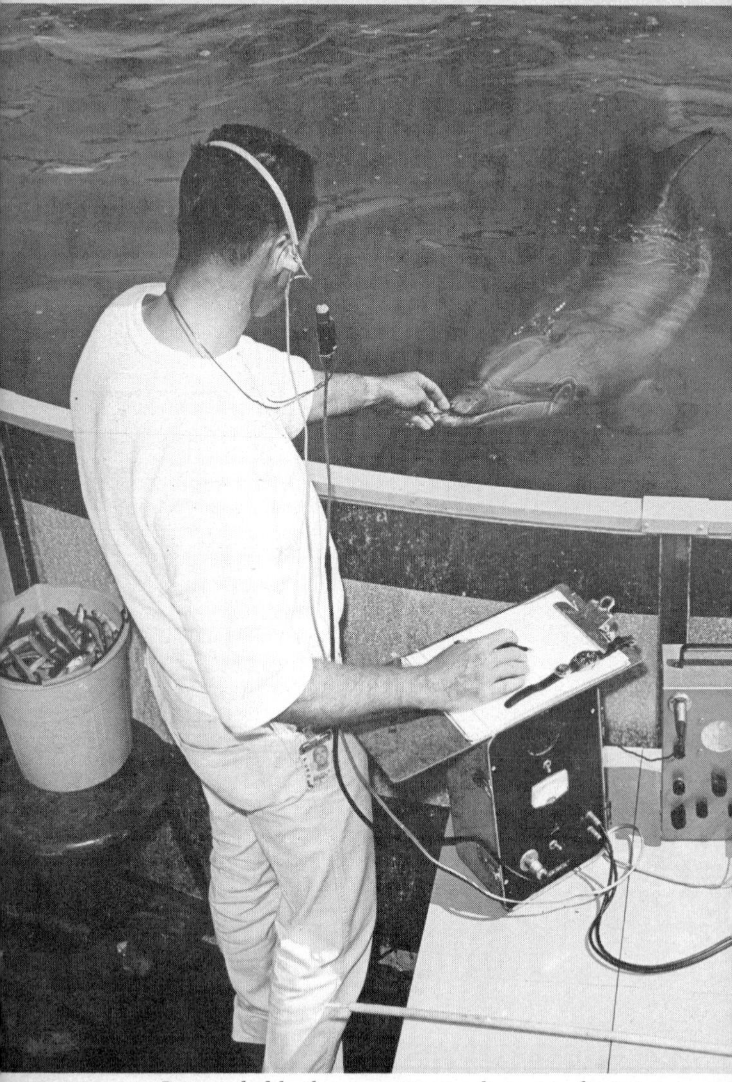

It is probable that a responsive language for human/dolphin communication will be devised. As we reach toward space it may be necessary to redefine our concept of intelligence. (U.S. Navy)

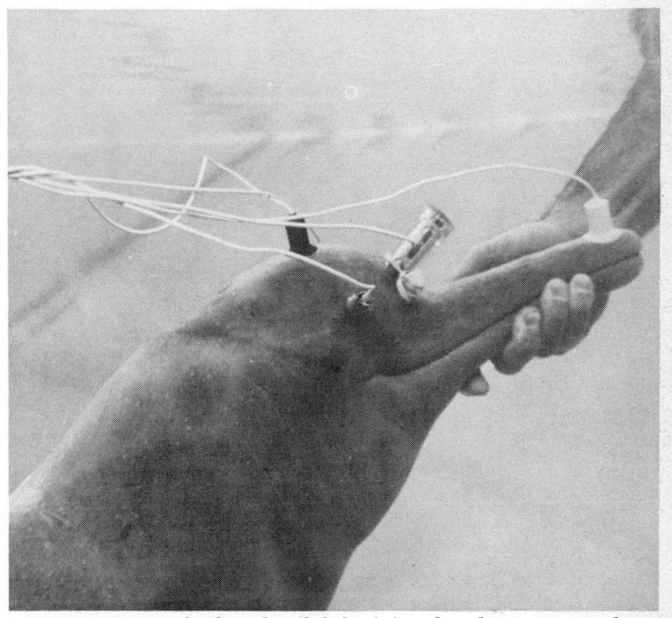

Sensors attached to this dolphin's head and snout record sounds during an echolocating experiment. Can the brain be used as a physical broadcast center? (U.S. Navy)

In 1931 Karl Jansky of Bell Telephone Laboratories accidentally discovered cosmic static or radio emissions from our galaxy—a realistic means of interplanetary communication! (Courtesy of Bell Laboratories)

On November 16, 1974 a message was beamed from the giant radio antenna at Arecibo toward a distant cluster of stars which described our earth and its inhabitants in bold graphic form. Perhaps extraterrestrial messenger probes can explain the history of mysterious radio signals. (Cornell University)

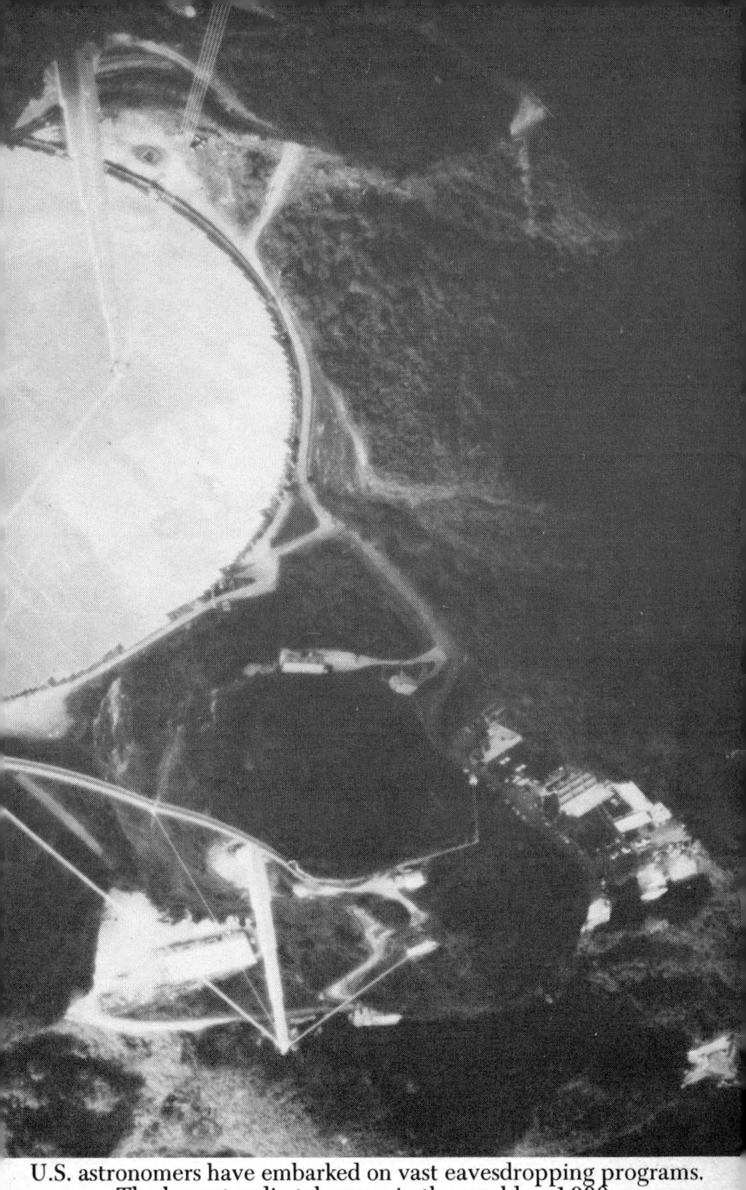

U.S. astronomers have embarked on vast eavesdropping programs. The largest radio telescope in the world—a 1,000-foot-diameter dish—is Arecibo Observatory in Puerto Rico.

The Arecibo Observatory is part of the National Astronomy and Ionosphere Center which is operated by Cornell University under contract with the National Science Foundation.

America's Orbiter 2 and Russia's Lunar 9 took photographs of monoliths on the moon's surface. They appear to be artificial. Are these a beacon for UFO spacecraft? (NASA)

The search for life beyond earth begins. We have just established a base on Mars from which we can conduct tests. Is there such a base already established here on earth by our galactic neighbors? (NASA)

Scientists in the Stanford/Nasa-Ames program have gathered to devise a system for detecting extraterrestrial life. The culmination was Project Cyclops. This is an artist's concept of the aerial view of the Cyclops system. Antenna array is about 16 kilometers. (NASA)

Starships of the Future

Should we try to duplicate the engineering expertise of UFOs? An alternative for the 1980s is the solar sail which would transform the sun's photon energy into usable spacecraft power. (Jet Propulsion Laboratory)

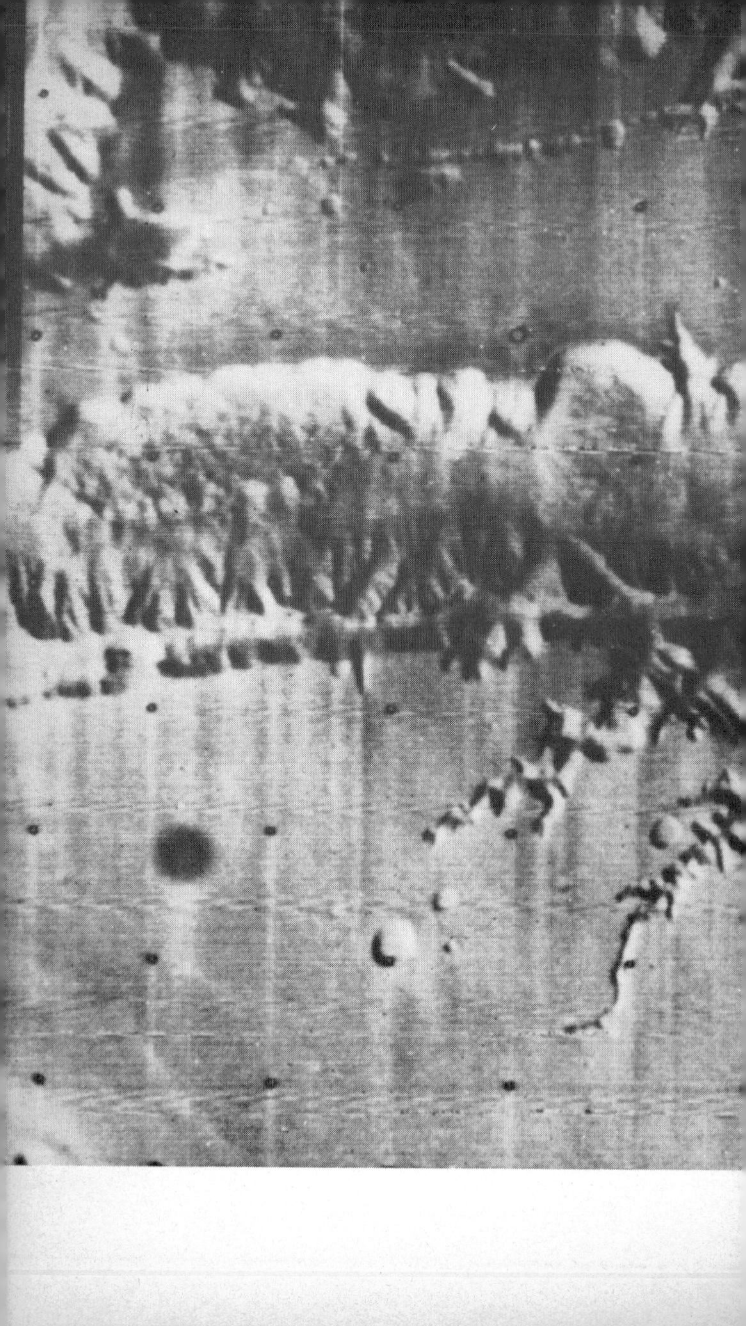

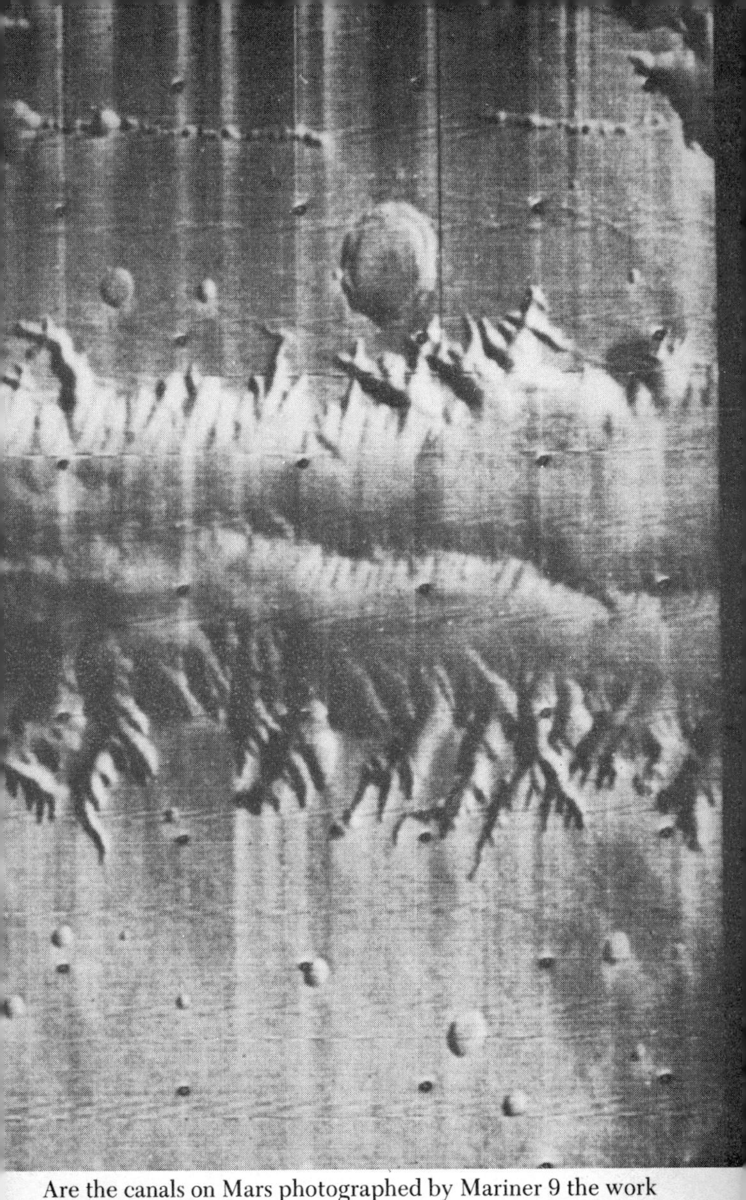

Are the canals on Mars photographed by Mariner 9 the work of intelligent creatures? (Jet Propulsion Laboratory)

Is Saturn next in the search for possible life forms? A mother spacecraft would carry a smaller orbiter-lander which would descend on Titan while the mothercraft would continue to study Saturn and relay data on both bodies back to Earth. (Jet Propulsion Laboratory)

An artist's conception of a likely candidate for a future space shuttle. The interstellar ramjet can travel the galactic highway unhampered by large cumbersome fuel loads. (Sechi Kiyohara, Hughes Aircraft Corporation)

I keep thinking about the man whose professional career was in advertising who discovered a revolutionary engineering concept for the design of airplane wings. He arrived at his discovery while making paper airplanes. I have often fantasized being such an inventor.

I do not believe it is necessary for an individual to have a long string of titles or degrees in order to be responsible for a profound new direction which deserves exploration.

Each spring I make a trek into the southern California deserts to camp out for a weekend. The cold night! The crystalline air and feeling that I can see forever are the parts of the experience I remember best. One night in particular stands out. We retired to our sleeping bags. The evening was moonless and inky-black and as I lay gazing at the star-dusted sky, a strange feeling of utter loneliness crept over me. Those who live in cities never see the sky as it was that evening. It was like an enormous intergalactic fireworks display—here and there a shooting star, whole whorls of many solar systems, distant suns and galaxies sparkling across the vast ice reaches of outer space.

The words of J. B. S. Haldane came back to haunt me. He once wrote, "Now, my suspicion is that the universe is not only queerer than we suppose, but queerer than we *can* suppose. I suspect that there are more things in heaven and earth than are dreamed of in *any* philosophy. That is the reason why I have no philosophy myself, and must be my excuse for dreaming."

The past fifteen years have reversed the thinking of the scientific community regarding extraterrestrial life, known as ETI. And while speculation about ETI has always been a heated one, today large segments of the scientific establishment are examining the hard probabilities that the universe is populated and that our galaxy is teeming with life. The problem—I should say challenge—is more "how" than "if." Science has always been very careful in the evaluation of data. Little models are constructed, formulas are worked out, tests are made, and the evidence finally evaluated. But as of this writing, there is really no practical proof for life in outer space other than the overwhelming odds that favor it.

Beyond speculation about ETI lies a great body of still-unanswered questions concerning our universe.

Let's consider for a moment whether the universe is finite or infinite. This brings us to a consideration known as Obler's Paradox. By mathematically calculating distances and numbers of stars, we should see more in the sky, but because of physical and technological hindrance, we don't. If the universe is infinite, the vast number of stars would provide more luminosity to the night sky. We know that not to be true. But if it is finite, there must be space beyond, which contains no galaxies and therefore no light. We also know that not to be true. What is the answer to Obler's Paradox?

Sagan and Shklovskii write in *Intelligent Life in the Universe* that "we may solve Obler's Paradox by assuming, instead of an end to space, a beginning of time. Thus, as we look to the most distant galaxies, we are seeing epochs further and further back into the past. If the universe began at a finite moment in time, eventually we would see at great distances to a point in space corresponding to the time of the origin of the universe. Beyond that, of course, there would be no galaxies. This is a possible solution of Obler's Paradox, but to many people it is an uncomfortable one. An apocryphal story relating to the life of Saint Augustine is relevant to this issue. Augustine was delivering an address on some of the same topics. A member of the audience objected: "Now, see here, Augustine. You have also told us that God is immortal, with no beginning and no end. What, then, was God doing before he created heaven and earth?" Augustine's riposte was: "He was creating hell, for people who ask such questions."

Despite Augustine's retort it is interesting to contemplate the possible form life might take. Professor Ronald Bracewell of Stanford University in *The Galactic Club* describes life forms which could have arisen on planets with surface gravity greater than earth's. He finds it very unlikely that intelligent life of this type would physically resemble man at all. Bracewell says that evolution there would favor creatures that crawled flat on their bellies and that found their ancestry in swamps where gravity could be counteracted by buoyancy. Instead of moving to the plains to become upright walkers like earth-niks, they might have moved from their place of birth to natural or artificial waterways.

Bracewell writes: "Perhaps there could be intelligent scum. After all, the size of the human individual has practically nothing to do with the size of his pyramids, cathedrals, oil tankers, rockets, and other products of technology. Had we been twelve-foot giants or three-foot dwarfs, would it have had any influence on the scale of such undertakings? I do not see why scum composed of single-celled plants, living on a water-air interface, possessing no resistance to wind or weather, could not attain technological control of the environment."

I wanted to return to the more conservative view of life as we know it existing on other planets. If there are six hundred billion suitable planets, and if we were able to reach any one of these planets, then what? If no one were there, we might establish a colony and develop a culture locally adapted. Our values would change; certain customs would alter. Perhaps slight differences in atmospheric conditions would slowly affect evolution, and natural selection would then change the physical look of the colonists. Gradually a new race of people would emerge, similar in general to humans, but different in detail. Has this already happened? Was this the reason for the humanoid stories? My work on *In Search of Ancient Astronauts* had convinced me that I should not ignore these possibilities.

I wondered. What if a space probe uncovered a strange form of matter unknown to life on earth? Could this be the product of a civilization which had moved on to colonize new frontiers in space? Thomas Gold, chairman of the Department of Astronomy at Cornell University, and director of the Center for Radio Physics and Space Research, suggests that advanced life in the universe may have evolved from cosmic garbage!

It was all so fantastic, and at the same time not so fantastic at all. Was all of this—the UFOs, the reported abductions, the humanoid visitors, the ancient records—from the dawn of history to the present, from the old science to the new science, a worldwide coincidence or hoax? And are the reports in some way linked to the reality of life existing elsewhere in the universe?

Certainly, life exists elsewhere in the universe. We now have a rather lengthy history of scientific attempts to communicate with extraterrestrial intelligences, the ETI. We have been trying to send and receive messages for some time. Listening to space isn't new. But it is based on the assumption that if in fact intelligent life did arise on other planets, it would want to communicate with us. However, this in itself is not a steadfast result of intelligence. It's merely a sequitur of intelligence which earth men have deemed inevitable. For as Bracewell states, "Preoccupation with technology might cease after some stage in a community's development, and intelligent life might become contemplative or turn more to philosophy and the arts. If the civilizations like this exist, they could be hard to detect." Communication with other civilizations might not interest such a highly advanced civilization. But I suspect that those civilizations aren't the only ones in space. The possibility that more technologically involved societies indeed exist has encouraged an increasing number of astronomers to turn to radio astronomy in an attempt to contact these civilizations.

7

Hello Out There

I have always had difficulty envisioning the mass actually represented by large numbers. For example, during the filming of a hive of bees, I asked the entomologist with whom I was working how many bees were in the colony. He told me that there were about fifty thousand. I tried to focus on that number by estimating how long it would take me to count them. I determined that if I set a rate of two bees per second it would take a little more than seven hours to do the job—with no time out for lunch.

Contemplating the numbers of stars and their plants has somewhat the same effect on me. Consider this question.

Of the six hundred million planets that might possibly be suitable for intelligent life, how many will develop a civilization capable of interstellar communication? Scientists have formulated the following equation: $N = R^* f_p n_e f_L f_i f_c . L$. The equation expresses a simple set of ideas. The letter N is the number of civilizations in the galaxy that are currently capable of communicating with other solar systems. The figures on the right signify factors affecting the number. R^* is the rate of star formation averaged over the lifetime of the galaxy: f_p is the fraction of stars with planets; n_e is the number of planets per solar system with an environment suitable for life; f_L is the fraction of suitable planets per solar system on which life actually appears; f_i is the fraction of life-bearing planets on which intelligence emerges; f_c is the fraction of intelligent societies that develop technical civilizations capable of interstellar communications; L is the lifetime of the technical civilization. L and f_c have the effect of securely limiting the total. Given these factors, the number N, advanced technical civilizations possessing both the interest and the capability of interstellar communication, is thought to be one million. To place that figure in perspective, it would take three and a half weeks of work to simply count that number.

I was beginning to understand why scientists were so optimistic about the possibility of contacting extraterrestrial life. The sheer weight of possibility is impressive. I find it possible to add in all variations that exist in the very means with which extraterrestrials might be contacted. Satellites, space vehicles, and radios are known and presently available instruments.

I realized, though, that the scientists who computed the one-million figure had interpreted intelligence and communication in a very restricted way. They assumed that the development of intelligent communicative societies always results in a technically advanced civilization. But is this necessarily the case?

I was reminded of the dolphin and whale communication research done some years ago by John C. Lilly of the Communication Research Institute in Coral Gables, Florida. The study focused on the brains of seagoing mammals. According to Lilly, the brain of the bottle-nosed dolphin is remarkable not only because of its size, which is slightly larger than that of an average man's, but also because of the density of nerve cells, which seems, under a microscope, to be comparable to that of the human brain. In fact, the cortex, or outer layer, of the dolphin brain is richer in folds and other structures than the equivalent part in the human brain.

The natural method of dolphin communication is in a frequency range far beyond the intelligibility level of the human ear. Lilly indicated that their intelligence is comparable to ours, but since we could not "hear" dolphin communication, we assume them to be of lesser intelligence. I knew what he meant.

I had been involved in a number of films which interpreted Dr. Lilly's work to television audiences. I remember the furor among his colleagues when he made his first pronouncements concerning the manner in which dolphins communicate. The fuss reached a crescendo when he announced the probability of devising a responsive language for human/dolphin communication.

Proof poured in from many centers once Dr. Lilly opened the floodgates when he stated that he truly began to understand behavior in foreign environment that was different than our own yet comparable in intelligence.

The dolphin's adaption to a liquid environment renders their bodies incapable of manipulative functions. Unable to use tools, dolphins did not build a technological society. Since they built neither monuments nor machines we placed them on a lower scale of life than our own. Yet they are capable of considerable social intercourse and detailed aural communication. I find it a source of some amusement that dolphins seem to be able to learn English, but we have not mastered dolphinese.

As we reached toward space, it may be necessary to redefine our concept of intelligence. Maybe advanced mental life or intelligence has its basis in the behavior patterns of the life form itself. The patterns are governed by the needs of the creature relative to its environment. Do all communicative intelligences have to develop technical civilizations that manipulate and sometimes destroy the environment? The answer is obviously no. The definition must be broader when we search the universe for intelligence.

If we are to communicate with extraterrestrial civilizations we must assume that there are receptors in existence and a means of interpreting the incoming signals. It is not farfetched to speculate on the possibility that communication may be achieved without the use of "machinery." Time and again recent experiments have confirmed the ability of the human brain to translate electronic impulses to imagery, or to emit electronic impulses when properly stimulated.

Not long ago I went to the San Diego laboratory of Cleve Backster and witnessed a fascinating experiment. Cleve is an expert in polygraph operation. One of the basic functions of the lie-detector is to electronically measure changes in the unconscious nervous system of human beings. Backster adapted the polygraph technique to measure the responses of plants to environmental changes. One of the startling possibilities he uncovered was that plants can react to acts that endanger their survival and communicate their "emotions" to other plants.

Backster also demonstrated the possibility that plants pick up and relay the emotional states of human beings. The experiment is simple. The lie detector is connected to a plant. A person is then asked to stand near the plant, and is told that as a part of the demonstration the person's hand will be superficially cut by a razor blade. The moment Backster tells the subject what will happen, the polygraph registers a distinct change in the response of the plant. It is Backster's belief that the plant responds to the apprehension of the subject. I tend to believe his general theory which I call plant E.S.P. His experiment reinforced the possibility of our being able to utilize the brain as a physical broadcast center. For this instant, we must look toward radio as the means of achieving inter-planetary communication.

The advent of radio marked the beginning of earth's recordable broadcasts. Marconi's coded telegraph message, broadcast more than three-quarters of a century ago is still outbound to the universe. Somewhere in space a dot-dot-dot-dash is drifting toward someone's receiver. The problem is that it will probably go unnoticed in the welter of electronic buzzing that surrounds all galaxies.

I am always a little uneasy about the outpouring of information emanating from our planet. Somewhere out there, on the road to infinity is a radio broadcast of a speech by Adolph Hitler, an episode of "I Love Lucy" and the children's chorus from "Howdy Doody." Hearing it all someone must say in complete bewilderment, "Who *are* those people?" I hope the signals we're sending out are clearer than the ones being picked up by modern radio astronomers.

Radio astronomy began in the 1890s as a theoretical notion accompanied by a few less-than-clear experiments. However, in 1931 Karl Jansky of Bell Telephone Laboratories accidentally discovered cosmic static or radio emissions from our galaxy. Prior to this discovery, our knowledge of the universe was limited to a list of visible objects photographed with traditional telescopes.

Radio astronomy helped peel back the limits of optical observation. Suddenly hidden presences revealed themselves through radio emissions. Radio telescopes discovered the spiral structure of our Milky Way galaxy, optically invisible due to galactic dust clouds. We suddenly had at hand a realistic means of interplanetary communication. Because radio waves are an extension of light waves into longer wavelengths, the discovery that part of the heavens "shine" in the radio spectrum portion opened a second window. In a relatively short period of time there have been improvements in the sensitivity of radio receiving apparatus. Two developments—the master (microwave amplification by simulated emission of radiation) and the parametric amplifier—eliminate almost all the usual receiver noise, increasing the possibility of radio contact with other civilizations. A relatively modest transmitter can send signals over distances of some tens of light years. We can begin to see hope of some contact. We have already made great progress. Artificial signals can now easily be distinguished from the thermal radio radiation of the local sun. The excellent frequency resolution of new radio receivers gathers information about distant planetary systems which will eventually lead to communication with intelligent life.

The average distance between extraterrestrial civilization is posing a critical obstacle. The length of time for a message to reach its destination is so long that our only hope for interstellar contact might be the use of automatic probe vehicles. On January 3, 1963, the Mariner II sent meaningful signals across 50 million miles of interplanetary space. Assuming the message reaches a planet 300 light-years away, it will take thousands of years to reach its destination, and still longer for earth to receive an answer. Ronald Bracewell writes of the problem: "One way or another, it is clearly possible in principle to pack an enormous amount of information into a modest interstellar probe, and to send it into the vicinity of a likely star. When the probe arrives, it fires a rocket and goes into circular orbit about the star in the middle of the habitable zone . . . ."

There are a number of advantages to probe contacts. An instrument package can be programmed to react to suitable environments. There are ways of allowing the probe to be triggered and powered by a local star, making its transmitted signal much more powerful. Moreover, and probably most important of all, the probe program doesn't depend on a specific choice of wavelengths as the terrestrial radio scopes do. Since we, ourselves, have had a relative amount of success sending Mariner II and Pioneer 10 into space, there is a great possibility that ETL probes exist. Perhaps extraterrestrial messenger probes can explain the history of mysterious radio signals.

Before the advent of radio astronomy in 1931, Tesla

and Marconi had experimented with electrical energy and believed they had heard signals from another world.

Nikola Tesla was the first to propose an effective way to use an alternating current (Edison vehemently opposed this scheme) which eventually made possible the harnessing of the power of Niagara Falls. He is apparently the first to use transmitting and receiving antennae tuned to the same frequency. One of his favorite theories was that power could be drawn from the magnetic field of earth in such stupendous quantities that it could be used to signal other planets.

In order to test this theory he set up a laboratory in Colorado Springs in 1899. It was equipped with a two-hundred-foot transmission tower and high voltage equipment designed to deliver a mammouth blast of manmade lightning which could be loosed across space in an intelligible sequence. He produced bolts of artificial lightning that rocked the countryside.

During the course of his experiments Tesla observed some electrical actions which he later reported to be signals, Tesla described them as taking place periodically and "with such a clear suggestion of number and order that they were not traceable to any cause then known to me." The feeling is constantly growing in me that I had been the first to hear the greeting of one planet to another." Tesla's report was not taken very seriously because of his rather extreme and well-known eccentric personality. He allegedly believed in mental telepathy, and unwillingly became a mascot for spiritualists. But his signals have never been explained or conclusively discredited. In fact, from what we now know, it seems that Tesla's contentions that he had been listening to extraterrestrial wireless signals was well-founded.

While Tesla was experimenting in Colorado, the Italian physicist Guglielmo Marconi demonstrated the capabilities of radio by transmitting messages across the Atlantic. In 1899 Marconi was tapping out the letter V; his partners fifty miles away finally succeeded in intercepting the signals. By 1901, he had broadcast the letter S across the Atlantic Ocean. The communication revolution had begun. In 1921, Marconi reported receiving strange, unidentifiable radio signals. He, like

Tesla, reported their bizarre regularity. The signals, he thought, represented some kind of unrecognizable code. But within the unrecognizable code was the letter V, which he had sent in 1899. The New York *Times* on September 2, 1921, reported that Marconi was convinced that some of the signals were from Mars. Little else was said about the matter and it was soon forgotten.

In 1924, David Todd, former head of the Astronomy Department at Amherst College, proposed an eaves-dropping program on Mars; the planet was then in close opposition to earth. He was going to use Charles Francis Jenkins' newly-invented radio-recording device. The Jenkins' radio-camera converted signals into pictures. Other nations participated in this widely publicized experiment by instructing their wireless stations to remain silent during Todd's experiment. Some of these stations reported results. None of the results were similar to those received by the Jenkins radio-camera. The New York *Times* reported on August 28, 1924: "Development of a photographic film record of the radio signals in a period of twenty-nine hours, when Mars was closest to the earth, has deepened the mystery of the dots and dashes reported heard at the same time by widely separated operators of powerful stations.

"The film . . . discloses in black and white a fairly regular arrangement of dots and dashes along one side, but on the other side at almost evenly spaced intervals are curiously jumbled groups, each taking the form of a crudely drawn face."

According to Frank Edwards in *Flying Saucers—Serious Business,* the scientists observed something even more mysterious than the faces. "They noted that there was an interesting chronological relationship between this flood of signals recorded in 1924 and the earlier experiments conducted by both Tesla and Marconi."

For example, in 1899 Tesla transmitted repeated pulses of radiation in a regular sequence while Marconi transmitted the letter V in Morse code. After a time lapse of twenty-two-years Marconi reported receiving unrecognizable signals accompanied by the V code. In 1901 he sent the first wireless message, (S) across the Atlantic. In 1924, within a similar twenty-two-year pattern, strange human faces were recorded on the radio camera. As Edwards pointed out, "Twenty-two years from our space signal experiments of 1924 brings us to 1946, the year the Unidentified Flying Object swarmed over the Earth, in this case over the Scandinavian countries and parts of Soviet Russia."

Carl Stormer of Norway and Balthasar Van der Pol heard another set of strange radio echoes in 1927, 1928, and 1934. These remain unexplained today. Their mysterious source caused Stanford's Ronald Bracewell to suggest that they might be typical of communication attempts by unmanned space probes. Van der Pol and Stormer began to study these strange echoes. In an article in *Nature,* 1928, they announced a change in the echoes of outgoing signals which had until then been regular. The time lag in the signal varied from many seconds to as long as a minute, suggesting that the signal was reflected from some object about one million kilometers from earth. Some people have thought that the signals were being reflected from clouds of ionized gas, but they have never been satisfactorily explained and remain a mystery.

Duncan Lunan, a fellow of the British Interplanetary Society, described the Stormer-Van der Pol experiment: "Signaling began on September 25, 1928, and no echoes were heard for sixteen days. On October 11, 1928, just after 3:30 in the afternoon, Hals telephoned Stormer to say that he could hear three-second echoes. Stormer went at once to Hals' home, about ten minutes away, and arrived just in time to hear the last-ever regular three-second echoes. Almost at once, the delay times began to vary from three seconds to fifteen. Caught by surprise, Stormer made only a rough record of the variations in delay time but he sent a telegram to Van der Pol announcing the extraordinary development. Van der Pol repeated the experiment that evening, increasing the spacing of his pulses to thirty seconds. The echo pulses did not immediately follow suit but ranged from three seconds to fifteen."

There is an "I shot an arrow into the air" quality about the reports of radio-signal experiments carried out in the late 1920s. Duncan Lunan has made an attempt to plot the echo patterns and deduce from the spacing the planet of their origin.

Intrigued with the theory of possible messenger probes already monitoring earth, Lunan researched the reports of Stormer and Van der Pol, hoping to assemble the pieces of the puzzle. He plotted Stormer and Van der Pol's reported delays on an E-Y recorder, a device that records the axis of two input signals. For graphic purposes he placed the amount of time the echo was delayed on one side and on the other the position of the echo in sequence. At first Lunan couldn't find anything recognizable, but in time he discovered that the recorder drew a map that remarkably resembled the constellation of Boötes—a double star system. Lunan believed that the map illustrated the star system as it was when it originated. He continued his work, plotting more echoes. Time and time again the plotted graphs not only depicted Epsilon Boötes but indicated the planets around the star. Lunan says that the logical sequence is so clear that it can be stated in standard, even colloquial English: "Our home is Epsilon Boötes, which is a double star. We live on the sixth planet of seven—counting outward from the sun which is the larger of the two stars. Our sixth planet has one moon. Our fourth planet has three. Our first and third planet each have one. Our probe is in the orbit of your moon." Lunan also found that Arcturus, the brightest star in this binary system, was in the place it occupied thirteen thousand years ago. It is possible that this probe could have been circling our moon for thirteen thousand years, and not have been noticed, even by recent radar scanning. Lunan's startling discovery has since been supported by a January 1974 account issued by Russian scientists. They also have been detecting similar signals. Has Lunan stumbled upon a signal from a civilization in distress? Was this extraterrestrial civilization searching for another home before its own planet burned up in the heat of its ancient expanding sun? Did they find a new planet in time? Do they know now that we exist?

The idea of an alien probe with a messenger isn't unique. On March 3, 1972, the United States launched

Pioneer 10 from Cape Kennedy to probe the environment of Jupiter as well as to explore the asteroids that lie between Mars and that Jovian planet. Pioneer 10 carried a message from earth. It was a six-by-nine-inch gold-anodized aluminum plate which described our earth and its inhabitants in bold graphics. Carl Sagan states: "The message itself intends to communicate the locale, epoch, and something of the nature of the builders of the spacecraft. It is written in the only language we share with the recipients: 'Science.' " It was the same kind of logic Lunan used to decipher the message from Boötes, only to be assailed by many astronomers as being "fanciful."

Electromagnetic interstellar messenger communication either by probe or earth-based radioscopes still leaves much to be desired. The communicants are far away, and the ability to find common language is slow and painful. Direct contact is probably the best of all possible worlds. But the distances which have to be covered pose an insurmountable obstacle. There is a solution. Halt the aging process of a human being and make it possible for him to survive a round trip to the galactic center which might take sixty thousand years. Cryogenics has fallen into some disrepute as a life-extender. For one reason existence in low temperatures for an extended period of time has never been accomplished. But recently a chemical formula was discovered which may radically slow the aging process in cell structure. It is now possible to contemplate an individual life expectancy of eight hundred years. The final processing of the new discovery will take some time, but the age of Methuselah may soon be here.

Even without chemical aging inhibitors, manned interstellar flight is feasible. The theory of relativity could play a major role in space flights traveling close to the speed of light. Passengers would travel over immense distances, at relatavistic velocities, and would age only slightly. Aboard an interstellar space ship, time moves more slowly for the passengers than people on earth. The explorers would physically move more slowly, their heart beat would slow and their awareness of time would retard. I wondered. The travel itself is a life extender. Have extraterrestrial civilizations, million of years more technically advanced than ourselves, already achieved this? Are UFOs and the humanoid encounter evidence of this?

Future think, the puzzling out of probabilities, may be a fascinating exercise, but I wanted to focus on realistic, at-hand alternatives.

Astronomers have embarked on vast listening programs. The United States has the largest radio telescope in the world at Arecibo Observatory in Puerto Rico. The thousand-foot diameter dish at Arecibo enables us to gather a wide spectrum of signals. The National Radio Astronomy Observatory in Green Bank, West Virginia has an eighty-five-foot-dish antenna. It was there that the first attempt to listen to signals from another world was made.

The real stimulus for present-day eavesdropping programs came from Giuseppe Cocconi and Phillip Morrison, both professors at Cornell University. Their work revived the prospect of interstellar radio contact. Shortly before their concentrated efforts to organize an eavesdropping program, scientist Hendrick Christoffel Van de Hulst made an important discovery. His work removed the major roadblock to using the radio's spectrum to intercept extraterrestrial signals. Unlike light, radio lacked the sharp emission or absorption lines that had proved so useful in astronomy. These lines were used to detect relative motion toward and away from the observer. Van de Hulst proposed that the clouds of individual hydrogen atoms should emit radio noise waves at a 21-centimeter wavelength. Since these clouds exist everywhere inside space there should be a sharp increase of cosmic radio noise at the magic 21-centimeter wavelength. He was proved correct. Suddenly the dust that formerly closed much of the universe to our telescopes became transparent by using 21-centimeter emissions as a guidepost.

The 21-centimeter discovery sparked a flurry of activity. Large antennae were put under construction or planned; radio waves from space now opened up myriad lines of investigation. Cocconi and Morrison jumped at the possibility of looking for signals for ETI. They wrote an article in *Nature,* hoping to publicize their ideas among reputable scientists around who were interested in searching for signals. "We shall assume," they wrote, "that long ago the ETI established a channel of communication that would one day become known to us, and that they look forward patiently to the answering signals from the sun which would make known to them that a new society has entered the community of intelligence."

Almost in tandem with the suggestion of Morrison and Cocconi a secret plan was being prepared to search for intelligent life. Directed by Frank Drake, it was called Project Ozma, in memory of the princess of the imaginary land of OZ—a place far in the distance inhabited by exotic beings. Drake selected two targets: Tau Ceti and Epsilon Eridani. They were eleven light-years away and probably observable with an eighty-five-foot dish generated by a million-watt transmitter operating through a six-hundred-foot antenna.

The National Radio Astronomy Observatory at Green Bank, West Virginia was the site of Project Ozma. Listening began on April 3, 1960. In a very short time, strong signals were heard. It seemed as if they had come from the control room. Everyone began looking for quirks in the circuitry that might account for the strange pulses, but nothing was found. Apparently, or so the public was told later, the signals were due to secret military experiments in radar countermeasures. Yet a strange thing happened after the first signals were reported. The Ozma search was abruptly suspended. No further explanation was given except that the telescope was needed in other projects. Whether the "secret military experiment" was indeed the source of the signals will never be known. But as Major Keyhoe notes, "If this had been true, Project Ozma could have continued with no excitement. It could not possibly explain the incredible actions which followed."

In 1971, twenty-four scientists and engineers in the Stanford/NASA-Ames Summer Faculty Fellowship Program gathered to devise a system for detecting extraterrestrial life. Dr. Bernard M. Oliver and Dr. John Billingham directed the group. They investigated the different aspects involved in making radio contact.

They studied the design and cost of large antenna structures, electrical transmission and control, signal processing and sensitive radio receivers. The culmination of the study was a 243-page volume entitled *Project Cyclops.* The Cyclops scientists established that radio is the superior means of contact, particularly into the microwave range of wavelengths from about 10 to 30 centimeters.

The entire proposed Cyclops system would comprise one thousand or more large radio telescope dishes spread over an area of up to ten miles across. I called Dr. Billingham to find out what the projected cost of such an "orchard" system of telescopes would be. He emphasized that there could be neither a fixed cost nor a fixed size. The size would be the size that it takes to detect signals. Cyclops, if it were to be built, would start very small and increase its size gradually.

Project Cyclops officially ended when the report was finished. But each summer since 1971, Ames Research Center scientists assemble to discuss certain aspects of eventual radio contact. In the summer of 1976 they studied the requirements needed to build a telescope that would photograph stars outside our solar system. The scientists at Cyclops feel that if funding were to materialize, and a sufficient amount of technology could be built, there might be a good chance of detecting life on other planets.

The present lack of funds and state of technology in the area of radio contact severely limits the possibility of new discoveries. Nonetheless, attempts are being made. The persistent and adamant belief in life on other planets and our ability to contact it has spurred the U.S. space program. In November 1974, at the Arecibo Observatory in Puerto Rico, Frank Drake sent the first and only intentional signal from earth to M-13. I called Dr. Drake's assistant and asked her why M-13 was the target. Apparently it was the globular cluster of stars which happened to be in the right position at the time. It will take 24,000 years for our signal to reach M-13 and another 24,000 years for an answer to return to earth. It's easy to understand why we are more intrigued with listening programs than making ourselves heard.

Scientists interested in using the Arecibo radio telescope for interstellar communication searches are severely limited. They can listen for signals only every three months for a thirty-hour period. So far, there are no questionable echoes. Until the time devoted to listening to signals increases, practical results will be few and far between. So, while we wait to listen, we doodle with the language we will use to "communicate" with ETL.

The question of language and message content is an important one, considering how close we are to encountering, voluntarily or involuntarily, the galactic club. Frank Drake went through a practice session by sending an enigmatic communication to the participants of the Green Bank conference held after Project Ozma terminated. He thought it might be the kind of initial message sent from another race of beings. His message triggered the question of how we might exchange ideas with those who are so totally different in physiognomy, and even possibly in methods of logic and thought.

Drake's message contained a series of pulses sent in a fixed rhythm, filled with many gaps. The pulses he wrote as ones; the gaps as zeros—a simple binary code commonly used in computers. Everyone worked on the message, but with little luck. Only one person was able to decipher it. Bernard M. Oliver simplified the message by expanding it so that the pulses and gaps eventually became dots forming a picture. The sun and planets of our solar system were represented. Marine life and water were shown, along with a manlike creature pointing to the fourth planet, where the civilization resides.

Drake's cryptogram stimulated some hard-nosed thinking about what we might include in a message, and how we might illustrate that message. Phillip Morrison suggested courses in anticryptography, or code design in easy-to-decipher language. He devised a scheme for coaching distant creatures in the establishment of a television link. All technologically advanced civilizations, he speculated, might have mathematics based on numbers as a common touchstone. Yet their mathematical logic may be radically different from ours. Oliver points out that, despite these handicaps, they most likely can see. Therefore, establishing television contact is very logical.

Morrison's method of establishing television contact is an elaboration of the "radioglyph." "Plus," "minus," and "equal" concepts could be symbolized by a distinctive signal—a radioglyph. I wondered if any of the answers were quite enough.

In 1880 an Austrian priest named Volapuk worked on a pure logic language. Seven years later Zamenhof developed Esperanto which finally did not prove to be universal enough. The effort to develop a purely logical language in which all mathematical reasoning could be expressed was also attempted by Giuseppe Peano at the end of the nineteenth century. Peano's work stimulated the *Principia Mathematica* developed by Alfred North Whitehead and Bertrand Russell. Then Hans Freudenthal of the University of Utrecht tried to expand Whitehead and Russell's logistic method to communication. He wanted to design language intelligible to creatures whose intelligence was their only common link. *Lincos: Design of a Language for Cosmic Intercourse* was the result. Lincos is expressed by unmodulated radio signals of varying duration and wavelength. These signals can combine to create words. The lexicon and syntax are established slowly, similar to the way in which we began to build our own vocabulary as children.

Lincos and radioglyphs are attempts to solve the problem of interstellar contact with a race of creatures vastly different from ourselves. In view of the recent increase in UFO landings, sightings, and the new trend toward UFO abductions, we seem to be precariously near the realm of forced communication with our cosmic visitors.

Aside from the possibility of involuntary contact, why should we attempt to contact them at all? The question is a very rational one. And it offers a fascinating field of contemplation and quiet reflection.

We have spent so much time debunking the possibility of cosmic visitation that we have not prepared ourselves for that eventuality. Hasn't the time come to begin?

Earth has just entered a technological phase capable of interstellar communication.

For more than fifty years, earth radio communications have traveled through space; we have been engaging in self-advertisement. These waves are now touching other planetary systems light-years away. Already a reply to our radio emissions could be traveling toward earth. Their response is forthcoming. Any day now our radio telescopes could reveal to all the world that human intelligence isn't supreme.

Even now there are unexplained space signals on record, evidence, perhaps, that advanced civilizations are aware of our existence and technical progress. Refusing to answer doesn't guarantee against space visitors. In fact, the UFO surveillance might just be a follow-up of attempts to communicate. The extraterrestrial hypothesis as a possible explanation of UFOs is becoming more and more inevitable. The earth's technology is in its infancy. We've been a technological civilization for a mere one hundred years, a minuscule fraction of the fourteen billion years since the planet earth was formed. Millions of stars and their planets out there are older and perhaps wiser. More than a million are thought to be much more advanced than earth. The likelihood that they have already developed the means to span the great galactic distances and directly contact us is almost a certainty. In our own short technological reign we are already sending space probes and contemplating the technical advancements required to achieve manned interstellar space flight. It's been seven years since we landed men on the moon! We have just entered the cosmic era!

But the question remains: How have the extraterrestrials spanned the galactic distances? How can we meet them directly on their own territory? A curious new space mystery has been discovered that might shed some light on these questions—the black holes.

8

Black Holes

A black hole is the condensed corpse of an exploded massive star. Nothing escapes from a black hole, not even light. Black holes are thought to be the ultimate relic of massive stars, which, having lost their energy, collapse, so that no light, matter, or other radiation can ever escape from them.

Black holes are tombstones. They signify the death of a massive star's life cycle. Black holes are the end product of an exquisitely complicated evolutionary scheme. They are the ultimate unknowable! If a star's development is traced from a black hole back through its minute globular beginnings, a very curious relationship emerges.

Star births generated the planetary beginnings of life. The creation story in Chapter 6 describes how planets were formed from the innards of stars. Atoms—the necessary components of life—were boiled and baked in the wombs of red giant stars like our sun. Ultraviolet light, thunder, and volcanoes generated by the radiation of the sun forced these atoms together to create complex organic molecules. Hence sunlight or starlight emerges as the ultimate energy source from which almost all terrestrial organisms live out their days. Life on earth is closely connected to stellar events. But our sun is approaching middle age and has only five or ten billion years of stellar life ahead until it becomes a shriveled white dwarf and eventually fades into the void. Long before the end, all earthly life will disappear.

One kind of star death interests astronomers in particular—total gravitational collapse, the death throes of a star more massive than our sun. The results of such events are black holes.

A star dies when its nuclear fires stop providing the heat needed to maintain the star's internal pressure. The heat has kept the star from collapsing under the weight of its outer layers. Hydrogen fusion produces energy for the star, but it cannot power the star forever. Eventually stars consume all their hydrogen fuel and reach the end of their existence. They enter the stellar cemetery, becoming haggard white dwarfs, neutron stars, or perhaps cadaverous black holes. The corpse that each star eventually assumes is dependent on its mass. A star with a mass equal to that of our sun becomes a white dwarf.

In about ten billion years our sun will have consumed so much of its hydrogen that it will evolve to a red giant. As a red giant it will expand to 250 times its present diameter, devouring any of its surrounding environment, including, perhaps, the earth. As it consumes more of the available nuclear fuel, the distended, swollen sun will reverse its expansion and contract its present diameter to become the size of the earth. It will then have evolved into a ghostly white dwarf, and its contraction will halt. As a white dwarf it will eventually blink out of the universe. Many white dwarfs have been observed. They are part of the evolutionary process of "normal" stars such as the sun. However, not all stars can find peace as white dwarfs. There is a size above which a star cannot sustain itself against further collapse.

A star with twice the mass of the sun will expand, like our sun, to an enormous size, after consuming almost all of its original hydrogen fuel. It will then contract. But unlike our sun, the larger star has no shrinking point that will enable it to settle down as a white dwarf. Therefore, it will collapse through the white-dwarf stage to become more and more dense. Due to the extreme temperatures and densities involved in this further collapse, it will explode catastrophically. A supernova exploding star will outshine a galaxy for several days.

I have often looked up at the sky and seen a burst of light flashing across the blackness, and wondered: What is it that shines so brightly? I had never realized that the streak of brilliance was the marker of death.

Ninety percent of the star's mass can be ejected during the explosion, leaving only a collapsed core of the previous star. The core is much too small to become a white dwarf, so it can find equilibrium only as a neutron star. Thus nature once more outwits the laws of gravity. Stars twice as massive as the sun can escape a journey into nothingness. The neutron or pulsar star remains. But again, as in the case of white dwarfs, there is a maximum possible mass above which a neutron star cannot sustain itself against still further gravitational contraction. The mass limit is probably not more than a few solar masses, and there are stars whose mass is more than fifty times the mass of the sun. What might be their eventual fate? What other types of concentrated matter could exist with densities greater than those maintained inside a neutron star?

Massive stars have two very interesting characteristics. They evolve very rapidly and thus burn up their stellar fuel very quickly. Once they have consumed all of their fuel, no forces in nature could stop the stars' disintegration. The internal pressure, combined with the external gravitational forces, causes the star to contract indefinitely and become what is known as a black hole. Kip Thorne of Cal Tech, world-renowned black-hole scientist, explains: "For a star to be stable, the total force of gravity pulling a star's surface inward must be balanced by the star's internal pressures pushing the surface outward. If the force of gravity is stronger, the star collapses; if the internal pressure is stronger, the star explodes. . . . For stars more massive . . . the force of gravity always wins and crushes stars into a black hole in less than a second."

The black-hole idea has a long history. Black holes were discovered as early as 1788, when Pierre Simon de Laplace predicted from Newtonian mechanics that a very massive and dense body would be invisible because the escape velocity at its surface would be greater than the speed of light. Therefore, nothing, not even light, could escape from this body. Laplace's theory was based on Newtonian gravity and his theory of light. Newton thought of light as tiny pellets with properties similar to small billiard balls. Since such pellets could not escape from the surface of a sufficiently massive body,

Laplace wondered whether space might be inundated with such *corps obscurs*.

Black holes are also the by-products of Einstein's general theory of relativity. The search for black holes has challenged scientists to explore the outer limits of Einstein's theory of gravity—a fundamental part of the relativity story. In 1916, shortly after Einstein's theory of gravity appeared, Karl Schwarzschild, the German physicist, described the nature of a black hole, at least in theory. However, he, like Laplace, was unable to verify whether such a point could exist in the real world. Then, in 1939, J. Robert Oppenheimer and Hartland Snyder showed, according to general relativity theory, that a cold and sufficiently massive star must ultimately collapse and become a black hole.

Black holes and Einstein's theory of gravity are tied closely together. According to the general theory of relativity, gravity is produced not only by mass but also by pressure. Thus, if the star's internal pressure is extreme, it gives rise to gravitational forces that overwhelm the internal pressure, and the star collapses. Depending on the size of the star, either gravity or intermediate pressures win the battle over the ultimate form of the stellar corpse. If gravity conquers, the fabric of space and time fold in on themselves and a black hole is formed. A black hole symbolizes gravity's victory in its role as the controller of stars' life cycles. Relativity theory says that space and time curve in upon themselves, and black holes are the logical results. But according to Kip Thorne, black holes were regarded as strictly theoretical objects for a long time. They were objects that could be formed by the death of a star but probably never were. Objects like black holes and even neutron stars were still too bizarre to fit comfortably into our complacent scientific model of the universe. But time passed, and soon our view of the universe began to change radically.

In the 1960's certain observational discoveries materialized. Exploding galaxies, quasars, cosmic microwave radiation from the "big-bang" explosions, and radio-telescope signals showed the scientific community how mysterious and awesome the universe really was. Then, in 1967 the pulsar or neutron stars were discovered. First, white dwarfs, then neutron stars—an evolutionary scheme seemed to be in the making. If neutron stars really existed, then surely black holes must exist as well. The search for black holes was on.

But how does one search for black holes? They are invisible and can't be optically detected except indirectly. One lead is the probability that black holes have a strong gravitational influence on the "companions." With this notion in mind, two Russian astrophysicists began the first serious search for black holes in 1964. Zel'dovich and Guseynov thumbed through binary-star catalogs looking for systems that might be black-hole and companion-star teams. If they found a double star system where a companion star could not be detected, the companion star might be a black hole. But the star catalogs are full of just such systems. So Zel'dovich and Guseynov went one step further. They investigated the mass of the dark companions and limited themselves to those dark companions with masses three times greater than our sun. They narrowed the number of possible candidates to five. But, unfortunately, there were alternatives to the black-hole theory that explained the action of these stars; many other explanations were just as feasible. The search seemed stymied.

One other hope remained. It was conjectured that a black hole in a two-star system might pull gas away from its companion star. As the gas fell into the hole, it would be heated so much that it would emit X rays. If X rays were ever detected, the supposition that a dark companion was a black hole would be more convincing. In order to conduct such a search, an X-ray telescope aboard an artificial satellite would be needed.

The first such telescope—the Uhuru satellite—was launched jointly by the United States and Italy on December 12, 1970. By 1972, Uhuru had gathered enough data to compile and catalog a list of 125 X-ray sources. An immense field of speculation and debate now presented itself for further scientific analysis.

The great hunt for black holes was begun. Astronomers and physicists probed the skies, playing what I considered to be a highly sophisticated game of blindman's buff. In some ways it was like finding the invisible man who had hidden in a totally dark soundproof room. You know he's there, but you'll never be sure you've found him.

There are traces that black holes leave, sort of a fingerprint by which we would know their passing. The gravitational field of the hole obeys the standard laws of Newton and Einstein. According to Thorne, the hole's attraction for an object is proportional to its mass. The existence of a black hole would attract material. Call it, for simplicity's sake, an invisible magnet exerting pull on various objects. The strength of the pull depends on the size of the hole. Second, a black hole creates a kind of suction that swirls and traps all approaching particles or gas into whirlpool orbits. Therefore, circular meteor tracks or light displays might be evidence. Next, black holes curve space and warp time in their vicinity. Typical black holes should have masses between three and fifty suns. A black hole has an "event horizon," a point of no return. Whatever goes past will never emerge again. I wondered what it would be like to enter a black hole. What if I were taking a mythic trip through space and suddenly found myself caught on the "event horizon"?

According to Harry Shipman, in *Black Holes, Quasars and the Universe,* the first noticeable effect a spacecraft might sense would be a relentless gravitational pull. It would begin to fall toward the black hole, getting closer and closer to the event horizon. The event horizon itself is the essence of the black hole. In order to escape the suction of this mighty vacuum, the spacecraft must be able to travel at the speed of light. Since a spacecraft cannot travel that fast, it cannot return to the outside world once it has crossed the event horizon, the edge of a black hole.

As objects approach the event horizon, another unusual phenomenon may occur. Black-hole gravity will distort time and prevent signal transmissions from objects near the event horizon. To an outside station, spaceships falling into the hole would appear to be frozen at the precipice. Observers would never see anything actually fall through the event horizon. Time would apparently stop, due to the perspective of the observer.

Shipman explains that if we could observe the formation of a black hole we could witness a similar story. At first the star's collapse would appear rapid, but as the star came closer to the horizon, the collapse would appear to slow down. The star's own gravity would cause everything to seem to happen in slow motion. It would first distort time, and then time would seem to stop. Hence the name frozen star. But as Shipman notes, this effect is again merely a consequence of the observer's point of view. The object, person, or star that gets too near the event horizon would indeed be sucked into its whirlpool.

Inside the event horizon, strange and frightening things are thought to occur. First and foremost, nothing can return. Second, in the center of the hole, a "singularity" exists. This is where Einstein's theory breaks down. A "singularity" is the point that contains all the mass of the hole. It is the point at which all matter is condensed into infinity or nothingness. Objects caught in the "singularity" would be crushed into infinity. Scientists feel that whenever a theory starts to suggest infinity, it has begun to break down. According to the experts, subatomic matter cannot be destroyed. Therefore, this "singularity" is thought to be merely a mathematical error in Einstein's calculations. In order to compensate for this oversight and get rid of the "singularity," we are faced with the intriguing new idea that multiple universes exist, through which any trapped spacecraft can surface, entering another part of the universe myriad miles away in a different epoch.

Science-fiction writers produced these "elevators to another world" many years ago. It seems incredible to me that science fact is making them a reality.

All of the fantastic phenomena are merely theories of what should exist if relativity is pushed to its limit. As passageways to other parts of the universe, black holes become a source of great credibility for explaining UFO behavior. In fact, UFOs seem to be not only a mild but also a logical phenomenon in comparison to the conjectures that black-hole theorists are presenting.

Even though the actual existence of black holes is still a matter of controversy and presently remains a theoretical concept, some astronomers believe they have detected black holes gravitationally. Moreover, the gravitational evidence that has been accumulating is leading more and more scientists to believe that strange stellar corpses, the ghosts of dead stars, are more than the products of elaborate theoretical surmise. I have talked to researchers who have turned up evidence that may pin down the elusive black hole.

One of the strongest candidates that the Uhuru satellite reveals lies in the constellation of Cygnus. It is called Cygnus X-1. Observations at the wavelengths of light, radio waves, and X rays from Uhuru indicate that the X-ray source Cygnus X-1 is probably a black hole in orbit around a massive star. The case for a black hole in the center of Cygnus is a pretty strong one, but some hard-nosed trackers will not be satisfied until they can calculate the properties of the X-ray emission in detail. Nevertheless, the evidence is very persuasive. Tables have been drawn estimating the X-ray output of a black hole. The Cygnus measurement fits the table very accurately. The way it works is that the gravitation field of the black hole continually pulls gas off the companion star and funnels it into orbit around the black hole. As the gas is sucked into the hole, it is heated and radiates energy, about 80 percent of which emerges as X rays. Presumably these are the X rays detected by the telescope aboard Uhuru. Scientists generally admit that the fairest statement of the current situation is that Cygnus X-1 is probably a black hole, but it has not yet been proved conclusively that it *must* be a black hole.

Some scientists at Cornell University believe that they have discovered black holes at the centers of globular clusters. (A globular cluster consists of approximately 100,000 stars.) The presence of a black hole should cause the distribution of the stars to change; their number density should increase as stars are destroyed and consumed by the suction pit. The Cornell scientists have observed just such a distribution change. The stars in these globular clusters seem to be getting closer together! I wondered if there might be a black hole in the center of our galaxy. What would that mean?

A black hole is thought to produce detectable quantities of gravitational radiation. In 1969 Joseph Weber set up a gravitational detector at the University of Maryland in order to find out whether our galaxy might possess any hungry, dark, invisible companions. The results of these experiments were quite alarming. Weber used aluminum cylinders that were suspended by wires in a vacuum. Any incoming waves would excite the cylinders, and these oscillations could be detected by the quartz crystals bonded to the surface of the cylinders. And in 1969 Weber announced that he had observed several hundred disturbances over several months, which could not be explained as chance fluctuations. These signals were most frequent when the detectors were pointed in the direction most sensitive to radiation coming from the center of our galaxy. The radiation consisted of a short pulse of less than half a second long about once every four days and was picked up at a frequency of about sixteen hundred cycles per second.

In order to explain Weber's observation, one suggestion has been put forward. It is proposed that the radiation is coming from stars near the galactic center as they fall into a large spinning black hole that forms the central part of our galaxy. A rotating black hole may be at the center of our own galaxy, causing the emission of the radiation. The evidence is not conclusive. But there is every indication that violent events of some kind do occur in all galaxies. Exploding galaxies, quasars, cosmic microwave radiation from the "big-bang" explosion, flaring X-ray stars—all point to a violent universe. Our galactic center seems to be full of activity; it might very well even harbor a black hole!

Frank Low of the University of Arizona has discovered five mysterious infrared radiation sources. These sources, whatever they might be, make up approximately 10 percent of the total luminosity of the galaxy. Could these be gas radiations from stars that have fallen into black holes?

On June 30, 1908, a giant fire ball exploded in Siberia's remote Tunguska territory. It scorched the ground for miles around, leveling trees, killing reindeer, and causing atmospheric shock waves that were detected around the world. It was suggested that a comet head or a meteorite could have caused this phenomenon. But astronomers and geologists failed to find a major crater of clearly identifiable meteor fragments at the site, and so the Tunguska event remains a mystery. A short time ago two Texas physicists, Albert A. Jackson IV and Michael P. Ryan, Jr., proposed that the 1908 explosion was caused by a black hole colliding with the earth. Ryan and Jackson proposed that their theory could be supported by a search of oceanographic records and ships' logs for any reports of strange doings in the North Atlantic on the day of the Siberian explosion. They believe that if the object was indeed a black hole, such disturbances would have occurred. Their theory has not been seriously challenged, although some scientists believe that the black-hole idea is at best highly implausible. I'm not so sure.

The actual physics of black holes is rather poorly understood at the present time. Therefore, I think it might be too soon to be cocksure about the invalidity of any hypothesis. Perhaps black holes will provide us with an answer to the UFO enigma. In fact, one highly respected astronomer conjectured that UFOs may have been trapped in these suction pits and are emerging now on earth—another part of their universe in a different epoch. Are we on the brink of an event that would stagger the minds of even the most imaginative?

One conjecture that has been made which cannot be disproved: black holes may be corridors to elsewhere. Perhaps, if we were to enter a black hole, we might surface in a different part of the universe in another epoch in time. It might be possible to reach other places in the universe faster through a black hole than by the more usual route. Sagan writes: "For all we know, black holes are the transportation conduits of advanced technological civilizations—conceivably, conduits in time as well."

The search for extraterrestrials may one day focus on the "event horizon" inside a black hole. Nothing could be more fascinating to learn than the fact that all of the rules we associate with time and space become inoperable when a black hole is present. They could be one-way streets that spacecraft from another galaxy enter, to exit in our galaxy. If that were the case, UFOs might then be simply spacecraft in search of bearings or information about where the tunnel has deposited them. It all sounds vaguely Buck Rogers-ish, but in the world of UFO-ology, anything is seemingly possible.

9

Designs of Spaceships

Slowly but surely I was gaining momentum in my search for evidence of extraterrestrials. I was gradually demystifying those parts of the puzzle that previously had eluded me. The spanking-new speculations now popping up in scientific journals had empowered my search with optimistic yet nervous excitement. It is practically a foregone conclusion that an enormous number of extraterrestrial intelligences exist outside our solar system. Radio communication with ETI is imminent, due at least in part to our recent inadvertent radio and TV signals. Black-hole gravity may explain how ETI travels at awesome velocities. We ourselves just landed the Viking probe on Mars. The age-long life-on-Mars puzzle should soon be resolved.

Still, I had not solved the question of extraterrestrials on earth. I wanted incontrovertible evidence that would point to one inevitable conclusion. More problems lingered, nagging for answers that would enhance and embellish the evidence.

The next question I wanted to tackle was directed to aerospace designers. In what kind of vehicle could ETI be arriving? I soon discovered that this particular question had to be phrased rather precisely. Aerospace designers, in general, were loath to discuss any advanced speculative designs for interstellar vehicles. The majority preferred to limit themselves to only those designs feasible within the next thirty years. I experienced a great deal of difficulty locating those rare engineers willing to speculate about the propulsion requirements and physical appearances of the best possible deep-space vehicle and landers which we hope someday to design.

I spoke to many engineers at NASA, Jet Propulsion Laboratory, Marshall Space Flight Center in Huntsville, Alabama, and the Goddard Space Institute. The list was endless, yet the responses were incredibly uniform. During the first weeks of traveling and interviewing it seemed as if the answers to my questions were all the same. For whatever reasons of national security or emotional security, aerospace engineers seem loath to deal with far-out speculation. Universally, they claimed that there were only five propulsion systems inventable within the next thirty years. However, these propulsion systems didn't differ too much from the propulsion system of the Viking probe already landed on Mars. The systems are limited. Their speed and cost make interstellar travel a rather unattractive goal. In fact, interstellar travel is so unattractive that neither the Skunkworks (future aerospace design team) at JPL nor the Ames Research Center at NASA is willing to admit they are even working on interstellar vehicles. They claim, to any unauthorized truth-seekers like myself, that they are still working on the interplanetary vehicles. A brief review of the five "very advanced" propulsion systems we have thus far imagined readily shows the wisdom of these publicly stated goals. (Pioneer X, our first interstellar probe, will reach only the nearest star, 1.3 light-years away, in 80,000 years.)

The propulsion mechanism that should launch and drive interstellar probes seems to be our main stumbling block. Rocket engines drive our present-day craft forward by throwing propellant particles out their exhaust in one direction at high speed, thus making the spacecraft respond by moving in the opposite direction. Today's interplanetary travel, as well as tomorrow's interstellar travel, is thought of in the same way. Both take advantage of a tried-and-true formula. If you push on something with a given force and it has a given mass, then the acceleration you get is proportional to the force. In essence, all of the five propulsion systems now envisioned for the future are based on this concept. They are all brute-force systems distinguished only from today's interplanetary models by more efficient propulsion systems with a better payload capability.

After talking to engineers, I find my notes and even my speech sprinkled with their jargon. I became deeply involved in phrases like "propulsion system." Translated, it's just another way to say "motor." But after a while the engineering vocabulary just takes over. I have tried to avoid "specialist" talk in describing possible deep-space ships.

One possibility is the nuclear-pulse propulsion system. It operates by jettisoning a nuclear bomb, exploding it, and absorbing some of the momentum and acceleration of the resulting nuclear debris. Needless to say, environmentalists do not look too fondly on such a system, and testing is rather awkward in light of the nuclear-test-ban treaty. The total fuel cost for this propulsion system is estimated at eighty billion dollars. Beyond the cost, the rather long flight time makes nuclear-pulse propulsion a discouraging proposition.

The prospect of controlled-fusion reaction is more promising but still a far cry from the kind of propulsion system that would permit practical rather than just theoretically possible flights. Another system might be the interstellar ramjet; unlike today's conventional craft, it would collect interstellar matter to fuel its rockets and thus eliminate the need to carry large quantities of fuel on board. But objectors to the ramjet say that the amount of fuel available in interstellar space is so low that the reactions used by the ramjet aren't feasible in space. Interstellar travel that uses beamed laser power is the most promising of the five concepts, but it requires an enormous amount of energy, which at the moment cannot be generated. And finally, huge engineering problems arise in the design of an engine that can convert antimatter energy into a direct thrust of the propellant.

The questions I asked the designers about interstellar travel were met with very few inspired answers. In fact, none of the engineers I talked to during the first part of this search were very excited about the interstellar prospect at all. They all summarized the five possible techniques. Some favored ramjets as opposed to nuclear propulsion, and vice versa. The uniformity of answers was rather astounding and very intriguing.

I pursued my list of aerospace designers. To each I queried: How would you design the best space vehicles and excursion modules? What would they do? How would they differ from what we already have? I was on the phone with Robert Wood.* His field is advanced systems technology in aerospace design. A few seconds elapsed between my question and Dr. Wood's response. I wondered what he was about to say. All the answers I had gotten prior to this seemed to come automatically—almost rehearsed. But Dr. Wood was taking his time. He began: "Well, the answer to those questions all depends on the assumptions you are willing to make. If you assume that they are inventable, then you get an updated model of the Viking system. The updated system would have a better, more specific impulse on the propellants. It would orbit the planet, slow down using atmospheric drag to reduce its velocity, and so forth. In short, it would operate the same way Viking does, but with more efficient components, so it could carry a larger payload for less fuel weight." He paused. I waited, wondering what he was going to say next. He continued. "If you invoke a new assumption about science which is as yet unprovable and try to design the best deep-space vehicles and landers possible, then you come up with a UFO. That is the best model we have, for a perfect interstellar craft. Either you assume something completely new or you play it safe and go with only what we already know. In the latter case, you come up with what we essentially already have." Now I understood why all the engineers I had previously contacted gave me such uniform answers. For them to imagine much more, or rather, shall I say, in order for them to truly answer my question, they would have to refer to UFOs as a possible, realistic spacecraft doing things that are completely incomprehensible and unrepeatable in terms of present technology.

The UFO prospect puts science in a rather uncom-

*of the McDonnell Douglas Corporation

fortable position. Robert Wood and other designers with a broad-vista approach were truly few and far between. Reaching into unknown and untried subjects, the researcher runs the risk of being wrong. Few take such risks. Dr. Wood elaborated. He said, "UFOs are stunningly different from our present landers. Their apparent antigravity allows them to accelerate and decelerate in an instant. They can do this without causing the occupants physical harm they would otherwise encounter without such gravity-interaction devices. UFOs seem to operate on a principle other than F = MA [Force = Mass times Acceleration]. Their circular shape denotes a conductive wire around the vehicle. The currents of this hypothetical wire flow around the disk and might somehow relate to controlling gravity."

Dr. Wood and I talked for a long time. He explained how the changing colors often observed with the UFO could be technically explained. They might be due to ordinary interaction of the vehicle with the atmosphere. Ionized air becomes red, or there might be a massive magnetic field in the vicinity of the object, which would cause excited molecules to manifest themselves in different wavelengths. He assured me that all this was speculation on his part.

Needless to say, Dr. Wood did not intimate that this was an easy task, but he did point out one very worthwhile analogy. He said, "If we make the assumption that it can be done—that it's possible—then we can try getting experiments done to test that assumption. We can direct these experiments toward discovering the principles behind the way these machines behave. Remember, as soon as the Russians knew it was possible to make the atom bomb, they made one in two years. The big gamble, then, is in the speculation that it's possible. The USA took the gamble, and we succeeded in producing the bomb. The key, then, is that if people know that it can be done, they will figure out how to do it. But for the most part, technological people have not been willing to make that assumption. They assume that gravity-interaction systems cannot be made. Hence they aren't working on them."

Dr. Wood's analogy helped me out a great deal. UFO debunkers are constantly pointing an index finger at any "wild-eyed" believer who is willing to assume that strange, unexplainable things that for the moment elude science, can possibly exist. Perhaps it's about time for the tables to turn. Aren't the hard-nosed technicians also assuming that strange things that defy the cautious goddess of science can't exist? Haven't they been surprised time and time again? Their surprise is rarely celebrated in the textbooks. I wonder how wise that really is.

How do UFOs behave? Why are they the best possible design for deep-space vehicles? What can they do? Well, in order to answer those questions, I made a brief survey of UFO behavior. UFOs appear to be weightless, yet radar often picks up their movements. Therefore, they were ostensibly physical phenomena distinguished on the one hand by frequent appearances and on the other by a strange unknown and contradictory nature. Their movements seem purposive, and internally controlled. They were highly maneuverable. They were mostly lens-shaped or circular when seen close up, and zeppelin- or cigar-shaped when seen at greater distances. They shine in various colors. But the most interesting thing from a technical point of view was that time and again eyewitnesses reported that UFOs start with blinding speed. This acceleration is such that if a man were to guide the craft, he would be instantly killed. UFOs make high-speed right-angle turns that seem possible only if the object observed were weightless. No exhaust fuel is visible, and nothing similar to a sonic boom accompanies these high speeds. UFOs can hover, circle objects and then dart off into space, never to be seen again. UFOs chase airplanes, but they also fly away from them. They have no apparent systematic plans for their flight. They behave like a group of boy scouts on a nature field trip, stopping wherever the spirit takes them in order to inspect various points of interest along the way. Mother ships, it is claimed, have been observed discharging the saucer-shaped excursion modules. They are either manned or unmanned, and sometimes appear to be remote-controlled. In general, UFOs seem to be masters of interstellar aeroacrobatics—a characteristic desirable for any aerospace design.

I wondered how far we were away from designing something like this without any new assumptions in science. Had anybody been working on that possibility? When you ask the question, you sometimes get an answer. Stanton T. Friedman is a nuclear physicist who had been working on such questions for fifteen years. He got involved in the UFO problem from an engineering perspective. He was interested in understanding how UFO maneuver and design could relate to our present knowledge of physics and energetics. In 1968 he submitted a paper before the House Committee on Science and Astronautics. I read Friedman's paper and decided to contact him to see if his views had changed substantially in the interim.

During our interview Friedman reiterated time and time again that designers should be looking at UFOs to find out how to design fast, efficient interstellar spacecraft. I tried playing the devil's advocate during the conversation and found that it only stimulated Friedman, rather than deterring or discouraging him. He was an experienced lecturer and clearly delineated the technical possibilities within our grasp. He was optimistic about our ability to soon duplicate the engineering expertise UFOs seem to manifest.

While we talked, I began to formulate some direct to-the-point questions for Friedman. His lecture series boasts of several years of full-time study of UFOs; he could answer the questions and doubts looming in the minds of his audience. "Don't UFOs do things that scientists know are impossible?" I asked. He had answered this question before. He didn't hesitate. "No laws of physics have been violated. The UFOs need great maneuverability. They have to be able to get home again." Then Friedman began to recount all of the craft's physical characteristics, backing each one of them up with a technical-design reason for their appearance. The saucer-shaped symmetric craft allows them to move in any direction. They don't have wings like our airplanes because wings would prevent them from such unidirectional maneuvers. Their glow suggests a plasma-ionized atmosphere. Their reported color changes suggest an electromagnetic field capable of interacting with that plasma. They land in football fields or large empty spaces in the Midwest; they have no use or need for metropolitan airfields bustling with people.

Friedman explained that none of the observed UFO maneuvers violated any laws of physics. They merely demand that we look at the present model of physics in a new way and perhaps add a few new conceptions. Friedman concludes that interstellar travel is indeed possible, with round-trip times shorter than a man's lifetime if fission or fusion propulsion systems are refined. But he also pointed out that these already envisioned methods of flight aren't the only possibilities. He explains how engineers accelerate things to high velocities. He states, "Physicists for years have been pushing particles of one sort or another to velocities close to that of light. We don't do this by physically or mechanically pushing the particles; we do this by electrically and magnetically controlling the acceleration, taking into account the relativistic change of mass of the particles. Perhaps it's time we started thinking of accelerating aircraft electromagnetically." He continues his argument, explaining that from a mechanical-design viewpoint it is standard practice to recognize that systems can stand much higher accelerations when they are subjected to them for a short time. The acceleration and deceleration of UFOs happen in an instant. Dr. Friedman suggests observing systems that, unlike airplanes, can go both backward and forward (automobiles, hummingbirds, and basketball players). They seem to perform this maneuver by interacting with the surroundings, not by swiveling an exhaust vent or moving an engine. He concludes from this that if what is wanted is a truly maneuverable craft for a flight in the atmosphere, or even for motion in water, then the answer lies in a system for interacting with the surroundings. The option is there to use all the available space and to have a system that is constantly exerting differing pressures. When one system stops the exertion of pressure, other systems can take over. In short, we are looking for instant switching of forces. Again, this suggests electromagnetic forces rather than mechanical forces. The analogy holds for something like the electromagnetic submarine. Friedman believes that electromagnetic propulsion systems could be an entirely new approach to high-speed air and space propulsion. The system could be developed using the interaction between magnetic fields with electrically conducting fluids adjacent to the vehicles to produce thrust or lift and reduce hypersonic flight problems such as sonic boom or drag. Much the same kind of system could account for the lack of sonic boom in the UFO phenomenon.

According to Friedman, electromagnetic propulsion systems have been developed. In his paper before the House Committee on Science and Astronautics, he says, "At Northwestern, turning on a magnet inside a simulated reentry vehicle with a plasma around it resulted in a change of color of the plasma and its location relative to the vehicle. However, an electromagnetic submarine has actually been built and successfully tested. . . . The EM submarine, which, incidentally, is silent and would be quite difficult to detect at a distance, is directly analogous to the type of airborne craft I envision, except that the shape of the aircraft would most likely be lenticular and the electrically conducting seawater would be replaced by an electrically conducting plasma of ionized air." As for how occupants could endure the high acceleration and G-forces of UFOs, Friedman says that a physicist has already published one paper dealing with the question of accelerations, concluding that UFO accelerations were not impossible for people to withstand. However, other scientists that I spoke with believe that if one could invent a gravity-interaction system, then this system might allow gravity to work equally on every atom of the body and protect it from the G-forces. Gravity interaction, along with electromagnetic energy produced by the UFO, might permit the various observed effects, such as unidirectional movements, color changes, and instant acceleration and deceleration, minus any disastrous results.

I called Friedman a second time for a bit more information. He told me that it was very important to distinguish the disk-shaped UFOs from the cigar-shaped vehicles. The saucer-shaped craft were earth-excursion modules analogous to our lunar-excursion modules

(LEM). He feels that this analogy between our own LEMs and their oddly dressed pilots and the observed UFOs on the ground is a real one. In both cases, strange-shaped (compared to airplanes) craft are able to land in unprepared out-of-the-way places. In both cases, the pilots have reportedly gathered soil specimens and artifacts, and appear to ramble aimlessly in an apparently childish fashion.

Friedman remarked that when he stood beside several symmetric Apollo command modules he was struck by how much more they looked like UFOs than like airplanes designed for much lower speeds. He was right. He had successfully reduced what hitherto had been weird sci-fi spacecraft maneuvers to quite understandable, mundane interstellar actions. The distinction between mother ships and excursion modules, analogous to our own staged vehicles, is very useful. Friedman has successfully created hypotheses to fit the data, rather than vice versa. I was glad I had located Friedman. He had cleared up a great deal of the mystery that surrounds the technological aspects of UFOs, for example, how occupants could make the interstellar trek in the vehicle the witnesses so often describe. The external appearance of the vehicle could give us some clues to the inside of the vessel. Many people who claim to have been inside a UFO remark that they didn't notice any signs of a door. Friedman says that this is quite expected, since the system would have to be leak-tight. Other design features—including round walls, a central hallway with special rooms to the side, light without light bulbs—are quite understandable if you compare the environment requirements of submarines destined for lengthy underwater jaunts. Perhaps the major part of the journey is done in the larger cigar-shaped vessels. The little UFOs might derive power from the mother ships and enter the earth's atmosphere with a storagelike battery. At any rate, the propulsion requirements would still remain the same.

I felt pretty optimistic about my progress so far. It took me a long time to discover engineers willing to go out on a limb in the hopes that their speculations might provoke new theories and experiments. It was a lonely, vulnerable place to be. Very few of us in any field are willing to risk the ridicule and accept the challenge of speculation. But this seems to be the only way new ideas have emerged. When history ends, the myths begin. These myths document man's hopes, dreams, and accomplishments. Yet, attempts to rob man of his dreams abound in history and science texts. Why? I wondered.

I talked to a few more scientists who told me that interstellar travel would have to wait for a breakthrough in science before it is economically wise for us to invest our time and funds in such projects. That is why radio communication, though a less attractive means, is a much more popular idea; we already have the Arecibo installation. We are going to have to discover a new physical phenomenon, probably related to the gravitational and electromagnetic fields in space.

I spoke to Dr. James Harder, a professor in civil engineering at the University of California at Berkeley. He agreed that the scientists at JPL and NASA are at the edge of what's technically possible. Harder thinks that if we could come up with a way to invent negative mass, then attaining velocity close to the speed of light would not have the same problems connected to it in terms of energy requirements. If you could mix negative mass and positive mass and get a total package of no mass,* then you would have a material that could travel at incredible speeds without requiring constant high energy input. I wondered if the more advanced galactic inhabitants had discovered how to do this. Was that how UFOs worked? I mentioned Bob Wood's analogy to Dr. Harder and asked him if he thought it held up. Would it merely take an assumption and a commitment to try to reproduce the technological feats of UFOs for eventual success? He said that the analogy stands for civilian scientists but not for government scientists. Government scientists take the UFO seriously. But the casual release of any information concerning the UFO phenomenon is very unlikely. Breakthroughs, if they come, would certainly be reported. Until then, we could expect to know very little. I ended my conversation with to find a UFO in design terms. Somewhere there had

*F. Winterberg, University of Nevada, has published technical papers on this subject.

to be a way to marry the eyewitness accounts of UFOs with technical knowledge.

John Schuessler* was a technical manager in cruise systems in Houston, Texas. I asked him how he would design the best deep-space vehicle and lander possible. What would it do? Schuessler responded enthusiastically. He seemed to trust me, and wanted to talk. He said he wanted to design a lander that could be used and reused. It wouldn't require a large amount of fuel for landing or taking off. He would like to invent a closed-loop system that would require very little outside fuel. This system would work within other types of fields. Besides burning fuel, it could perhaps crush gravity. But he assured me that these are only his dreams. He doesn't know how to invent such a system. I asked him how he got interested in such way-out ideas. He laughed and said that as a designer in cruise systems he had read the reports of observed UFO maneuvers and knew that that was the kind of spaceship he would like to design. They did everything a designer could ask for. He slowly became more and more involved in the UFO subject.

We chatted for a few more minutes. Schuessler was friendly and very easy to understand. His jargon was not the usual jawbreaking stuff that I had often encountered. A film producer could understand him. Then, amid our chatter, Schuessler told me of his pet idea: Project Visit. He was one of about fifteen engineers who had decided to get together to try to recreate a UFO device! They were going to design a questionnaire aimed at extracting technical data from people who had observed UFOs in close-up detail, including those contactees who claimed to have been on board. This questionnaire, they believe, will transform what is essentially poetic description into hard technical data. I was fascinated. It sounded like the first time a group of aerospace designers had ever attempted such a thing. How did they come up with the idea? Why? Schuessler said that a contactee named Herb Schirmer had undergone regressive hypnosis and Dr. Harder. I was chasing a ghost, of sorts. I was hoping had sketched in detail the inside of the UFO he be-

*of the McDonnell Douglas Corporation

lieved he was on. The sketches were so full of potential technical information that Schuessler and a few of his engineer partners wanted to extract more information from Schirmer and others in order to determine how such a craft could be built. They devised questions as to the temperature, movements, and noises outside a craft that contactees might have readily felt or seen. The questions are arranged in categories in order to provide engineering-design details as well as environmental factors in the UFO cabin. Questions concerning noises, lighting, air flow, odors, equipment appearance, and occupants' clothing are included in the questionnaire. The questions are to be asked during regressive hypnosis by a qualified psychoanalyst. The Visit team would then try to re-create the situation, putting the answers through a computer in order to first build a mathematical model and later a physical model, provided the information was extensive enough. I immediately wanted to participate. Perhaps we could document in film some of these experiments. I told Dr. Schuessler my idea, and he agreed. I had to call Mr. Schirmer.

Mr. Schirmer lives in British Columbia. I telephoned him first to see how my film idea sounded to him. I also wanted to have his story for this book, so I asked him if he would recount some of the results of his hypnosis sessions. He didn't want to tell me anything over the phone. He told me that if I wanted to know anything at all, monetary compensation would be required. I have always felt uneasy when I am asked to pay a person to relate an experience. As a TV documentarian I have on occasion presented honoraria for extraordinary cooperation, but outright payment seems to turn information into a packaged commodity designed to suit the buyers' needs. I decided to decline.

It was sad to have to tell John that the film experiment with Schirmer was rather unlikely, since it had been Schirmer's sketches that had inspired the birth of Project Visit. There were other contactees. I intended to contact them for the Project Visit experiment. The film idea would have to wait a little longer than I had initially expected.

Before we finished talking, John told me that I

should contact one more person. It seems that James McCampbell is an engineering physicist who just wrote a book called *UFOlogy*. He has attempted to explain how the propulsion systems of UFOs might relate to the electromagnetic radiation effects usually accompanying a landing. McCampbell uses the close-encounter cases described by Jacques Vallee in his book *Passport to Magonia* as a data bank of the various physical effects associated with such cases. I called Mr. McCampbell in northern California and asked him to tell me about his findings. He said that it's possible to assess some technical clues that can tie all these strange effects together. He believes that UFOs are pumping out copious amounts of electromagnetic radiation similar to radar in higher-frequency ranges. This radiation, McCampbell feels, is probably part of, or evidence of, the propulsion system.

If we study its effects on the environment, we can begin to gradually pin down the nature of this radiation. It causes gases in the atmosphere to luminesce. Various gases have different characteristic colors. The color changes are coordinated with vehicle maneuvers; as the object goes from a dead stop to movement, the gases go through a series of changes. The contactee unconsciously feels certain sensations that could also provide information as to the nature of the radiation. In fact, we have learned that this radiation is pulsed and that its pulse rate is in the low audio range. We know this because the humming noise often associated with UFOs is heard in the head, not in the ear. It produces heat on the face and arms. And it looks as if the longer wavelengths penetrate the body, activating the nerves, to cause temporary paralysis. Electromagnetic effects have caused auto engines as well as radio and television sets to stop functioning. Interference with power transmissions in police radios is well-documented. All of these effects lead McCampbell to believe that UFOs are relying on emission of radiation in their power systems. UFO behavior patterns, according to McCampbell, indicate that these extraterrestrial craft can somehow tamper with their own mass. They understand time and space better than we do. McCampbell has been trying to interest the aerospace industry in forming design teams around the country to work on these engineering mysteries. But at the present he isn't having much luck. However, he is very optimistic, and predicted a breakthrough in ten years if we would just make the assumption that such a system or concept could be discovered. In fact, he said that a group in France is working on part of the problem right now. Claude Poher's group got interested in the problem because of Mr. McCampbell's book. Furthermore, the French government is supposedly funding part of their experiments.

The Poher group is working in magnetohydrodynamics. They are trying to send a plasma current or electromagnetic field around a disk-shaped object to see if it can move around the object without causing shock waves. The experimenters might be able to duplicate in theory, the UFO power system. Needless to say, more work needs to be done before any conclusive results can turn up.

I had gathered enough information for my files. It was a fascinating subject area. But probably the most interesting fact I discovered amidst all of the technical ifs and buts was the conclusion itself. If we were to design the best possible deep-space vehicle and lander, they would probably turn out looking like the UFOs everyone seems to be seeing in the backyard! Surprising? I don't know anymore. All I am certain of is that the search will continue.

10

Astronomers' Views

It was again time to assess all of the information I had gathered. Where and how did it all fit against today's technologically stained backdrop? My goal was to seek evidence that extraterrestrial intelligences exist, that traces of their presence could be found on earth. It was time to begin assembling astronomers' past and present views on the subject of UFOs and their origins.

It was August 1976. Viking I had just landed on Mars and was sending back astounding data concerning the atmospheric conditions on that planet. The preliminary results from Viking's mini biology laboratories boosted scientists' speculations about extraterrestrial life. Now more than ever before, scientists were overwhelmingly optimistic about the possibility of life on Mars.

On November 16, 1974, the giant radio antenna at Arecibo, Puerto Rico, beamed a message toward a distant cluster of stars at the Milky Way's edge. This signal can be converted into a television picture that will explain to the watchers that a planet called earth is dominated by a species whose genetic makeup is mediated by the chemical molecule known as deoxyribonucleic acid—DNA.

The next part of my quest was obvious. How would today's astronomers handle the UFO phenomenon when I placed it in apposition to the celebrated ongoing search for extraterrestrial life and the possibility of interstellar flight? How would they connect these ideas? What coordinating conjunction would they employ in such a statement? Or would they even coordinate or connect them? What rationales would they use to describe and account for their views? Moreover, I wanted to know if there had been any change since the last survey was taken. In order to save time, I would survey the astronomical viewpoint by phone. But first I wanted to know what the last such survey had disclosed.

As recently as 1972, Franklin Roach had divided astronomers' views into two categories: "One view is that all could be readily explained as 'natural' phenomena if we had better data. The other extreme leads to the hypothesis of extraterrestrial visitations." However, according to my telephone survey, things seem to have changed since 1972. The spectrum of viewpoints had expanded, allowing the entrance of what previously would have been considered maverick opinions into the scientific mainstream. The last systematic attempt by the U.S. government to investigate UFOs was conducted by the Air Force Project Blue Book. When it ended in 1969, the Air Force had investigated 12,600 UFO sightings and could not explain almost 700 of those cases. The records are now available to researchers at the National Archives. Today most investigators agree that at least 20 percent of all reported cases are totally unexplained.

In order to obtain statements from busy astronomers, I was going to have to design just the right question format. Through practice I found that the best way to approach the problem was to formulate the question in two parts. The first part asked for the astronomer's off- and on-the-record speculations about the existence of advanced extraterrestrial intelligent life; the second part of the question was designed to elicit their official and unofficial views on the connection UFOs might have to that speculation. It's interesting to note that no one admitted having separate off- and on-the-record thoughts. Even though I promised not to disclose any names, I still received only one statement to cover both viewpoints.

I collected many interesting responses. But I will share with you only those answers that represented either new or psychologically intriguing points of view.

The famous New Mexico astronomer Clyde Tombaugh was first on my list. He had discovered the planet Pluto and was one of the few remaining visual astronomers who still physically peered at the celestial horizons through a telescope. He had also seen his own UFO—a sighting that has remained a classic up to the present day. In August 1949 he observed a flight of rectangles of light arranged as if they were "ports" on an elliptical object. I wanted to speak to Dr. Tombaugh and try to update what his views were.

Dr. Tombaugh answered the phone. After I told him my business, he politely and quietly refused to make any statement whatsoever. He was very apologetic but firm about his refusal. I asked him why he had taken a position of silence on the matter. He told me that he had received so much backlash from previous statements that he no longer wanted to be involved with such an emotional topic. It caused him more grief than he felt it was worth. He told me that he had precious little time left to investigate those things that mattered to him and that a statement would only encourage a replay of a familiar and painful barrage of positive and negative feedback. He didn't have the time or the inclination to get involved. He kept apologizing for his refusal to answer my questions. In fact, his apology was so sincere and unceasing that I had the feeling I could have ultimately obtained a statement had I remained on the phone. However, my heart went out to Dr. Tombaugh; I empathized with all he had gone through and understood his refusal completely. He had risked his career when he had acknowledged the 1949 UFO sighting. I felt he had. He was more than entitled to a bit of "free time." And anyway, his refusal to comment was statement enough. It demonstrated just how emotionally charged the entire subject has been in the past and remains at the present. It provides a clue to the inconsistencies of thought and frequent blatant lack of imagination and nerve that sometimes accompany scientific discussions on the UFO subject.

Everyone I interviewed suggested that I obtain Frank Drake's views on the subject. You will remember from the previous chapter on radio communication that Dr. Drake was instrumental in initiating the search for extraterrestrial life through the use of radio telescopes. He is presently the director of the National Astronomy and Ionosphere Center at Cornell University. Dr. Drake has been asked about UFOs on more occasions, perhaps, than any other astronomer in the country. He spoke slowly. "With regard to the possibilities of there being intelligent creatures elsewhere in the universe, I think that all of the information we have from astronomy, biology, and the evolution of intelligence and technology on the earth would indicate that it is certain that there is intelligent life and indeed civilizations elsewhere in space. Their numbers may be small and their manifestations on an astronomical scale very faint. Therefore, the question is not whether they are there—they are—but rather, how difficult it is to detect. My own belief is that it is indeed a very demanding enterprise to detect the manifestations of other civilizations and it will require an effort on our part which is of the same order as the largest scientific undertakings that we have so far pursued."

Dr. Drake was very familiar with his subject. He had pushed for a concentrated search for extraterrestrial life and was a convinced exponent of the exobiological thesis. He continued, "In the matter of UFOs, I have followed the subject for years and investigated personally many UFOs. I have never seen evidence that would convince me that UFOs are an indication of extraterrestrial intelligent activity. The evidence just has not been delivered, in any case." That was it. He asked me if that was all I wanted, and then cordially bid me good day. I had my statement—short and sweet. There weren't any separate official or unofficial speculations. Yet, something in Dr. Drake's statement, and others like it, puzzled me. It will thus serve as an example of the liberal declaration.

As disarmingly simple as it appeared at face value, Drake's total statement offered an extremely tantalizing and rich field of study. As far as I can recall from my research, the probability of extraterrestrial life—that is, the estimated number of existing intelligent civilizations—is based on quite a few near-fact assumptions. Nevertheless, they are still just assumptions waiting to tread the hallowed ground of fact. The connection between extraterrestrial life and UFOs is one more step down the scale. The acceptance of the link depends upon subjective frames of reference. Some people were willing to extrapolate from one assumption to the other, until they ended up with the extraterrestrial hypothesis. They would go no further until steel-hard sharp evidence emerged. *In Search Of . . .* seeks to catalog the daring extrapolations of many scientists who pride themselves on their prophetic foresight—black-hole transit systems, other universes, gravity interaction. But in the realm of UFOs, few boast so boldly. The discrepancies are becoming transparent. I somehow detect an inconsistency in the tenor of these liberal arguments.

What was it about the UFO phenomenon which placed such absolute limits on so many scientists' imaginations? Had the lunatic fringe tainted the problem that much? Conservative or establishment scientists, as well as liberals, have tried to explain the unexplained before. But the UFO problem precludes and inhibits any such attempts. Except for a relatively small handful of brave souls, most scientists shied away from any speculations; they did this almost unconsciously. When I would ask them to let their imaginations fly, they would reply that they couldn't do that, yet a moment before, they had raptured in glorious, scientific abandon about the ultimate possibilities for finding ETL. When the UFO problem emerged, though, they were at loose ends to try to explain what was going on.

Views were changing. During my survey I found that more and more "conservative" scientists as well as "liberal" scientists acknowledged the existence of UFOs as something unexplained but real. Was this the beginning of a new trend? Would this acknowledgment challenge scientists' previous dogmatic refusal to deal with the UFO subject? Would "liberal" statements on the possibilities of communication with ETL begin to accommodate or accept other "extreme" hypotheses—like the extraterrestrial origin of UFOs? Or is consistency of thought a factor at all in such an emotionally charged area? I'm not sure. But the questions stimulate my search for answers. Dr. Leonard V. Kuhi provided me with one more clue.

Dr. Kuhi was formerly chairman of the astronomy department at the University of California at Berkeley. He is now the dean of physical sciences. I talked to Dr. Kuhi for a long time and found him to be a very candid, refreshing astronomer, an appropriate candidate for my survey. When I asked him about his position on the possibilities of extraterrestrial life, he told me that he was an optimist on that subject and said that it was very likely that there would be other sources of life in our galaxy. He also felt that the number of these civilizations would be large. However, he didn't think the possibility of communication with other civilizations was too likely. As he put it, "The possibility of communication with civilizations around other stars is a long shot in the dark." I asked him why he felt that way. He said that the distances involved in communicating between the stars were too great. They put a damper on detecting intelligent life. As for the connection UFOs might have with the extraterrestrial theories, Dr. Kuhi states, "I'm not willing to take the step that UFOs represent space probes from other civilizations. I don't believe that at all. What I do think, however, about UFOs is the following: there are so many professional people—pilots, for example, I think, constitute the biggest majority, and air-traffic controllers, and other people, including astronauts—who have seen strange things in the sky. I think the phenomenon is a real one and that it should be investigated. I think Allen Hynek makes a valid point that we shouldn't dismiss these things seen by people we have no reason to doubt. You see, I'm trying to separate the fact that there probably is some very real phenomenon that needs investigating, which we don't understand, from the connection that many people make—that these UFOs are really spacecraft from another civilization. I just can't make that connection; it's too big a leap for me." He paused. I asked him what was stopping him from going one step further, for it really was just one more step. He said that the big problem was the time scale that it would take. According to the laws of physics, nothing can travel faster than the speed of light. Even traveling at the speed of light, Dr. Kuhi wonders where and how we could get the energy to accelerate something that fast. "That's a hang-up I have." I knew what he was saying. He was not optimistic about our ability to communicate with other civilizations because of the distances involved, nor was he willing to connect UFOs with ETL, for essentially the same reasons. At least Dr. Kuhi was truly consistent. He was willing to go just so far in both realms. The UFO stigma did not seem to faze him. Even where and when it was safe and acceptable to tread, communication with ETL—black-hole technology—he chose to stay behind the threshold.

I respected Kuhi's consistency and learned a lot from our conversation. It looked like even "conservative" scientists were willing to admit that some kind of unknown phenomenon was taking place. That was new and daring in itself!

I have spent a great deal of time on the telephone interviewing various astronomers on the subject of ETL and the UFO connection. Astronomers' views have changed. Franklin Roach's 1972 survey was passé and needed expanding and renovating. Exploration of Mars, Arecibo radio communication attempts, interstellar ramjets—all of these things contributed to and indicated the inclusion and addition of a third category. Now astronomers' views on UFOs can be divided into three major categories. 1. All UFO sightings can be explained by natural phenomena. This view seems to be on the decline. 2. A small number of UFO sightings cannot be explained and remain a mystery. This view is increasingly being shared by both conservative and liberal scientists. 3. The unexplained UFO sightings are accountable to the presence of extraterrestrial visitors. Only the most romantic observers are willing to accept the extraterrestrial conclusion.

The second category is the newcomer. It is the maverick, almost neophyte opinion now come of age. It represents most of the views I obtained in my survey. Because not only the most liberal but also the most conservative scientists I interviewed entertained the second notion—that UFOs are probably very real, unexplained phenomena—this second category is not only new but also psychologically interesting.

An amazing number of shock waves have buffeted twentieth-century science. As new discoveries wiped out traditional theory, concepts that were considered fundamental to a scientific discipline were dropped. Never was the process peaceful or without pain. For the most part, new ideas were battered by endless gauntlets of established thinking. And then a break would come. Certain truisms exist when it comes to UFOs. Communication with galactic neighbors was unlikely because of distance. The possibility for interstellar flight was remote because of those same distances and energy requirements. Therefore, it logically followed that UFOs could not be explained by the extraterrestrial hypothesis. This opinion may result from a "failure of imagination"—a term coined by Arthur C. Clarke. But it is thoroughly consistent and lucid and does not contradict itself. It certainly isn't breathtaking or flashy, but it is sound, solid, and steady. In general, each of these positions follows the conservative thought.

"Liberal" statements were prone to list the beyond-a-doubt likelihood not only of extraterrestrial life but also of a manned interstellar probe, the possibility of eventually harnessing black-hole power, signaling and monitoring extant galactic civilizations through radio communication, time-space warps, and last but not least, other universes. I appreciate every bit of imaginative speculation. But so many experts seem to stop abruptly and arbitrarily. They withhold comment on UFOs. They are quick to point out that the extraterrestrial hypothesis is irresponsible; it is not respected, and thus smacks of lunacy. I find this intellectual gap both amusing and perplexing.

I'm not saying that liberal, farsighted, imaginative scientists must necessarily end up with the ETL hypothesis. I only wonder why they mock those scientists who have chosen to see their ofttimes highly publicized futuristic scenarios one step further. The range of fact and speculation is the same in both cases.

The "liberal" viewpoint seems to be suffering a "failure of nerve"—another term coined by Arthur C. Clarke. I empathize with Clarke in *Profiles of the Future* when he says: "The great problem, it seems, is finding a single person who combines sound scientific knowledge—or at least the feel for science—with a really flexible imagination." This chapter documents exactly that same problem, especially if I replace the word "sound" with "consistent."

11

The Viking Mission

My search for extraterrestrials was drawing to a close. I had one last bit of information to record, and then I knew I would have to conclude the book. Writing a book is sometimes frustrating. It seems like I should and could go on forever, amassing data in support of the goal. But the book has to end at some point in time, and when it does, it should reflect the context of time in which it was written. It was August 1976; the Vikings were landing!

THIS MONTH, MARS. That boldface, rather electrifying headline appeared in the Los Angeles *Times* of August 11, 1976. However, as I was browsing through the paper that morning, it passed right under my nose without a second glance. And when I got to the office, one of my researchers had faithfully placed it on my desk for my edification. She was not as blasé. So there it was once again staring me in the face—both challenging and celebrating my nonchalance. It was three weeks since the Viking I lander had touched down on Mars. And already THIS MONTH, MARS had entered the collective consciousness (or unconsciousness, as the case may be), to become part of the routine vocabulary. The common psyche had already absorbed the exhilaration of this extraordinary achievement. I thought I had better ponder the significance of that headline before dismissing it so quickly.

I was writing *In Search of Extraterrestrials* in the context of our recent achievements in space. The Viking I landing on July 20 was seven years to the day after the first men walked on the moon. Mars—the search for life beyond earth had begun. Prior to this, I couldn't have written the same book. Our space programs had blazed the trail for my current search. I wanted to include a brief survey of the Mars monitor mission in my search for extraterrestrials in order to place the book in the proper perspective. The red planet has a fascinating history.

Amateur and professional stargazers claim that Mars is visible from high, remote areas. I have always lived in the city and have never seen Mars. But people say that it is distinguishable from the other stars because it is brighter, and unlike the stars, it does not blink. Even though I have never seen Mars, I've forever been fascinated by its history of riddles and myths.

Mars has always bristled with symbology. Except for

the sun and the moon, it has stimulated man's imagination more than any other heavenly "corpus." Its ruddy hue led the ancients to associate it with fire and blood. They christened the planet Mars after the Roman god of war.

Galileo invented the astronomical telescope in 1608 and opened a new era in planetary observation. Now, instead of appearing as a small glowing disk, Mars's surface features emerged, opening a new observational field for ancient stargazers.

In 1659 Christian Huygens drew the first sketch of Syrtis Major Region ("giant quicksands"). Huygens observed one specific feature on Mars's surface and was thus later able to show that Mars rotated on a north-south axis like earth, producing a day that was about thirty-six minutes longer than earth's.

In 1666 Giovanni Cassini, the Italian astronomer, sketched the martian polar caps. Early-eighteenth-century observers noted various changes occurring in the surface appearance in a matter of hours. These changes were probably due to dust storms, now known to rage periodically. In 1783 William Herschel noticed that Mars's rotational axis was inclined to its orbital plane at roughly the same extent as earth's, revealing that long-term changes could often be associated with seasons that would result from such inclination.

That Mars and the other planets were inhabited was commonly accepted in the seventeenth and eighteenth centuries, but the real excitement and romance began when Italian astronomer Giovanni Schiaparelli reported seeing an extensive network of "canals" or channels covering the length and breadth of the planet. As a result of extensive observations, Schiaparelli constructed detailed maps with many features, including these dark, almost straight "canals" hundreds of kilometers long. Because the word "canals" implied intelligent life capable of constructing artificial waterways, the idea of extraterrestrial civilized societies began.

American astronomer Percival Lowell elaborated on this misnomer. He was of the firm opinion that the canals weren't natural phenomena but the work of intelligent creatures similar to us in spirit but not in appearance. His beliefs nourished the burgeoning mystique surrounding the red planet. He wrote of dead-sea bottoms and life-giving waterways on a desertlike dying planet. To pursue his interest in the canals, he established the Lowell Observatory near Flagstaff, Arizona, in 1894 and devoted the rest of his life to the observation of Mars. His writings about the canals and their relationship to life on Mars created a welter of public excitement near the turn of the twentieth century.

Speculation about intelligent life on Mars abounded through the first part of the century, lacking the possibility of any sort of conclusive resolution. Slowly though, a gradual skepticism began to develop among scientists concerning the likelihood of martian intelligent life. The martian myth suddenly lost its glamour. No astronomer could successfully duplicate Lowell's sighting of waterways constructed by intelligent beings. Furthermore, through investigation of the planet's surface conditions, it was learned that Mars lacked an appropriate habitable atmosphere as we know it. Attitudes changed. Scientists were no longer optimistic about the possibility of life on Mars, or, for that matter, extraterrestrial life in general. The search for extraterrestrials was in for a long wait.

Scientific skepticism was further reinforced by the results of the Mariner flyby missions in 1965 and 1969. Limited coverage of only 10 percent of the martian surface by flyby photography revealed Mars to be a lunarlike planet with a uniformly cratered surface. The Soviet Union dispatched at least eight spacecraft between 1962 and 1973. Several of them vanished without a trace, but five of them sent back rather interesting data with varying degrees of success.

Then, in 1971–72 the Mariner 9 orbiter was launched, and a new and strikingly different face of Mars was revealed. Scientists' attitudes toward the possibility of ETL began to soften, and the exobiological field was revived once more. Whereas the flyby coverage had seen only a single geologic feature in the cratered highlands of the southern hemisphere, Mariner 9 displayed gigantic volcanoes, a valley extending one-fifth of the way around the planet's circumference, and slight evidence of flowing liquid water sometime in the remote past. Mariner 9 photos also revealed polar regions with layered terrains and the effects of dust blown by winds several hundred kilometers an hour.

In short, Mariner 9's seven thousand detailed pictures disclosed a dynamic, evolving Mars radically different from the lunarlike planet suggested by previous evidence. Mariner 9 revealed a ripe and rich subject for scientific study.

Of special interest is the question of water on Mars. Scientific literature abounds in speculation. It is known that there is water in the martian atmosphere, but the light pressure of the atmosphere will not sustain any large bodies of liquid. The braided channels found in the Mariner 9 photographs suggest to many geologists that they are the result and evidence of previous periods of flowing water.

Volcanologists are now interested in the high concentration of volcanoes clustered near the Tharsis ridge, missed by the three previous flyby missions. Volcanoes are thought to be the source of the atmospheric gases and water in the ocean; they may have played a catalytic role in the formation of organic molecules in the seas and thus have huge implications for the origins of life.

Scientists' attitudes toward the possibility of ETL have been changing since the Mariner 9 photographs were returned. Henry S. F. Cooper, Jr., in "A Resonance with Something Alive" (*New Yorker*) cites Bruce Murray's statement in "Mars and the Mind of Man": "When the photographic evidence of these huge volcanoes first came in, I simply couldn't accept its significance. I too was a victim of the very process of being so captured by the prejudices that had grown up in my own mind about the planet as to have great difficulty in accepting and understanding the significance of new data when they arrived." Cooper continues: "With respect to internal activity, Mars appeared a lot livelier than the moon, though a good deal less lively than the earth—a reasonable state of affairs, inasmuch as Mars is midway in size between the two. . . . Most striking from a Lowellian point of view, when all the data were in, Mariner 9 showed that both poles, while overlaid with frozen carbon dioxide for most of the martian year, which is six-hundred and eighty-seven days long, had permanent 'summertime' caps that apparently contained some frozen water."

Mariner 9 photos laid the groundwork for the search for life in the Viking mission. It's interesting to note the attitudinal changes Viking scientists have undergone just prior to touchdown and immediately after the first biological test results had been returned.

The *New Yorker* article by Cooper charts the diverse feelings that the scientists held prior to the first photographic returns. There was a buzz of excitement created by statements issued from stalwart exobiologists like Carl Sagan. Geologists and meteorologists feared that Sagan's statements were irresponsible and lacked sufficient observational data. Very few scientists ventured speculations as to what kind of life forms might be found in the martian microenvironment, much less the macroenvironment. For the most part, they left that kind of showmanship to Sagan. In fact, as Cooper states, "Many biologists deny that Viking's chief purpose is to find life or that their package was ever conceived as any sort of *raison d'être* for Viking; they point out that they are just one of Viking's thirteen scientific teams, and the one cubic foot allotted to their biology package is no more than the space given to other instruments. . . . Whatever the case, almost everyone connected with Viking believes that there would have been no exploration of Mars if it weren't for the search for life; one biologist has said, 'You don't seriously think Congress would have spent a billion dollars just to do geology on Mars!' "

Then, on July 20, 8:12 A.M., EDT, Viking touched down on Mars's Chryse Planitia (golden plains). *Time* magazine reported the excitement in the control room at JPL. "For the first time, through an obedient and ingeniously contrived robot, man was about to gaze at a Martian landscape, to begin sifting through Martian soil for evidence that life exists beyond earth." As I read those words, I wondered how many people actually realized the significance of our most recent space accomplishment.

That night I watched on television the first color-picture returns of the Mars surface. It was shaded a deep sienna, littered with rocks and pebbles, reminiscent of deserts in Arizona and New Mexico. That round glowing ball orbiting in space had a surface that looked like a desert here on earth! I had believed in the possibility of ETL for a long time, but this remarkable physical similarity drove the point home more strongly than ever. The sky was surprisingly bright, causing some scientists to say that the atmosphere might be richer than expected in light-diffusing particles. I remembered that the lunar sky looked black, due to the fact that it had no atmosphere. But Mars looked incredibly different from the moon. It looked so earthlike that I half-expected a reptile to slither into the picture at any moment. But after the initial excitement caused by the view of the martian environment, the reality of exobiology is that Mars looked lifeless. Strangely enough, however, scientists were not daunted in the least by these first surface glimpses of a seemingly lifeless planet. And some of their statements were rather refreshing and amazing in view of their past reticence on the subject.

Carl Sagan noted that nothing in the pictures had ruled out the existence of life on the planet. And G. Soffen, Viking project scientist, added that the lander's immediate vicinity held several niches in which conventional life forms could be found. "The microbes of Mars are within our grasp, if they are there. There could be cockroaches under those rocks." In fact, *Time* magazine reported, "In the early flush of excitement about the landing and the first photographs, none of the Viking scientists seemed particularly disappointed that the pictures showed no obvious signs of life—no lichen, bushes or trees, nothing even remotely resembling an animal or the monsters or little green men beloved by generations of science-fiction writers." Experts such as Harvard physicist Dr. Michael McElroy see no reason to exclude, from everything we know, the possibility of the evolution of life on Mars. Statements of that sort are beginning to be the rule rather than the exception. And as the biological test results began to be returned, more and more scientists were willing to venture some speculations.

The Viking lander biology instrument was built by

TRW (a defense and space systems group) and houses forty thousand components, thereby resembling a biology lab in capability but not in size. It is made up of three separate experiments to test soil samples in incubation chambers. The mini biology lab is designed to find evidence of living organisms, based on the assumption that to be alive an organism must consume something and leave some sign of having lived, breathed, eaten, excreted, and reproduced. It seems that all of the scientists are aware of the limitations that these assumptions impose upon their search for life. They repeatedly state that even if the Viking I and II landers find no life on Mars, the possibility of life on that planet is by no means ruled out; it just may be that we designed the wrong tests. I don't know how the reader will react to that kind of policy statement, but it pretty much came as a shock to me and my production team. After having logged in a vast amount of time encouraging speculation on the relationship between ETL and UFOs, and encountering nothing but disclaimers and disqualifiers, I was partially gratified by the sheer number of exobiologists who emerged with candid opinions. It looked like exobiology had a future after all.

The Viking landers provided some of the most fascinating television viewing since the first astronaut took that "one small step" onto the surface of the moon. I am dazzled by the speed with which we have begun to assimilate data about the surface properties of Mars, but I cannot resist a momentary flight of pure fancy wondering how the population of Black Rock, up there in Canal Country, Mars, has taken this "invasion from earth." Now that martian UFO-ologists have finally been vindicated—I mean, now that living proof is right there in the desert that those twinkles in the sky *were* space-flying chariots—how well the martians treat the activities of our Viking I and II. Imagine what it looks like—these spidery apparitions whirring and buzzing, lights flashing on and off, and primitive metal mandibles reaching out with spastic thrusts to scoop up a handful of sand! "Sand, by golly," the martians must say. "That durn thing eats sand. It must be some kind of cockeyed lizard." Whatever the country folk think, what really bothers the newscasters is the terrible problems of getting out to the desert observation platform to watch the "earthling." I mean, after all, it's winter.

One final fantasy I have about the "star" we've caused on Mars is the vision of a martian astronomer saying, "We're not sure it is an extraterrestrial."

More seriously, I suppose, the Viking landers are sending back experimental results. The mission program is turning up new information.

The first of the three biology experiments is called pyrolytic release. It searches for signs of a life process called photosynthesis—the process by which plants on earth remove carbon dioxide from the air and through the sun's energy then convert the carbon to organic matter. Martian microorganisms will be offered an atmosphere containing carbon dioxide and carbon monoxide, spiced with a radioactive tracer. Any life present in the soil sample should assimilate the carbon and the radioactive tracer. Then, after a period of incubation, the soil sample is cooked to release whatever carbon 14 or radioactive tracer has been assimilated during the incubation period. Pyrolytic release tests martian organisms on their ability to perform photosynthesis.

The second experiment searches for signs of metabolic activity. All terrestrial organisms break down and consume nutrients and then release waste products and gases; this process is called metabolism. The experiment is called labeled release. Martian soil will be moistened with a nutrient broth loaded with vitamins and amino acids as well as radioactive carbon 14. The experiment will monitor the soil sample to see if any organism that functions by metabolism is likely to consume the nutrient and release gases that contain radioactively labeled wastes.

The third experiment checks the environment offered to the microorganism to discover if it has been altered by the presence of living things. This is called the gas-exchange experiment. The martian soil sample is placed in a sterile solution for an incubation period. Then, if traces of methane or hydrogen or oxygen, etc., are found—and the same mixture is not found in the "cooked" control sample—something, indeed, may be alive in that soil.

While I am writing these words, test returns from the biology experiments have been coming in. And the results are very intriguing.

Two of the biological experiments seemed to have yielded evidence of what could be microbes in the martian soil. In the gas-exchange experiment, a soil sample had produced fifteen times as much oxygen as had been expected. Scientists now are faced with the task of finding either a chemical or a biological explanation for the data. If they come up with a chemical explanation, it will be "pretty fancy chemistry," claimed one scientist. Another scientist cautioned against separating chemistry from biology, since biology is chemistry. The labeled-release experiment, which uses radioactive tracers to look for signs of metabolic activity, showed a very strong response. During a Viking press conference concerning these results, Dr. Leslie Orgel, a member of the molecular analysis team, said that he didn't know whether it is going to be surprising biologically or chemically. He said, "Six months ago, we were talking about the potential dangers of bringing back material from Mars and somewhat rationally I said that if someone would care to bring back a sample, I would be happy to eat it. Now, I must say that in the light of what Viking I has found, I will withdraw that offer." That is a pretty descriptive statement of the present state of affairs in the JPL testing labs. No one was willing to say much more until the control tests were in. But on the other hand, scientists repeatedly emphasized that negative results would not imply the absence of life: we may simply have landed in an area where life is sparse. Joshua Lederberg, Nobel Prize biologist at Stanford University, stated: "The earth proves the possibility that there are living and nonliving portions. If I go into Kilauea Crater during a period of its activity, I don't think that there is any life in that lava. I stay at a safe distance. So, plainly, there are habitats on any planet that might be too hostile for life to survive there. There is little if any life at altitudes of over one hundred miles on earth, for example." I was glad to hear someone of Lederberg's caliber affirm the coexistence of both biologically active and barren terrains on the same planet. I had heard that argument used at least a hundred times in the process of researching this book. Dr. Lederberg's forthright position was a refreshing change of pace. For me it expressed the essential change of attitude I had been witnessing ever since Viking's moment of touchdown.

I hesitate to include much more of the test results, because none of them are really conclusive, insofar as they are all pending the second and third control cycles. Furthermore, the touchdown and soil testing of Viking II in the Utopia area are still undefinitive. There are some early results that encourage exobiologists.

The labeled-release experiment had gone through a sterilization or control phase and received very different results from the first round of experiments. This difference between the two experiments did not rule out biology but narrowed still further the range of possible chemical reactions. You might say that the biology experiment had received a booster. One scientist noted that if these same two tests were performed in the JPL parking lot and yielded the same results, we would conclude that life was present. He apologized, however, for their cautious statements regarding life on Mars and claimed that because we were on Mars and not in the JPL parking lot, we cannot rely on the magnitude of difference shown between these two tests.

Even more surprising was the way scientists acknowledged test results that failed to show the presence of organic compounds. The GCMS—gas chromatograph mass spectrometer—was chosen for the organic analysis. It so far had shown no evidence of organic compounds. The results really weren't positive or negative. It could be that the soil on Mars was not able to hold hydrocarbons for any appreciable length of time. The identification of organic substances present in surface material is a complex task because so little is known about their overall abundance. Any one of thousands of organic substances, or any combination thereof, could be present. As time went on, I was really beginning to feel like I had exchanged roles. Previously

I had had trouble just getting most people to imagine the entire range of possibilities contained in any evidence at hand. Anything in the extraterrestrial realm was taboo for all but a few radical trailblazers, and even then, those few trailblazers refused to enter the neck of the woods that smacked even slightly of UFOs. I wondered if that was about to change. Was the Viking mission going to affect the scientific psyche? Already there had been some speculation as to the temporary presence of ozone in the atmosphere at high altitudes during winter. The winter atmosphere would be optically thick enough to shield the surface from ultraviolet rays. An increasing number of scientists were even speculating on the history of water on the planet and the abundant water that is presently bound in rocks. Scientists are encouraged by what they are finding on Mars and will admit that they didn't expect to see all that they are seeing.

One scientist at the August 10 Viking press conference at JPL summed up the situation. He said, "Lest you go away from this conference feeling that we're all agreed that there is either only biology or only chemistry going on on Mars, that the answer will be either only biology or only chemistry going on, let me say again that we are planning a long investigation, and it is not inconceivable, it is entirely possible, that we will see further data of a biological nature, or a more biological nature than what we've seen. In other words, there may be this active chemistry going on, and there may be buried in that signal other information which we may be able to pull out before this is all over with, indicating that despite the active chemistry, or maybe because of the active chemistry, there's some biology. It's not going to be necessarily one or the other." That is the most apt status report I can hope to provide before this book goes to press. I'm quite sure that it will stand the test of time, no matter what the final outcome of the Viking mission. More important, though, it marks a concrete change in the attitudes scientists now have toward life on other planets. The Viking mission seems to have stimulated their imaginations for the present time.

The Viking monitor mission to Mars provides the

context in which I conducted my search for evidence of extraterrestrials. The Mars mission documents our belief that there is advanced life to be found in the cold icy reaches of space. It also demonstrates the capabilities of a rather tender, young technology; we are approximately fifty technological years old. What magic can extant technologically more advanced galactic civilizations perform?

We, planet earth, have just established a base or beachhead in space from which we can now conduct soil tests and monitor surface and atmospheric changes. Is there such a base already established here on earth by our galactic neighbors?

12

Why Bother with Life Out There?

In September 1971 a symposium was held at the Byurakan Astrophysical Observatory in Soviet Armenia under the auspices of the Soviet and U.S. academies of science. The symposium was attended by distinguished scientists—including two Nobel laureates. The question was raised: Should mankind try to listen in on extraterrestrial communications between life forms in other planetary systems, in other galaxies? A proposal was issued: "It seems to us appropriate that the search for extraterrestrial intelligence should be made by the representatives of mankind."

But why bother searching? Any reasons that may be suggested are based upon the assumption that mankind will be on this planet for a while to come. I assume, and hope, that we will survive as a social and scientific race. Of course, if this is not the case, there is simply no reason at all even to try. But I hope that we will not exhaust our natural resources, overpopulate the globe with starving children, poison earth itself, or vaporize ourselves in a nuclear way. If after almost five billion years we have reached the end of the line, there is no reason to do anything. Except, as Dr. Bernard M. Oliver who headed Project Cyclops puts it, "drink our nepenthe, turn to a life of sensuality and subjectivity, and occasionally weep for glory unattained."

But putting that aside, let us assume that man will be around for some time to come. In fact, it would probably be safe to postulate that if we can survive, more evolutionary development awaits us. We are almost certain not to have reached the top of our evolutionary scale.

How do we ensure that mankind will evolve even more? Of immediate and foremost importance is the determination to solve our ecological situation. The earth must be washed, population must be brought under control, and mankind must learn to live and work together. Otherwise we are doomed.

It is well within our grasp to restore ecological balance to the earth again, and, at the same time, search the stars. And in a broader view, this interstellar quest cannot help but give even greater meaning to our survival and thereby place even more importance on our ecological situation.

The two are truly as one. For if we can survive, it means that the probability that other cultures have also survived is even greater. In the long run, this would significantly reduce the actual probability of making contact a reality.

Civilization has all but forgotten the excitement and cultural stimulation brought to societies by the discoveries of the fifteenth, sixteenth, and seventeenth centuries. Man discovered new worlds. He traveled around the globe, exposing himself to cultures that were new and different. From these new worlds he learned alien languages, alien customs, and alien philosophies, and he ate alien foods. How different were the stone pyramids of the Yucatán from the manicured lawns of Buckingham Palace. How different were the religions of the Chinese from the beliefs dictated by the Vatican. From this contact there evolved a period of cultural enrichment, growth, revolution, and the inevitable rise of a high technology.

Although the tradition of cultural exploration and expansion is deeply rooted within us, new geographic or cultural frontiers have all but vanished. Does this leave mankind with a frustration that has not yet surfaced and now lies barely submerged in our own consciousness?

At the beginning of the space race, the hopes were high that not only would we put a man on the moon before the Russians, but also that our interplanetary probes would bring us some confirmation that a primitive form of life existed somewhere in our solar system. No one had ever seen the other side of the moon. Venus was a planet covered by clouds. And Mars, the planet closest and most visible to earth, may be veined with canals to distribute water from the martian pole. These questions, and the expectation that they would be answered, led most of us to enthusiastically support the space program.

But many illusions were shattered when Mariner gave us a closer look. Venus was found too hot to support life. The moon was barren and lifeless. Mars was a bleak, pockmarked rock, and the great canals of Giovanni Schiaparelli were nothing but illusions. Earth, as seen from space, was an incredibily breathtaking sight—so unlike the scarred landscapes of neighborhood satellites and planets. Hanging in space like a shimmering turquoise globe was man's home. Fragile, delicate, and in danger. Then, with that perspective, the clamor for ecology grew and the support for the exploration of space withered.

Let us suppose that man and his technology are able to restore a proper ecological balance to earth. Let us suppose that man's inventions can recycle our wastes, develop new sources of energy, and control our birth rate. Then what? Will we accept forever a status of zero population growth? Will we be satisfied to wait alone in the universe, knowing only ourselves? Perhaps that is good, but perhaps such a condition will drain the blood from our veins, sap us of our lust, and tranquilize our dreams. What then?

Of course, there are many things we can do. Continue to probe the universe, the atom, and ourselves. But as long as we limit ourselves to earth-based life alone, many enormously exciting and very fundamental questions will remain unanswered—perhaps forever. It is most likely we will find the answers not in ourselves, but in the stars.

As we have seen, the foremost and overriding question is simply: Are we alone? Is earth singular in the solar system, the galaxy, the universe? Has some cosmic miracle caused just one speck of dust to bear life? Are billions of other stars and their planets without any form of biological intelligence?

We have mentioned that only very recently have we signaled our presence in the universe because electromagnetic communication has been with us less than a century. But we too are able to detect such signals, so any race we contact will be at least as technologically sophisticated as ourselves. Indeed, it is likely that they are more so.

Therefore, there are some immediately valuable benefits to science and technology from contact with other cultures. However, such an exchange could not be in the form of a dialogue, for the distances are much too great, with delay times likely to be a century or more. So most likely there will be no question-and-answer transmissions, but a series of simultaneous transmissions, each a documentary about the society involved—its planetary data, its life forms, its age, its history, and its religious beliefs. And so, over a period of a century or so, we might receive a tremendous amount of information that would enable us to build a model of the other race. It is not impossible that we could even gain access to an alien data bank.

If we do succeed in establishing interstellar contact, it is also highly possible that we are not the first civilization to have done so. In fact, it may well be that such communication has been taking place ever since the first civilization evolved four or five billion years ago.

We would literally be given an enormous body of knowledge, knowledge handed down from race to race, from culture to culture, from planet to planet. In this galactic heritage we may find the total histories of countless unknown planets and their inhabitants. We could receive astronomical data dating back aeons, perhaps pictures of our own and neighboring galaxies taken by races that have long since vanished. We would have at our disposal a sort of cosmic archaeological record of a galaxy.

If such a heritage exists—and it almost certainly does—then it can only serve to illuminate our past, present, and future. It could serve to give us the social forms and structures most suitable for self-preservation, genetic evolution, and ecological repairs. It could give us access to new art forms, artistic achievements and other endeavors. It could give us answers to those branches of science, technology, and medicine that still elude us. It could mean the end of the cultural isolation of the human race. We would be proud of our species and no longer engage in childish rivalry. We would find ourselves cast in a larger role than we could ever construct for ourselves or even visualize, one that would offer us a cosmic future and a reorientation of our philosophies. The cost would be less than a month of warfare.

What are the possible dangers of such a venture? What risks would result from contact with extraterrestrial intelligences? If we expose our existence to an alien civilization more advanced and therefore more powerful than ours, are we placing ourselves in even greater danger?

Although the invasion of the earth by hostile aliens has been a cloying theme in science fiction, it seems that this possibility is extremely remote. The annihilation or colonization of the earth by hordes of superior beings would be a very impractical venture for any advanced culture. Interstellar travel is enormously expensive, and only the most extreme crisis would ever justify a mass interstellar exodus. In fact, if a culture did need, say, additional living space, it is more likely that a civilization capable of interstellar travel could well have solved its population problems by internal means long ago. Or if not, such a race, to avoid extinction by means of a mass exodus, would almost certainly seek an uninhabited world rather than face the additional problems that invasion would bring. And to such an advanced race, likely worlds would most probably have been cataloged far in advance of any planned departure date.

The theme of exploitation has also been touched on by imaginative writers. In such stories we may appear to be so primitive that we would be candidates for some galactic zoo, experimental organisms, or even a gourmet delicacy—although the differences in biochemistry may make us poisonous. The arguments against invasion are even stronger here. And from an anthropocentric point of view, that intelligence is positively correlated with compassion, empathy, and respect for life itself.

Or perhaps an alien culture would attempt to subvert us, under the guise of benevolence. But there is no logical reason to believe that this would aid an intelligent culture in any way. Giving the imagination full run, there is no limit to the kinds of treachery that could confront us, and our only defense would be appropriate security measures and a high degree of suspicion.

So it seems that the greatest threat that contact with an extraterrestrial civilization could bring to bear is not to man's body and environment, but to his psyche. There is the distinct possibility that the cultural shock could produce in many a retrogression rather than a cultural advance. The concept, of course, is anathema to many religions, and man, with his long heritage of Judeo-Christian culture, may not be able to cope with a reexamination of God-created universes. Also, as sociologists are quick to point out, contact between two different cultures has always resulted in the domination of the weaker by the stronger.

On the other hand, there is no precedent of such a contact being made by radio alone. Physical contact has always been the case in point, and without aggression on the part of the more advanced cultures, the lesser cultures have often benefited and prospered. For example, the natives of many South Sea islands have greatly improved their status, health, and skills through outside help.

While it is true that interstellar communication is not totally devoid of risk. I am quick to suggest that the benefits far surpass those risks. We cannot logically conclude that our civilization would be placed in danger by radio contact alone, although the subject should be debated and resolved at a national level.

In the case of interstellar contact, the long delays required and the remoteness of the contact should allow most of us to readily adapt to the realization that we are not alone in the universe. Generations would be required for a dialogue. But the knowledge derived from a civilization that has solved its problems could be of great help to mankind.

Perhaps it could teach *us* the secret of survival!

13

Conclusion

I was at the end of my quest. I had traveled hundreds of thousands of miles searching for evidence that extraterrestrials exist, that traces of their presence could be found on earth. My production team had recorded hundreds of incredible stories told by extremely credible people. The *In Search of . . .* television series and the *In Search of . . .* series of books would be my contribution to these credible, sometimes bewildered people. I wanted to give them a vehicle for expression.

I had talked to hundreds of experts and eyewitnesses in the field. Every interview I obtained propelled my search forward. I had decided to ask some ordinary questions. Every answer I received prompted me to ask more extraordinary questions in a myriad of disciplines —ranging from radio astronomy to archaeoastronomy, from black-hole science to aerospace design. Each question and each astounding answer goaded my search into new directions. The questions invented the search. And the answers revealed and exposed a dazzling patchwork of evidence. I now face the task of piecing together the puzzle parts. The inevitable questions sallied forth.

How do you explain away all the different kinds of evidence incessantly reported by eyewitnesses? I was asking myself the same question that UFO researchers like Hynek had asked me many months ago when I had first begun to search for answers! But now I had gathered all that evidence myself. And there it was ogling me—challenging me to dismiss it as a result of mere mass hysteria or a widespread hoax. But there is so much. There are radar/visual trackings; many good photos: physical traces at landing sites; animal reactions; electromagnetic interference; soil luminescence tests; occasional direct gravity effects; and some, though infrequent, nuclear radiation reports. There's a profusion of evidence. If I were limited to only eyewitness sightings and a couple of polygraph tests, I might not be so overwhelmed by the mysteries in the skies. But I have more than just eyewitness testimony. And anyway, how would I explain away the eyewitness testimony I have recorded on tape?

The Baker family of Mellen, Wisconsin—a story depicting quiet fields and quiet people and the one night that something incredible happened. The night of March 13, 1975—the night the Baker family saw a UFO on the town road. Then later undersheriff George Ree and seven deputies from two neighboring counties raced across country roads following bright celestial objects. And to this day no one knows what it was that George Ree and those other men chased that night. Something remarkable happened on the Mellen town road, something that would have seemed unbelievable if it hadn't happened to people as down-to-earth as the town of Mellen itself. How do you discount the stories of the Baker family?

That kind of eyewitness testimony would stand as evidence in a court of law. Do attorneys hold the monopoly on the right to establish witness credibility? For it's one of the principal means of establishing whether we should reasonably believe witnesses' allegations. Lawyers establish the reputation and caliber of the witnesses as well as the quality of their affidavits.

Are there apparent motives for distortion or prevarication? Was there preexisting knowledge of the thing being reported? Were there multiple witnesses? How did the witnesses react? An attorney uses these factors to establish witness credibility. But critics say that such eyewitness testimony is not conclusive evidence in the case of UFOs. As I looked over the testimonies of the Bakers and the Kay family, George Ree's statements, the polygraph tests of Critchfield, and all of the many other stories I had recorded, I knew that they would stand up in court. But good court evidence was not enough in the case of UFOs. The subject area was too sensitive. Perhaps the implications of a superior race from another planet are too traumatic.

Anyway, the people who were spotting UFOs and filing reports came from all walks of life. An astonishing cross section of people has seen UFOs. Housewives, farmers, and policemen are as reliable as other, more technically trained witnesses such as airline pilots and astronomers. So the question still remains: How do you explain all these reports away? Many people have tried to, but with very limited success.

The Air Force's Project Blue Book investigation committee tried to and couldn't. They couldn't explain almost 700 of the 12,600 cases. And according to Dr. Allen Hynek (the Air Force's official astronomical consultant to Project Blue Book), some of the most intriguing cases are those the Air Force claims it had identified but actually hadn't. Now that the Air Force has declassified the PBB files, the public will be able to review the remaining 11,900 mysterious cases. Hynek claims that some of the 700 cases were solved because of insufficient data, but there was never any attempt to get sufficient data. So there you are. The number of unidentified flying objects lacking any natural explanation is growing.

The majority of scientists I interviewed admitted that there is something going on up there that they cannot explain at the present time. Most will go no further. Some "fringe" scientists will make the next leap and explain this mystery as an extraterrestrial flying machine. Others, like Jacques Vallee, who is an astrophysics and computer scientist, say that UFOs represent a different order of reality—a psychic reality. He thinks that UFOs may constitute a control system. The "liberal" prophetic scientists will speculate on the possibility of radio communication with outer space but refuse even to venture the extraterrestrial hypothesis for the UFO phenomenon. They seem to be suffering from a "failure of nerve." As defined by Arthur C. Clarke: "Even given all the relevant facts, the would-be prophet cannot see that they point to an inescapable conclusion." Every time I encountered this sort of inconsistency, I was both confused and compelled to take my search further into those various disciplines these would-be prophets had touched upon. I wanted to turn up all the circumstantial evidence and facts surrounding the extraterrestrial subject: radio science, aerospace design, potential black-hole technology for acceleration of interstellar travel, the overwhelming odds favoring extraterrestrial life, hoaxes, the Sirius connection, disk-shaped objects sighted in the past, and last but not least, the Viking mission to Mars. And everywhere I delved, I found surprising answers. I was not out to prove anything either way. I just wanted to expose all of the issues surrounding the UFO subject and extraterrestrials in general. I wanted to expose the issues that most people refuse to examine.

I guess I wanted to see what happens when someone attempts to explain the unexplainable. For me it proved to be an exhilarating exercise in both detachment and passion. The attempt to explain the unexplained unites these two opposing qualities, so critical to any sort of exhaustive search.

For others, like sociologist Dr. Richard E. Yinger, the attempt to explain the unexplained marked the beginning of a new field of sociology called exosociology. Exosociology views the UFO as an indicator, a code, part of a puzzle, a vehicle for intellectual travel into new idea spaces, ultimately dealing with the most profound issues of life and the nature of the universe. This exciting new discipline was recognized by the Pennsylvania Sociological Society in 1974 and the American Sociological Association in 1975.

The National Aeronautics and Space Administration's launching of the Viking Mission to Mars marked the beginning of the search for life beyond earth. After reading scientists' speculations on the possibility of life on Mars just prior to touchdown, I had agreed with Sagan when he wrote: "They [scientists and newspaper editorialists] are sometimes found supporting the curious principle: 'When faced with two alternatives in a subject about which we know nothing, choose the least interesting.'" But after the biology test results were returned, attitudes were remarkedly different, especially during the Viking press briefings.

Just before I handed this chapter to the publisher, I decided to conduct a test. I wanted to know how many probes to how many systems we would have to launch in order to conduct a systematic search for extraterrestrial life. I asked William Baity of the University of San Diego to calculate this equation for me. He is currently working in X-ray astronomy there. Baity interpreted Ronald Bracewell's calculations and found that if we were to estimate that there were 10,000 superior civilizations to be found among one million stars likely to have planets, then we would need to send 100,000 probes in order to locate just one of the 10,000 superior civilizations within an average of one thousand light-years' distance from each other. I think it's safe to say that that number coincides pretty well with the number of UFOs we are seeing. Is there some conclusion to be drawn from this? Well, I certainly think it has to be included in the evidence I have so far amassed.

The evidence in favor of the extraterrestrial hypothesis is strong—almost overwhelming. Furthermore, whatever the ultimate explanation for the UFO phenomenon may be, I must concur with Robert Wood in "Testing the Extraterrestrial Hypothesis" when he writes: "The challenge to science offered by UFOs is not to the methods of science, but to the present models of science, which are inevitably doomed anyway."

The evidence seems to point to at least the theoretical possibility of extraterrestrial origins for UFOs. And as Arthur C. Clarke so beautifully states: "Anything that is theoretically possible will be achieved in practice, no matter what the technical difficulties, if it is desired greatly enough." An advanced extraterrestrial civilization could indeed have mastered interstellar travel. And UFOs could be their craft. This theoretical possibility cannot be refuted or dismissed as being simply the wild, irresponsible meanderings of a lunatic fringe. The evidence is available for any who wish to examine its significance and meaning. We have to avoid that "failure of nerve" for which, as Clarke states, "history exacts so merciless a penalty—we must have the courage to follow all technical extrapolations to their logical conclusions. Yet, even this is not enough. To predict the future, we need logic; but we also need faith and imagination, which can sometimes defy logic itself. . . ." And anyway, "the real future is not logically foreseeable."

Yes, even though UFO maneuvers seem illogical and silly at times, the time has come when we can no longer smugly ignore the evidence at hand. For "any sufficiently advanced technology is indistinguishable from magic," writes Arthur C. Clarke. And who knows, we may be witnessing just this kind of magic. For something indeed is truly happening. Something unexplained, but not unexplainable.

Epilogue

I had journeyed virtually around the world in search of extraterrestrials. I was convinced that UFOs had touched planet earth as a part of the universal investigations of ETL. But I had no proof. I was left with single recollections that contributed to my suspicion that UFOs exist. In the final analysis, it was the people I had met who had witnessed landings that provided the most convincing evidence. People like Jan Maddox and her friend Richard Gustafson.

The place was White City, Kansas. Jan worked for the local newspaper, the White City *Register*. Sweet, young, blond, and dedicatedly honest, she told a most convincing story. In her words: "It was about a quarter of eight on July 19, 1975. We were into daylight saving time, and it was still light out. There wasn't a cloud in the sky. Richard Gustafson picked me up, and we were on our way to Junction City. We were going past the Skiddy Cemetery and we saw this object in the sky, a large object. It was very shiny. I noticed that it had three cylinder-shaped objects in a straight line, parallel to each other, and one right below the middle one of the three. We just viewed it for a little while, and I noticed that it didn't look like an airplane. About that time, it came down, straight toward the earth, at a fast rate of speed. I estimate it took anywhere between three and five seconds for it to come to the ground. Our first reactions, Richard and I, was that a plane had crashed. We hurried up to the site. When we got up over a rise, the field was on fire and I just knew that a plane had crashed. There wasn't anything in sight, no metal or a plane where it had crashed or anything. There was nothing. There was nothing on the ground. I was scared, because I've got a real weak stomach and I was afraid if that was a plane crash I was . . . wasn't going to be of much help. I was just gonna faint or something. In a way, I was really relieved there wasn't anything there.

"I couldn't say much. I was just . . . I was really shocked. It scared me, and if you want to know the exact words, I said, 'Let's get the hell out of here. Something's landed here, and I don't want to stay around until it comes back.' 'Cause I was really scared. There were three rings of fire all burning separately in the grass. They were about five feet in diameter and about fifteen or twenty feet apart from each other in a triangle shape. Two men came out in a truck and they had gunnysacks and they were gonna put the fire out, but other than that, there wasn't any other people.

"After we looked at the fire, and while the other men were putting the fire out, we got back in the car, and I was shaking. Richard said he was going to go over to this farmhouse right across the road and ask a friend of his if he'd seen anything. We went over and talked to the man. And I talked to his wife, too. She said she wished she would have known that it was there. She was out in her garden, and she said if she would have known it was there she would have run into the house, 'cause she was just as scared as I was. I hurried on up to the sighting, and there was smoke coming up, so I knew that something had crashed. We turned down the road and we got to the sighting and jumped out, crossed the fence, and walked right up to where this was. But there was nothing there. The . . . the ground was just on fire. The first thing I thought of, it might have been a UFO. I've never seen one before, but I've heard people talk about 'em in different places. I wasn't prepared at all for this when it happened. I was shaken by it. I'd seen programs on UFOs, and the movies that are out, and I've read stories about 'em, and I just felt that I'd never see one. You never really do believe in something, truly believe in it, until you've seen one yourself. Well, I believe in 'em now, because I believe what I saw was a UFO. This has affected me quite a bit. I've become more aware of things around me. If somebody says, 'I saw something funny the other day,' I don't just say, 'Oh,' I ask them what they saw."

When Jan finished telling her story, I asked Richard Gustafson to go over the details with me. Here's his version of what happened that night.

"I'm Richard Gustafson, from Skitty, Kansas, and I'm a farmer. I raise hogs. It was a Saturday evening. We were on our way to Junction City to celebrate Jan Maddox's parents' anniversary. I picked her up and we were a couple of miles west of Skitty, heading north, when we saw this object in the air. All of a sudden it was there, and it was kind of strange. The first thing I thought of, it was a large aircraft heading straight toward the ground. And I told Jan that it looked like an aircraft to me that's gonna crash. We'd better get up there and see what we can do to help out. Anyhow, we watched it for a little bit. I was kinda stunned. I didn't . . . I didn't know exactly what to do. Pretty soon I saw a couple of guys coming in a pickup with a couple of gunnysacks. They saw the fire, but they came up to put it out. I asked them if they had seen anything laying there, and they said no."

Richard then told of visiting his friend at a nearby

farm: "When we pulled out of Ray Weber's yard, we noticed that they were getting the fire under control and everything and they wouldn't need any help. So on the way to Junction City, I decided we'd better go and tell some authority what we had seen. We'd better report it. So we went into Junction City, and I stopped at the Junction City Police Department and I told them the story. They just laughed at us. They didn't take us serious. They didn't think we were . . . well, I don't know what they thought, but they just laughed at us. They didn't take the matter on any further. They said . . . well . . . 'Thank you,' and that was it."

I remembered, as Richard spoke, the most important fact about UFOs that Allen Hynek had given me. "The one absolutely incontrovertible fact in the whole UFO situation is that UFO reports exist. Not just in the United States, but all over the world." You may say, "Well, so what? Reports are cheap!" Then one has to examine, and that's what I did as I sorted out my last notes on UFOs. I reviewed the people, the highly credible people I spoke to in the course of crisscrossing the country.

I recalled Janet, Jerry, and Helen Kay and the story of their sighting in Medford, Minnesota. It was on the night of November 2, 1975. Janet remembered doing her homework, and then, as she put it, "I looked up in the sky across the street, and there was a great big orange-red glow in the sky. I didn't know quite what it was. I kept staring at it, and it just kept on coming down slowly, and it had fire coming off the top. My mom was in the room right next door, and she, she looked out the window, and she kind of said, 'Wow.' We just both kind of stood there. As it was coming down, it went behind this one building. We ran outside and we jumped in the car to follow it. We wanted to go over to the site and see what had gone on, if it was a plane or something, 'cause we didn't know quite what it was. So we went over there, and by this time, there was nothing there."

Janet did not make up the story. She's a bright, well-adjusted young woman who clearly knows what she saw and what she did. Helen Kay, her mother, concurs. And adds to Janet's narrative what happened the next day, when she heard that something had marked the site where the UFO had apparently come down. "It was burned," she said, "burned by heat. Just like you would take a torch and . . . and burn the grass. You could pick the grass up. It was just powdery. It was so burned that you could just rub it between your fingers, it would just disintegrate. It was just powder. It was that dry.

"The whole football field was in real good condition. There were not any bare spots. It was all green, and this spot lined up perfectly with the plane we saw go down. That's where the burned spot was, right in line with our window that we saw it out of."

Soil samples taken at the site were tested in the aerospace lab at the University of Kansas by Dr. Edward Zeller. He explained the test examination he made this way: "If a soil is subjected either to radiation or to heating, these heating or radiation effects leave a characteristic signature in the luminescence properties of the soil. Now, almost all crystalline or glassy materials—window glass, crystal, and sand, anything, normal rocks in soils—will show a certain amount of luminescence if you heat them on a hot plate in a dark room. If you just throw them on a hot plate in a dark room and allow your eyes to adapt, you can see it yourself. It's nothing very mysterious. If they're strongly irradiated, they show less luminescence. What we're dealing with here essentially is a phenomenon which allows us, when we make the measurements, to determine whether the sample has either been subjected to radiation or been subjected to heating. In this case, if you expose the soil to radiation, the luminescence properties of the soil change and the soil becomes more luminescent. And the more radiation it's exposed to, the more luminescent it becomes. On the other hand, if by some means you heat the soil, then the soil loses its luminescence properties and becomes less luminescent. And the increase in radiation is exactly what we measure."

I asked Dr. Zeller to describe the results of the Medford test. "At the Medford site," he went on, "some of the samples show almost ten times the amount of luminescence that others do, and that's unusual. We wouldn't expect that level of variability in soil samples that, under the microscope, look very similar. We don't find large differences under the microscope, and therefore the Medford-site samples were fairly good in the sense that they looked to us to be quite uniform initially, and therefore we would have expected them to have similar luminescence properties.

"When we look at them, when we look at the glow curves, we find large-scale variation in the glow curves but no large-scale variation in the microscopic appearance of the samples. The only thing we can say is that these high-variability conditions are . . . are unusual, and exactly what they mean, I can't tell you. I cannot say. In the case of the Medford site, the only thing I can say is that the variability is extreme, and I would not expect that in samples that have just been lying in a field."

I thanked Dr. Zeller, because I know we had reached the limit of his desire to comment on what might have happened at Medford. And definitively, all we can say is that a UFO landed. We use Allen Hynek's criteria. As he says, "To be a true UFO, the report and the content of the report must remain unidentified and unexplained, even after severe technical scrutiny by experts."

Sometimes an investigator runs into the stone wall of embarrassment that follows an individual's belief that something has been spotted. Dr. Hynek reports: "UFOs have been subjected to such a barrage of buffoonery in the last twenty-five years that people are reluctant to report. When I give talks on the subject, at the end of the lecture I will say, 'Okay, now, how many people in the audience, come on, confess, how many people have had what they consider an actual UFO experience?' And invariably I will get 10 to 20 percent of the people to raise their hands. Then when I ask, 'Okay, those of you who raised your hands, how many of you reported it either to the police or to the Air Force?' I'm lucky to get two or three hands. They just aren't convinced. There's a reservoir of unreported instances, and it's logical, because if somebody reports something, they're apt to get ridiculed."

I understood what he meant from having scoured

Meadowview, Virginia, to assemble the report of the night the town sought a UFO. It all started on January 18, 1976.

At approximately eight P.M. a brilliant ball of light was sighted about two hundred feet off the ground. It landed in rolling fields. The incident was witnessed or heard by a number of people. The fire department was called out to investigate, because an explosion and a fire accompanied the landing. No trace of anything was found. The terrain where the object landed is mostly cornfields. The Langley and Seymour Johnson Air Force Base said they knew of no military operations in or around the area.

I started my quest in Meadowview with Betty Barrett, a housewife who first saw the object.

"It was a real light night, the full moon was out," she said. "I had just got settled with the kids, and I saw a car going by the house, and it was going real slow, so it kinda got my curiosity up. I went to the kitchen window and looked out to see if it had pulled in, and it went on up above the curve, and that's when I saw a great old big shining light, it would hurt your eyes to look at it. I went outside. I didn't hear a bit of sound or nothin'. I took off to my neighbor's house. I rung the doorbell and asked her to come and look. I felt foolish, but I mean if I hadn't saw it, I guess I wouldn't have believed it either, but it was the brightest thing that I'd ever saw."

Helen Counts continued the story for me.

"Mrs. Barrett rang my doorbell and asked me to come out, that she'd seen this thing that she's scared of, and it landed over in the field, and I went outside, and when I looked I couldn't see anything. And she turned to go back to her house, and about that time something exploded, and it sounded like a dynamite, and fire just flew up everywhere. I called Central Dispatch. They're the County Sheriff, the Fire Department. I thought it was an airplane."

The story was then continued for me by Dan Ryan, assistant chief of the Meadowview Volunteer Fire Department.

"Around eight-ten I got a call which said there were fires on the top of the hill; by eight-thirty we was on the scene in the area where this plane was supposed to have crashed. I'd say twenty-five of us with three vehicles. And we searched the area with those trucks and lights and then the chief and about four or five men walked the area that night and that was just about it."

And Jim Booth, a free-lance photographer, filled in other details.

"I got to the scene about an hour and a half or so after the explosion. It was extremely cold that night, so I thought rather than just going out and freezing to death, we'd just let them do the search. I would estimate that there were at least . . . there were between twenty and thirty people involved in the search. They finally decided to end the search—that was sometime after midnight—and resume it again the next morning. We searched just about every square inch, unless it was in a wooded area that was just so dense that we couldn't see through it with the tremendous spotlights. The next day, several ground-search parties went out and went back over the areas they'd searched. They didn't go back over the fields, because they were relatively clear, good visibility, and they just went around the perimeter of the field, and could find nothing. No debris, no sign of any explosion or any fire."

A hoax, perhaps? A fraud? A flight of fancy? I didn't know until I talked to Helen Farmer.

"We went to church at Chestnut Grove. Just as we started to get out of the car, I saw this big ball fall from the sky, and I told my husband, I said I seen a ball of fire fall from the sky, and he said, 'Oh, you didn't see anything.' I said, 'Yes, I did, too.' And about that time something busted like a gun went off, and sparks flew from it. Really, we didn't know what it was."

I talked, as well, to Becky Thompson, the Central Dispatcher, and to Charles Seagar, a man who lived near the site of the incident. From all the interviews I conducted, this is the story: A fireball landed, then disappeared. It left no trace of its passing except in the minds of those who saw it. It is real. It fits Dr. Hynek's description. "Remember," he said, "the U in UFO simply means 'unidentified.'"

Have we been visited from outer space? Is that great void the origin of UFOs? I don't know. I will accept

Allen Hynek's summary: "Maybe the whole phenomenon is as mysterious as . . . asking Ben Franklin, 'What makes the sun shine?' How could Ben have known that the sun was a nuclear reactor?" In other words, it could be that the UFO phenomenon is so strange that it may signal a domain of nature that we have not yet explored—in the same sense that a hundred years ago we knew nothing about nuclear energy, for instance. Most people like this idea of visitation from outer space, and that may yet turn out to be the answer. But as I tell my students at Northwestern: if you know the answer in advance, it's not research.

For my part, I have marked the UFO story in my files "open," to be continued.

Bibliography

Arnon, Shlomo, *UFOs Are a Scientific Fact.* UCLA thesis paper.

Bracewell, Ronald, *The Galactic Club.* San Francisco: W.H. Freeman and Co., 1974.

Cameron, A.G.W., *Interstellar Communication.* New York: W.A. Benjamin, Inc., 1963.

Clarke, Arthur C., *Profiles of the Future.* New York: Bantam Books, 1958.

Cooper, Henry S.F., Jr. "A Resonance with Something Alive," *New Yorker,* June 21, 1976.

———, "Profiles Carl Sagan," *New Yorker,* June 28, 1976.

Dole, Stephen H. and Isaac Asimov, *Planets for Man.* New York: Random House, 1964.

Edwards, Frank, *Flying Saucers—Serious Business.* New York: Lyle Stuart, 1966.

Festinger, Leon, *When Prophecy Fails.* Minnesota: University of Minnesota Press, 1956.

Fuller, John G., *Aliens in the Skies.* New York: G.P. Putnam Sons, 1959.

Gold, T., "Cosmic Garbage," *Space Digest,* Vol. 3, No. 5, May 1960.

Gwyne, Peter, "Visit to a Small Planet," *Newsweek,* August 2, 1976.

Hyde, Frank W., *Radio Astronomy for Amateurs.* New York: W.W. Norton, 1962.

Hynek, J. Allen, *The UFO Experience, a Scientific Inquiry.* Chicago: Henry Regnery Co., 1972.

Jung, C.G., *Flying Saucers, a Modern Myth of Things Seen in the Sky.* New York: Harcourt Brace, 1959.

Keyhoe, Maj. Donald E., *Aliens from Space.* Garden City: Doubleday & Co., 1973.

Leslie, Desmond and George Adamski, *Flying Saucers Have Landed.* London: Werner Laurie, Ltd., 1953.

Lore, Gordon I.R., Jr., and Harold H. Deneault, Jr., *Mysteries of the Skies.* Englewood Cliffs: Prentice Hall, Inc., 1968.

Lorenzen, Jim and Coral, *UFOs over the Americas.* New York: Signet Books, 1968.

Los Angeles Times, "Two Viking Labs Report Unusual Soil Findings," August 1, 1976.
Los Angeles Times, "Mirror to Man," August 9, 1976.
Los Angeles Times, "May Be Biological Fool's Gold," August 9, 1976.
Lunan, Duncan, *Interstellar Contact.* Chicago: Henry Regnery Co., 1975.
Michell, John, *Flying Saucer Vision.* London: Sidgwick and Jackson, Ltds., 1967.
Moulton, Richard G., *Ezekiel, The Modern Reader's Bible.* New York: Macmillan, 1897.
Newsweek, "Viking Finds Some Hints of Life on Mars," August 9, 1976.
Sagan, Carl, *The Cosmic Connection.* Garden City: Doubleday & Co., 1973.
Sagan, Carl (editor) and Thornton Page, *UFOs, A Scientific Debate.* Ithaca: Cornell University Press, 1972.
Shipman, Harry, *Black Holes, Quasars and the Universe.* Boston: Houghton Mifflin, 1976.
Sjklovskii, I.S. and Carl Sagan, *Intelligent Life in the Universe.* San Francisco: Holden Day, Inc., 1966.
Smith, Ronald, "The Abdication of Human Intelligence," *The Humanist.*
Sullivan, Walter, *We Are Not Alone.* New York: McGraw Hill Co., 1964.
Thomsen, Dietrick E., "Black Hole Power," *Science News,* Vol. 105.
Thorne, Kip S., "Gravitational Collapse," *Scientific American,* November 1967.
———, "The Search for Black Holes," *Scientific American,* December 1974.
Time, "Mars: The Riddle of the Red Planet," August 2, 1976.
Time, "Viking: the First Signs of Life?" August 9, 1976.
Vallee, Jacques, *Challenge to Science.* Chicago: Henry Regnery Co., 1966.

ABOUT THE AUTHOR

ALAN LANDSBURG is a successful film and television producer, heading up his own production company in Los Angeles, California. He was instrumental in bringing the von Däniken phenomenon to the attention of the American public through TV by producing "In Search of Ancient Astronauts." Alan Landsburg is also the author of *In Search of Ancient Mysteries* and *The Outer Space Connection.* He is currently working on a weekly television series, "In Search Of . . . ," which has been on the air since September, 1976. *In Search of Extraterrestrials* and *In Search of Lost Civilizations* and four future books on magic and witchcraft, monsters, special phenomena and people, are based on this series.